Winfried Gödert, Klaus Lepsky
Information Literacy and Autonomy

Winfried Gödert, Klaus Lepsky

Information Literacy and Autonomy

———

A Cognitive View

Translated by
Tina Mengel

DE GRUYTER
SAUR

ISBN 978-3-11-161964-4
e-ISBN (PDF) 978-3-11-069374-4
e-ISBN (EPUB) 978-3-11-069383-6

Library of Congress Control Number: 2023936225

Bibliographic information published by the Deutsche Nationalbibliothek
The Deutsche Nationalbibliothek lists this publication in the Deutsche Nationalbibliografie;
detailed bibliographic data are available on the internet at http://dnb.dnb.de.

www.degruyter.com

For Gilda, Kristina, and Micha

Preface

Today, the concept of information literacy is diversely used and has therefore become an increasingly fuzzy term. The discussion that has been going on for years about the side effects of digitization and information technology, or in other words, the "internet age", is much about competent acting, but without addressing its requirements or conditions. We think that the concept of information literacy as a mere set of criteria for dealing with information systems falls short and thus hinders the urgently needed discussion of the consequences that the "internet age" will have for us as individuals and for society.

We therefore prefer a concept we call information*al* literacy. We start from the notion of human beings as acting subjects, even more, as autonomously acting individuals. Acting autonomously means acting on the basis of informational processes, which can be described as cognitive processes in humans and through their relationships within the world—to other communication partners, but also to external sources of information.

We look at informational literacy as lived informational autonomy and from this perspective develop consequences for a future image of the human being in a world dominated by information technology.

It is the central cognitive abilities such as abstracting, analogizing, reasoning, checking for plausibility, and creativity that are essential for autonomous informational action. We will explain how humans, starting from the physiological processes of sensory perception, are able to develop abstract concepts such as prime numbers, quarks, DNA, money, or justice, to think about them, and to communicate, write down, and reinterpret the results of these thoughts; and to do so on a global scale and over long periods of time.

This explanation is only possible by including several scientific fields, primarily cognitive science, computer science, and philosophy. We are not experts in these areas. However, a complete picture cannot emerge without compiling results from all of these disciplines and their various methodological approaches. Thereby, terms are introduced and used that may be understood differently even within the disciplines themselves and therefore cannot always be brought into congruence. We have strived to use our own understanding of these terms as consistently as possible. A glossary at the end of the book shall serve to explain some of the particularly important concepts.

It will not be possible to address each individual issue with the depth that would normally be expected from a single discipline. Likewise, original sources cannot always be cited; in these cases, secondary sources are used as a substitute, with all the known problems associated with them.

https://doi.org/10.1515/9783110693744-202

We can only apologize for the resulting shortcomings in our presentation. We believe, however, that the importance of the topic warrants such a broad presentation and, if necessary, also the acceptance of inadequacies.

Probably, with this approach we will disappoint all those who expect quick and easy answers to questions about information literacy or even instructions for its acquisition or teaching. Nevertheless, we strongly believe that any misguided discussion about information literacy must precede an in-depth look at the interrelations thereof. For this purpose, we want to raise and provide answers to the essential questions that offer clues for the human individual to shape free social communities while preserving informational autonomy.

Over the years of the book's genesis, the issues discussed have increasingly become the focus of public debate. What is striking here is the discrepancy between the media excitement and the seriousness with which topics such as "artificial intelligence" or "media literacy" are treated.

We can only hope that the great attention given to all information technology innovations in today's rapidly changing societies will equally lead to an increased interest in the role of humans in this process. In the midst of this current imbalance in the debate and the ever-growing faith in technology, this book wants to point out consequences for an informationally self-determined behavior in a civil society that is committed to the principles of equality, freedom and solidarity.

Erfweiler and Kronberg, March 2023

How Long Did You Sleep?

Dare you do this —
open your eyes
and look around?
Yes, you're here
here in this world,
you're not dreaming,
it's just as
you see it, things here
are like this.
Like this?
Yes, just like this,
not otherwise.
How long did you sleep?

Olav H. Hauge[1]

---

1 Poet and fruit grower in Norway (1908–1994); quoted from Hauge: The dream we carry, p. 119.

Contents

1 Information Technology and the Human Image

If a machine is expected to be infallible, it cannot also be intelligent.

Alan M. Turing[2]

1.1 Informational Autonomy at Risk

For several decades, we have been regularly confronted with characterizations of a new society that has supposedly dawned as a result of innovations in information technology. Typical labels for this are: information society, knowledge society or even the *Google* society.

Each of these allegedly new forms of society also holds promises for us humans. The greatest leaps in innovation are expected in the fields of work, education, recreation, and health. The trend to "get smarter" is always a part of this, and is only too willingly accepted.

However, before it becomes clear what concrete consequences there will be for the individual, the current model is already being replaced by a new one. Despite wide-ranging discussions, to date no halfway stable image of the human being as a responsible individual in a civil society dominated by information technology has emerged. Ideas about the future development of humans are changing like passing fads. What the models still have in common is the focus on humans as individuals and thus at least the conviction that the structures of society are shaped by acting subjects. The changes are supposed to bring relief and improvement, just as newly designed human images are to embody good influence.

Yet, that might change. The era to come will possibly be accompanied by fundamental reversals of the traditional image of man, for movements (pseudo-philosophies?) such as dataism or transhumanism regard humans as functionalized objects rather than as creating subjects. In this scenario, humans are only legitimized by their contributions to the data stream of a universal network and the resulting calculations to derive rules of behavior. It is not astonishing that such ideas are being developed and disseminated; what is more astonishing is the response to them, which sees them as a quasi-inevitable consequence of the advancing developments in information technology. In *Homo Deus*, touted as the cult book of a new age, *Yuval Noah Harari* sketches the less than friendly vision of the future under the conditions of a data religion:

---

2 Turing: Lecture to the London Mathematical Society on 20 February 1947, p. 124.

https://doi.org/10.1515/9783110693744-001

Dataism is neither liberal nor humanist. It should be emphasized, however, that Dataism isn't anti-humanist. It has nothing against human experiences. It just doesn't think they are intrinsically valuable.[3]

Dataism declares that the universe consists of data flows, and the value of any phenomenon or entity is determined by its contribution to data processing.[4]

Dataism is the first movement since 1789 that created a genuinely novel value: freedom of information. We mustn't confuse freedom of information with the old liberal value of freedom of expression. Freedom of expression was given to humans, and protected their right to think and say what they wished—including their right to keep their mouths shut and their thoughts to themselves. Freedom of information, in contrast, is not given to humans. It is given to *information*.[5]

Regardless of how much significance or realistic future prognosis is attached to these views, it is still absolutely necessary to address them. Characteristic of the debate is the fundamental disagreement of those for and against, and this pronounced polarization presumably also results from the fact that the substance of the vision is so intangible. Proponents see freedom of information as the ultimate victory of democracy. As everything and everyone becomes transparent in the data stream, the assumption is that all the evils of our time are automatically robbed of their business basis. This vision has become a message of salvation. The opponents see in this vision rather the beginning of a new totalitarianism that can be described as a situation in which there are no longer any rights of freedom of the acting subject (the human being), but only the functionalizing submission to mass trends and nontransparent algorithms.[6]

In his book *Life 3.0*, *Max Tegmark* looks at the living conditions of tomorrow under the influence of artificial intelligence. He believes that artificial intelligence is (or will be) able to make decisions on a rational basis while respecting moral and ethical judgments. This would be the first time that humans would face competition in an area for which they had previously claimed a monopoly. For this world shaped by artificial intelligence, *Tegmark* designs various scenarios:

Conquerors:
AI takes control, decides that humans are a threat/nuisance/waste of resources, and gets rid of us by a method that we don't even understand.

---

3 Harari: Homo Deus, p. 393.
4 Harari: Homo Deus, p. 372.
5 Harari: Homo Deus, p. 388.
6 See Pauen/Welzer: Autonomie.

Enslaved God:
A superintelligent AI is confirmed by humans, who use it to produce unimaginable technology and wealth that can be used for good or bad depending on the human controllers.

Reversion:
Technological progress toward superintelligence is prevented by reverting to a pre-technological society in the style of the Amish.

Self-destruction:
Superintelligence is never created because humanity drives itself extinct by other means (say nuclear and/or biotech mayhem fueled by climate crisis).

Egalitarian Utopia:
Humans, cyborgs and uploads coexists peacefully thanks to property abolition and guaranteed income.[7]

Tegmark leaves out a scenario in which one group of people succumbs to the temptations and, out of convenience, enters into a self-generated informational dependence and another group functionalizes this behavior for its own benefit within the framework of totalitarian structures. This scenario of a new formation of elites is considered by *Harari*:

> The third threat to liberalism is that some people will remain both indispensable and undecipherable, but they will constitute a small and privileged elite of upgraded humans. These superhumans will enjoy unheard-of abilities and unprecedented creativity, which will allow them to go on making many of the most important decisions in the world. [...] However, most humans will not be upgraded, and they will consequently become an inferior caste, dominated by both computer algorithms and the new superhumans.[8]

Even if one does not share the views of *Harari* and *Tegmark*, possibly even considers them to be exaggerated thoughts of technology driven fantasists, one must take note that there are many such and similar representations. Forecasts about the changes to be expected as a result of advancing information technology are booming. This often produces a kind of mental short-circuit between four concepts:

Information – Information technology – Progress – Future

In shaping the future one ability must not be lost: The ability to distinguish between future problems that are imperative to be solved and problems that are less important.

---

7 Tegmark: Life 3.0, p. 162, Table 5.1 Summary of AI Aftermath Scenarios.
8 Harari: Homo Deus, p. 351.

Today, the mere mention of an educational understanding of information seems to be enough to be seen as a preservationist or a worrier rather than someone who is shaping progress. Who wants to see oneself in the role of a fun killer, when almost everywhere the terms future and information technology are used quasi synonymously?

Information technology is always tied to computer-based processes. Since the advent of artificial intelligence computing, this fact has more than ever been infused with mythological meaning. The computer metaphor then becomes an expression of faith. But is this really sufficient for shaping the future? Rather not. If shaping the future is regarded as a human task, it is hardly appropriate to reduce human cognitive information processes, being the conditions of thinking and acting, to a model of technical information processing.

Often in this debate a vocabulary is used that relativizes the position of being human either as threatening or promising. There is talk, for example, of human-machine convergence, of emotional computing as a liberation technology, or of "affective computing" without empathy.[9] Typically, it is expressed that, as a result of the progressive development of information technology, humans will lose or have already lost their former unique position for performing superior cognitive tasks. The spectrum of performances is no longer limited to rational intelligence, but now also includes the emotional level, consciousness, and even the soul. It seems to be only a question of time until the unique characteristic of rationality, emotion, and consciousness that are currently still respected in humans will be completely abandoned and replaced by single components or attributed as a characteristic to machines as well.

It should be of particular concern that machine-related descriptive features are used as a computer metaphor and thereby characterize human cognitive performance. Especially in the context of the idea promoted by artificial intelligence of replicating the functions of the human brain, cognitive processes are described as being based on a model that separates the functions of hardware and software.[10] However, this idea is in no way supported by current brain research. *Thomas Metzinger* notes:

> The computer metaphor of the human mind is dead. The idea that mind and brain relate to each other like software and hardware and can be clearly separated as two layers is no longer pushed by anyone in cognitive science.[11]

---

9 See Benedikter: Digitalisierung der Gefühle.
10 For a recent example, see Thielicke/Helmstaedter: Ein völlig neues Kapitel.
11 Metzinger: Ist das Gehirn mit einem Computer oder einer Festplatte zu vergleichen? (author's translation).

Looking at the role emotions and sensations play for the fundamentals of thought and consciousness provides further justification that the analogies hardware ↔ brain and software ↔ mind are inaccurate. The following questions do not make much sense under the assumption of hardware and software being separated:

How does it feel to drink a beer?
How does it feel to be an Olympic champion?
How does it feel to prove a mathematical theorem?

What sensation is triggered by the color blue?
How does the color blue taste?
What smell is the color green?
What feeling is associated with wetness?

The same applies to estimations, beliefs, preferences, desires, in other words, to the entire spectrum of qualitative experiences in general. Thereby the concrete answer (or statement) doesn't play such a big role, just as little whether others would give the same answer. What is important is that the question triggers a process for which the experience of the unity of body and mind is a prerequisite for finding the answer.

Therefore, all concepts that assume an exchange of memory contents between natural and artificial systems or the possibility of a direct connection between the two must be regarded as highly questionable.

This anticipation of the computer metaphor is already leaving memorable marks in the professional world, for example when job applicants are asked which tasks they can perform better than a computer. In fact, this question creates a defensive situation for the applicant by establishing a context that assigns the computer the role of a subject and no longer just a tool. Why else would you ask so generally what someone can do better than a tool?

Where does the fascination with transhumans come from? Is it about feeling like a creator and seeing in it ways of increasing one's power? After all, the quite understandable desire to gain knowledge cannot be the only reason, considering all the self-sacrifice and doom scenarios that are offered along with it. What is it about transhuman rationality that makes it better than evolutionary rationality for ensuring the continuation of life? Isn't that more like admitting your own inadequacy?

Even pioneers of artificial intelligence—and these include not only declared critics like *Josef Weizenbaum* or *Hubert* and *Stuart Dreyfus*—have been quite cautious about what to expect from it. For instance, *Roger Schank* declares:

> The general approach of AI today [1984, author's note] should be to discover the thought processes that humans use for various intelligent activities and to program computers to perform these processes.[12]

Accordingly, we should exactly not judge humans by how far they live up to the ideas of artificial intelligence. So it is quite typical that the hype and the exaggerated expectations are in many cases promoted by people whom *Roger Schank* characterizes as follows:

> Is AI just a subject for pointy-headed academics, or will every person need some understanding of AI and computers in general just to be able to cope? These are the issues that now are discussed by newspapers and by people at cocktail parties. On the one hand, it is nice that people care about such things. On the other, it seems a bit odd that so many people want to discuss their opinion about a subject on which they have so little concrete information.[13]

It may always have been controversial whether humans have souls that distinguish them from all other living creatures. However, it is widely believed that there are mental states that are not compatible with algorithmic thinking and thus cannot be explained. Even the greatest sympathy for rational thought and decision processes cannot prevent us from remembering both good feelings and those we could very well live without.

So, before the path to informational immaturity is perceived as something attractive, it might be worth examining whether the following is true after all, namely that informational autonomy is so firmly bound to the basic characteristics of the human being that it cannot be given up at all. Two frames of reference would have to be connected: first, the bond of humans as social beings to communities based on common action, and second, the individual's cognitive-psychological basis of thought and action.

1.2 Rationality and Cognition

The ideas of the Enlightenment paved the way for humans seeing themselves as living beings with an understanding of self, regardless of their background or social class. Therein, human thought and action are characterized by rational considerations to such an extent that emotions can be controlled. This idea has continued in modern democracies and liberal civil societies, which consider the understanding of the responsible subject as an essential part of what constitutes a

---

12 Schank/Childers: The cognitive computer, p. 37.
13 Schank/Childers: The cognitive computer, p. xii.

modern society. Thanks to the achievements of psychology and modern cognitive research, we are able to understand how rationality, basic biological functions and emotional factors interact as a unity in any individual who thinks and acts consciously and autonomously—and who is thus an individual capable of shaping and participating in social structures. Assuming that these achievements are to be preserved and advanced in principle, the question arises with regard to the acting subject to which extent informational autonomy will play a role in this.

Humans are information-processing beings; this applies both to their individual thinking and acting and to their interactions with others. Views on the nature of human information processing are remarkably diverse and have undergone a number of changes throughout history. Decisive variables of information processing are sensory perceptions and their subsequent cognitive processing operations. In this context, comparing existing structures, adapting them, and building new structures play a central role for all performances associated with knowledge.

A model of knowledge acquisition in the context of solving tasks is sketched in Figure 1.1.[14] It represents a cycle in which externalized knowledge, i.e., knowledge made retrievable, from an information system or cognitive knowledge of an expert is queried, retrieved, and processed to solve a task. Depending on the success, the cycle is completed and either new knowledge is externalized for later use or a modified query is made. A case of complete failure is not specifically represented in the model.

Outlining a comparable model for general knowledge acquisition that encompasses all forms of knowledge (including procedural and emotional knowledge) is not that easy. It is widely agreed that transferring knowledge, neither from person to person nor from medium to person can be seen as a process of a mere transfer of data and saving those data unchanged. It is always the processing in the recipient's cognitive structure that leads to the individual's knowledge. A royal road to knowledge acquisition that works with equal efficiency for all individuals does not exist. This may come across with general agreement in the case of complex contexts, but not in the case of supposedly simple data or facts. It should be taken into account that data and facts are always found in a theoretical context and that the completeness of comprehending data and facts correlates with the completeness of knowing the context.

---

14 We base the illustration on a well-known model proposed by *Probst* et al. for application to the corporate context, but correct and supplement it to account for as many forms of task-oriented knowledge acquisition as possible. For consistency reasons we use the terms "cognitive" and "externalized knowledge" instead of "implicit" and "explicit knowledge" (Probst/Raub/Romhardt: Managing knowledge).

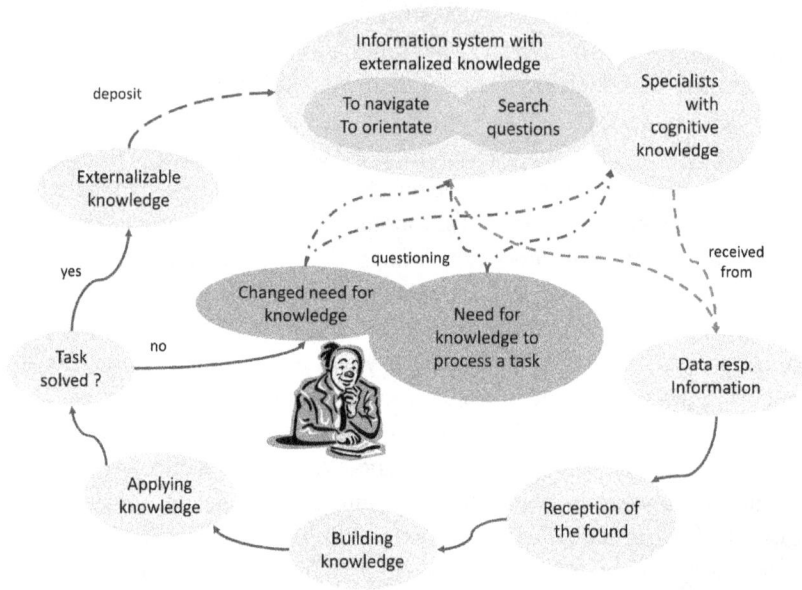

Fig. 1.1: Knowledge acquisition.

Currently, the so-called computer metaphor is used to establish a link between cognitive processes and artificial intelligence and the world of data networks as a new carrier of intelligence. The term computer metaphor shall be used here as a placeholder for all attempts to interpret the nature of human information processing by comparing it to a computer-algorithmic understanding of information. Undoubtedly, a creeping reinterpretation of established terms is taking place here under the premise of information technology processing, whereby the significance of the computer metaphor is assessed quite differently. The spectrum ranges from descriptions of an ongoing and inevitable developmental process to a manipulative tool for reinterpreting the fundamental value of cognitive performance.

It is worthwhile to look at the historical emergence of the computer metaphor, which can be traced in *Norbert Wiener's* book *Cybernetics or control and communication in the animal and the machine.*[15] In it, the term "cybernetics" is used for the first time to describe self-regulating systems of servomechanisms. There are linkages to automated navigation techniques, reliable communications technology, and artificial intelligence. Interesting is also the early parallelism of "living being" and "machine".

---

15 Wiener: Cybernetics or control and communication in the animal and the machine.

The importance that a metaphor can attain for the subject it interprets should not be underestimated. This can be illustrated by an example that has taken on a completely different dimension as a result of technical developments than the term still often used for it would suggest: tapping a telephone call. Analog telephone calls used an independent low-current power supply and could be seen as a temporary but proprietary connection between two subscribers, established via switching centers, first mechanically and later automatically. A considerable technical effort was necessary to realize the interception of such an analog telephone call. The situation is quite different with digital telephony via servers, where the data is available in storable form and is in this form part of the communication process. In this case, the data must be explicitly deleted or destroyed to prevent subsequent interception by third parties, which means that the effort is now to "avoid" a possible interception.

Basically, it can be assumed that the general understanding of technical processes always lags behind their development and is overlaid by their historically outdated metaphors. *Richard Sennett* points out the significant role of metaphors and their formative impact on imaginative and judgmental processes:

> Put another way, a metaphor creates a meaning grater than the sum of its parts, because the parts interact. The terms of a metaphor have meaning in relation to each other which they do not have apart. This is how metaphors may establish social relationships: the parts of the metaphor may be different social classes, or different roles in society. The whole creates the special meaning for the parts.[16]

Central to our discussion of the computer metaphor is the concept of information. Expressions formerly used rather metaphorically, such as knowledge storage, knowledge organization, or knowledge management, are given a direct information technology meaning here, which has led to the fact that today we speak of storing, retrieving and processing information in the brain. From this point of view, cognitive information processing is understood as a process just as it could be performed by computers using the *Turing model*. Consequently, there is source data that is input and then processed by an algorithm to generate the data to be output. The modification of the data here is done by the algorithm, which is the carrier of "intelligence" in the process. The data input and output operations themselves are generally not considered to be data modifying.

For communication processes, the computer metaphor results in a sender-receiver model that is in principle suitable for transmitting source data to the receiver without any affect on the data itself. Deviations here represent either in-

---

[16] Sennett: Authority, p. 78.

tended technical results or errors that can be avoided by taking suitable measures. This idea is most strikingly expressed by the so-called *Turing test*. In this test, questions are answered by an unknown entity. This entity can be a human being, or it can be a computer. If the interrogator is not able to identify from the answers given whether the conversation partner is the human or the computer, the computer is also assumed to have intelligence. Using such a criterion seems tempting at first glance. However, if this criterion is applied to living beings that participate in spatio-temporal events independently and in very individual ways, one may question whether this represents the entire spectrum of what intelligence is about.

Ergo, the computer metaphor does not work for cognitive processes. A brain, as already illustrated, cannot be considered as a system separated into hardware and software.

The dubiousness of taking the *Turing test*, based purely on behavioral observation, as a marker for attributing intelligence has been exposed by *John Searle* through his *Chinese room*[17] thought experiment. In this variant of the *Turing test*, the communication process is performed with a hidden communication partner in Chinese language. The hidden communication partner does not know Chinese, but has a set of rules which enables him to find and give out the correct answers. The set of rules, the "algorithm", creates the impression that the communication partner speaks Chinese, and the interrogator consequently assumes that the "system" really knows the language. In fact, it is the (human) creator of the set of rules who is proficient in the Chinese language, but not the one who gives out the answers.

The thought experiment exemplifies that a purely symbol-based manipulation is not sufficient to draw conclusions about content-related understanding or even the development of consciousness. In this sense, the *Chinese room* represents a clear refutation of the classical interpretation of the *Turing test*: semantic understanding (comprehension, insight, consciousness) cannot be inferred from witnessed behavior or syntactic manipulations.

The question of how meaning can be created from words is generally linked to the presence of consciousness. Without consciousness, symbol-based manipulation remains a mere syntactic process at the data level and does not produce any profound structured meaning. This, however, is repeatedly postulated by representatives of artificial intelligence.[18]

---

17 Searle: Minds, brains, and programs.
18 See on this question the video: On consciousness [YouTube].

Also frequently used are variants of the classic *Liar's paradox* "A Cretan says: 'All Cretans lie'" to sound out the possibilities and limits of artificial intelligence. A well-known variant of *Bertrand Russell* reads:

A man says, "I am lying."[19]

The correctness of the statement is as undecidable as all propositional paradoxes or antinomies. Does the issue of decidability have any relevance to the discussion of artificial intelligence? Actually, no. For if the system knows about the logical pitfalls of the paradox, it does not have to fall into despair, contrary to what some fictional or cinematic representations would like us to believe. Like us humans, an AI system can take on the attitude: All well and good, but where does it affect us? Logical arguments or scenarios of fundamental non-decidability cannot be invoked to counter the use of AI systems.

1.3 Intelligence and Artificial Intelligence

The linguistic proximity between the terms "intelligence" and "artificial intelligence" easily leads to the assumption that there is a close connection between the two in the sense that artificial intelligence is merely a specific manifestation of general intelligence. In fact, however, it is not about intelligence in general, but about "human" intelligence. We regard artificial intelligence and natural human intelligence as two independent phenomena whose relationship should be examined more closely in the context of addressing informational autonomy.

In many expositions of visionary promises about the potential of artificial intelligence, it is admitted that one cannot do justice to the concept of intelligence by one-dimensional descriptions or even by a single key value. At the same time, however, a narrowed interpretation is then made to bridge to artificial intelligence more easily. For example, the well-known AI advocate *Max Tegmark* has a characterization that seems quite innocuous at first:

Intelligence = ability to accomplish good goals[20]

---

19 "The simpliest form of this contradiction is afforded by the man who says 'I am lying;' if he is lying, he is speaking the truth, and vice versa." (Russell: Mathematical logic as based on the theory of types, p. 222).
20 Tegmark: Life 3.0, p. 50.

Here, the concept is broken down and thus limited to only one criterion: action-orientedness. Even the focus on problem solving, a quality that AI proponents used to emphasize, can be at best labeled a "good goal". This reminds us of the *Turing test*, which has an important meaning as a food for thought. This may be sufficient for the definition of machine intelligence, but not for the definition of the complex concept of intelligence related to space- and time-bound living beings with their individual experience spaces.

Other factors, for instance emotional ones, which are meanwhile regarded as being constitutive for the definition of a comprehensive concept of intelligence, remain unconsidered by such a view.[21] It is only consequent when artificial intelligence is then no longer explained as task-oriented or functional at all, but simply understood as "non-biological" intelligence.[22] Thus, it is easy to understand that no effort is made to arrive at a specific understanding of information.[23] The alignment with digital data storage or biological genetic material in the sense of "storing and reading out" is deemed to be sufficient for cognitive information processing.

Figure 1.2 illustrates the influencing factors, which, by interacting, reveal the similarities and differences between the two concepts of intelligence and artificial intelligence.

For human intelligence, two paths of influence can be identified, which, and here the figure must not be misunderstood, are not disjoint to each other, but interact with each other depending on the initial situation. There is one path that uses logic and rationality for knowledge acquisition and thus represents the type of intelligence which is used for action. The second path uses results of prior learning and experience; learning and experience may themselves be associated with logic and rationality. The action enabled by logic and rationality can also be influenced by emotion and empathy. Rational intelligence and emotional intelligence can thus be interconnected for a single action. In both cases, a processing of cognitive information takes place.

Artificial intelligence is, on the other hand, created and influenced by logic, rationality, and algorithms. If artificial intelligence is learning-based, perhaps even experience-based, the results obtained will be incorporated into the coded information, which will then cause the action to be executed.

The analogies made in the context of artificial intelligence between the brain (cognition), artificial neural networks, and *Turing machines* use the computer metaphor to neglect the peculiarities of biological systems and thus reduce cog-

---

21 See Damasio: Descartes' Error.
22 Tegmark: Life 3.0, p. 39.
23 Tegmark does not take "information" into account for the "terminology cheat sheet", which is intended to provide a clarification of the key terms discussed (Tegmark: Life 3.0, p. 39).

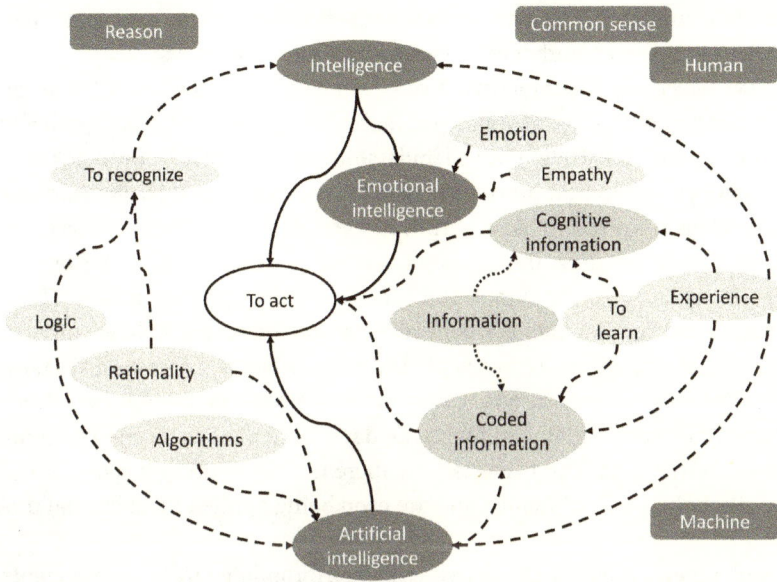

Fig. 1.2: Cognitive functions.

nitive functions to a function that can be considered purely mechanistic. Again, *Tegmark* can be quoted here:

> As mentioned earlier, Turing also proved something even more profound in that 1936 paper of his: that if a type of computer can perform a certain bare minimum set of operations, then it's *universal* in the sense that given enough resources, it can do anything that any other computer can do. He showed that his Turing machine was universal, and connecting back more closely to physics, we've just seen that this family of universal computers also includes objects as diverse as a network of NAND gates and a network of interconnected neurons. Indeed, Stephen Wolfram has argued that *most* non-trivial physical systems, from weather systems to brains, would be universal computers if they could be made arbitrarily large and long-lasting.[24]

What is suggested here is the equation of a computer, in the sense of the universal *Turing machine* (and based on binary logic), with a biological brain (which has neural connections and is connected to other vegetative systems), the justification of which we have already rejected. Regardless, however, it is questionable whether human—or more generally—biological cognition is controlled by the brain alone,

---

24 Tegmark: Life 3.0, pp. 64–65.

which would completely disregard neural connections with other organs. It must be left to further research and development which view will prevail.

For now, we can only summarize: Even if the neural basis of cognitive information processing of biological organisms (according to *Tegmark* metaphorically the hardware or the "substrate") can be understood in terms of a *Turing machine*[25], this would not yet mean that processing also takes place as in a *Turing machine*. A *Turing machine* is known to use algorithms. Even if these are regarded as trainable and capable of learning, the direct comparability would result only from the ability of self-organization, or autopoietic behavior of biological organisms. These concepts and resulting viewpoints will be revisited and discussed in later contexts.

Here, we first stay with the concept of algorithm, which has become a key term for artificial intelligence and the application of the computer metaphor. The advent of the algorithm went hand in hand with the development of automated computing systems. Today, algorithmic models are increasingly entering discussions of cognition, thought, and rationality, and are even being applied to emotional processes.

Many of our everyday familiar activities can be formulated by the components of an algorithm: Complex processes can be broken down into defined individual steps, and the conditions for the defined individual steps of the process can be precisely queried. Algorithmic processes are often associated with the idea of optimization and efficiency. Following the steps specified by the algorithm is supposed to ensure the least amount of time, the shortest path, and the lowest resource usage while maintaining the system's full reliability.

People are increasingly confronted with the idea of efficiency, especially in their professional lives, and may transfer it consciously or unconsciously to everyday activities, this leading to a fatal development: The personal claim to perform every action under efficiency aspects works against a balanced and happy life, also because it is precisely the breakouts from the idea of efficiency that offer room for happiness, and creativity.

An example: Imagine the domestic preparation of breakfast for several people, say, for a family of five. The process requires that a sequence of individual steps be followed, and personal preferences must be respected, or queried. Once the steps are recorded—it can be a delightful exercise to try this in detail one time—the same pattern could be followed every morning, creating the illusion of being able to act absolutely "error-free" from now on. The fact is that modifications would be un-

---

25 It is significant that at this point it is terminologically necessary to resort to a computer metaphorical expression, as for physiological processes no differentiation into hardware and software can be made (see Kluge/Singer: Hirnforschung).

avoidable: Let's say some of the food supplies have run out and need to be refilled, or a new jar of jam needs to be opened. Besides, not all family members are always present, or guests may be invited for breakfast, resulting in a higher number of people to be served. In addition, breakfast preferences may have changed. Something may be spilled that has to be wiped up first, or breakfast may take place in a different environment. In all cases, the algorithm must be adjusted. And yes, for all these cases one could make adjustments or extensions in the algorithm, but never reach a final state of the algorithm, because only already known or predictable conditions and elements can be incorporated and only certain considerations regarding probabilities can be made.

In reality, the property of cognitive plasticity, meaning the changeability of brain structures within dynamic boundaries (Chapter 2.2) enables us to deal with deviating situations, even without having to have integrated them into the process by prior interrogation. Characteristics and their specified boundaries are known to create order. Recognizing and including the in-between or the context are an important basis for dynamics and creativity, and thus a basis for neural plasticity as well.

As shown by the breakfast example, a particular value of the algorithmic approach can be seen in understanding the sequences of actions and their underlying decision logic. The introduction of computers into everyday school life was originally intended to promote precisely this value. As we know today, this did not quite work out. What was promoted was not so much thinking in algorithms, but above all using algorithm products in the context of an IT (entertainment) infrastructure. It is to be hoped that this experiment, which can initially be described as a failed one, will find a turning point with the upcoming generation of digital natives—new pedagogical approaches do exist. This would be necessary to ensure that the principles of algorithmic and logical thinking become firmly established in everyday thinking and can thus be regarded as a reliable basis for developing information literacy.

There is no need to mention that humans do not depend on the existence of formulated algorithms. Currently, however, there is a discussion about whether human actions are possibly based on internal, i.e., "mental", or even "emotional" algorithms. This would mean that a present particular situation (like making breakfast) triggers a cognitive processing routine that takes into account all the necessary steps and translates them into the actions required. If this were the case, the routine would be showing a degree of flexibility that algorithms aren't typically ascribed. In a complex process like preparing breakfast, there are modules that allow one and only one order; for instance, you open the refrigerator "before" you take out the butter and pour coffee into a cup "before" you drink the coffee from it. However, there are modules where the chronological sequence is not mandatory, for example, taking cups and plates from the cupboard, taking cutlery from the drawer, or preparing boiled eggs. Do you always use your left hand or your right hand for a single task? Do you let spontaneous circumstances influence your task? Those who often prepare breakfast will have experienced that interchangeable modules are indeed interchanged every now and then, and different people will follow different procedures anyway. Also, every now and then you will have found yourself choosing an order that is actually inappropriate. How unpredictable situations are integrated into such an internal algorithm also requires some explanation. Whether all this speaks for or against the idea of existing mentally triggered, internal algorithms will not play a further role at this point.

Basically, an algorithm can be characterized by: generality, clearness and unambiguity, feasibility, finiteness and termination, as well as determinacy. These properties may formally define what constitutes an algorithm; however, what this implies for the computation of complex problems remains an open question—a question that is also central to the performance of artificial intelligence systems. *Roger Penrose* denies the possibility of algorithmizing processes of understanding: "Real understanding is something outside computation."[26] He relates his answer to *Gödel's* incompleteness theorems and to the role of consciousness for a general understanding:

> [...] but I had this nagging feeling about Gödel's theorem, which I'd heard a little bit about before, and I thought it was saying that there are these things that we can't know. Then when I heard this lecture it wasn't that at all: he said you can know these things, it's just that you can't know them simply by following the rules of some formal system. You have to have some method of getting at truth which is reliable, but different; you have to bring your consciousness, your understanding, to bear on the problem. So it's not following the rules: it's knowing why the rules work which gives you an insight beyond the rules itself.[27]

An essential part of algorithms is the querying of conditions to get to a set of branches through which it is possible to successfully handle different challenges. The simplest pattern used in this process is a yes/no decision. The planning of such a decision tree requires a thorough analysis of the expected scenarios. In view of the effort required for this, it is not surprising that great expectations are placed in concepts dealing with the ability of algorithms to learn—and for which a variety of methods and techniques have been developed in the meantime.

It is also these learning algorithms that deserve special attention in the context of informational autonomy. More crucial than the question of trainability of the situations to be detected is whether the algorithms can improve themselves in their

---

26 Blackmore: Conversations on consciousness, p. 173.
27 Blackmore: Conversations on consciousness, p. 175.

range of actions. In this context, self-improvement does not only mean that the existing programming code is free of errors, but also that new performance features are created by new programming code for cases that have not been considered so far. Learning would thus allow the algorithm to decide on its own to make changes to the programming code already in place.

The computer metaphor seen as a tool for reinterpreting established concepts also has consequences for the meaning of "learning" in phrases such as "learning algorithm" or "deep learning". Combining "learning", "genetic", and "adaptive" with "algorithm", "neural network", or "programming" yields a number of other common expressions, including "neural Turing machine" (*DeepMind*).

In classical computer science, a program is defined as:

Program = algorithm + data

When speaking of the learning ability of algorithms, this traditional scheme is extended:

Program = algorithm + data + domain knowledge[28]

Here, domain knowledge is not bound to cognitive properties—we will later refer to this as "context" again—but is explicitly seen as dependent on formal data modeling. The application of background knowledge, in the form of a suitable data structure, can be seen as essential in this regard. Machine learning can be characterized in more detail by considering the components of the systems involved. For example, in addition to processing algorithms internally, programs for action control must have the ability to interpret their external world, to receive, process, and send signals, and they must be able to influence the external world through actions. We identify the following principles for algorithms:

– Besides the programming code of the algorithm and the data, domain knowledge is represented in specific schemes, respectively.
– Algorithms are processing rules, which include, in particular, a query logic.
– To process the queries, entered data is read or conditions detected by sensors (patterns, behavior, etc.) are recognized.
– By using neural networks or other deep learning methods, the range of conditions to be recognized is increased.
– The processing of the conditions for the queries results in steps for the execution of an action.

---

28 For background on this approach, see Kókai: Erfolge und Probleme evolutionärer Algorithmen, p. 17 (author's translation).

- There are options for planning and changing the strategy in order to achieve a predefined goal.
- There are options which allow the programming code to modify itself autonomously and to save the changes for future operations.

For each of the principles, it needs to be clarified whether learning ability can be coupled with it. This will determine how they can contribute to an overall system which, in the sense of an autonomous machine, not only processes specialized tasks, but can also move in a complex environment with self-generated and growing performance. The most far-reaching learning ability would be to achieve artificial creativity.

When applying the computer metaphor, human thought and action processes are simulated by algorithms, with the algorithms either supporting them or replacing them completely. We are increasingly influenced by these processes in our everyday lives and tend to be less and less aware of it. However, this fact should not mislead to the converse argument that the algorithmic approach represents a serious model for cognitive processes.

1.4 Informational Autonomy and Freedom

What can be stated about the position of thought leaders and advocates of modern humanism toward the ideas of transhumanism? So far, the statements of these groups have been rather reserved or even dismissive. Instead, a digital humanism is proposed—or should we call it humanistic digitalism? In an interview, *Julian Nida-Rümelin*, a German philosopher and Vice-Chair of the *German Ethics Council*, notes:

> Question: With AI, we are on the threshold of becoming godlike creators of new beings. Are we able to do that and should we be allowed to do that?
>
> *Nida-Rümelin*: We don't, nor can we, and if we could, we wouldn't be allowed to. It is the software developers themselves who are usually convinced that artificial intelligences, including humanoid robots, have no mental properties, do not pursue intentions, have no desires, do not feel pain, and do not even recognize or decide anything.[29]

Maybe this is an expression of a well-considered socio-philosophical position. But perhaps it is also evidence of misjudgment in the face of an interest-driven dynamic

---

29 Koch/Riecke: Deutscher Wirtschaftsbuchpreis (author's translation); see also Nida-Rümelin/ Weidenfeld: Digitaler Humanismus.

to establish new social structures with significantly less humanistic elements. Yet there is no clear sign of transhumanist ideas as a dangerous path with the potential to prepare totalitarian structures. The question of what drives social progress is often either not asked for, or is answered implicitly in favor of digitization with all its inhumane side effects.

Roles and functions of people in information technology contexts can be described as creators, contributors, beneficiaries, or victims. Through the Age of Enlightenment, people acquired a self-understanding in the sense of being autonomous subjects with an ego comprehension, tying decisions and actions to rational thought; this would particularly emphasize the role of the creator or contributor. The shift currently observed in favor of individuals who are being functionalized as part of a swarm formation would more likely emphasize the role of the beneficiary or victim. Freely acting subjects would become objects, and this might even pave the way for a totalitarian view of man.

There has always been a willingness to let others do the thinking and doing for oneself. Until now this leaning could be seen as a kind of convenience and mostly understood with the reservation of later accountability.

However, recent trends signal that a new level may have been reached where decisions are voluntarily and consciously delegated to machines and algorithms. Why is there this tendency, both by the individual and by the envisaged developments in information technology, to voluntarily give up informational self-determination, when informational self-determination actually has an explicitly high legal status? Is a foreign determination by machines and algorithms perceived as less alarming than a determination by other humans? Remarkable is that not even insufficient knowledge of the algorithms involved—whether at the basic functional or the decision detail level—changes anything about this attitude.[30]

Ethical considerations related to the question of responsibility quickly skip the fundamental level and focus on comparatively artificial decision-making situations, such as weighing human losses in risk situations posed by autonomous vehicles (stroller or senior).[31] Such views and approaches open up a field of conflict between cognitive informational autonomy and the state which we will later characterize as informational totalitarianism.

---

30 See O'Neil: Weapons of math destruction; see also the contributions of the platform *Algorithm Watch* (AlgorithmWatch [Website]).

31 See the recommendations of the German *Ethics Commission on Automated and Connected Driving* (BMVI : Bericht der Ethik-Kommission). Here, for example, the weighing of the value of individual lives was initially prohibited, but not the weighing of which action has the higher probability of minimizing casualties. See also the activities of the *German Ethics Council*: Deutscher Ethikrat [Website].

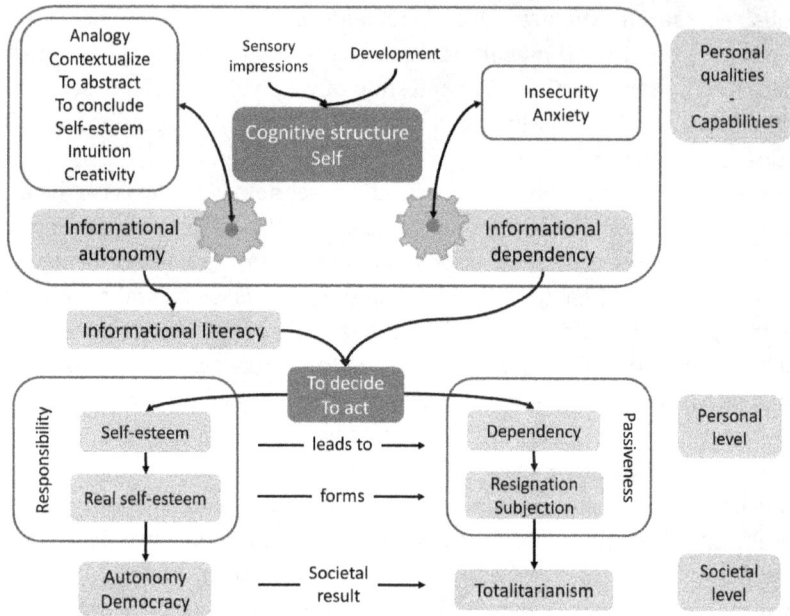

Fig. 1.3: Informational autonomy.

Figure 1.3 provides an initial overview of the connections between various key concepts. We will discuss the individual elements in more detail later in this book.

2 Cognitive Information and Knowledge Processing

> Neither does knowledge consist of a mysterious physical substance called information, which is arbitrarily transferred back and forth between differently structured systems, nor do these systems simply store knowledge, nor does it make sense to regard knowledge and information as raw materials or even commodities. Knowledge generates, by cognitive and communication means, the framework of meaning for the phenomena we encounter in the world.
>
> Jürgen Riethmüller[32]

2.1 Dimensions of Information

The concept of information knows many fields of reference and contexts of use. Information plays a role in cognitive psychology, media and communication theory, information technology, and biology, among others. Today, it is no longer clear whether it is still "one" concept with "one" core meaning, or whether it has already become a homonym with different meanings. A common "core" meaning is at best still recognizable etymologically or metaphorically.

Information Theory

Just as information technology has become more and more influential, the idea that information is something measurable and quantifiable has also become more important. This idea traces back to the research of *Shannon* and *Weaver*, who studied the properties of signal transmission in communications already in the 1940s.[33] In their well-known information theory, the possibilities and limitations of the transmission of information are explored, including conditions when channels are noisy or bit patterns are not completely transmitted. Information theory uses mathematical methods, in the sense of probability interpretation, to calculate the content level of a transmitted information. The theory is not making any statement about a single message, or a single piece of information, or the isolated state of an information system, and certainly not about its meaning. Rather, it always looks at multiple states of the system and makes statements about the transition from one state to another. The goal is to minimize the effort required to successfully transmit

---

32 Riethmüller: Der graue Schwan, back cover (author's translation).
33 Shannon: A mathematical theory of communication, Shannon/Weaver: Mathematical theory of communication; see also Capurro: Theorie der Botschaft.

https://doi.org/10.1515/9783110693744-002

information while maximizing the probability of sending it without errors. The digital world of global networks that we live in would be inconceivable without information theory.

Thus, it seems obvious to apply the information-theoretical inventory of sender, receiver, and message transmission to human communication as well. Very quickly, however, such attempts lead to rather simplistic models, which are sometimes characterized as "pipeline metaphor".[34] According to the pipeline metaphor, the information to be sent is transmitted using language as the information carrier; in other words, communication connects two brains ("containers") via the transport system of language. Successful communication thus requires the correct encoding of information into speech on the side of the sender and the correct decoding of information from speech on the receiver's side. Other influencing factors are not significant for the process.

What the model of the pipeline metaphor suggests is that there is a substance "information" that can be extracted from cognitive structures, transmitted more or less without loss, and then reloaded into other cognitive structures.

However, in our view, it is an unacceptable simplification to regard information as a quantifiable substance and to treat information transmission merely as a transport problem. The following example will illustrate that the pipeline metaphor ignores essential factors; in particular, it disregards the importance that context has for any kind of encoding/decoding of information. A schematic drawing is to be made to describe a route from the central station to the theater in a foreign city. On a city map, this could look something like in Figure 2.1. By specifying the sequence of digits

    10111100

with the meaning

    1 = turn right
    0 = turn left

the route from the station to the theater can be fully described. Without the specified context, though, the sequence of digits "10111100" is meaningless or at least open to interpretation, i.e., based on a different reference model, a completely different message could be transmitted with the same sequence of digits.

---

34 Antos: Mythen, Metaphern, Modelle, pp. 96–99. Note that we use conduit metaphor and pipeline metaphor synonymously.

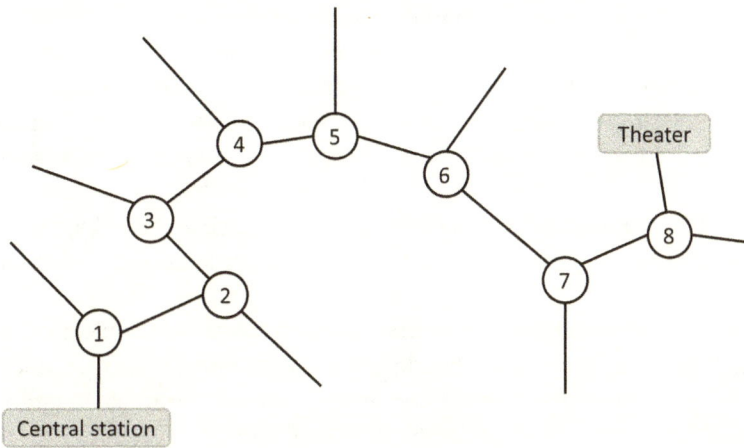

Fig. 2.1: Route from the central station to the theater.

Information in other Related Fields

In addition to the communications-technical or information-theoretical scope of the concept of information, there are other fields of reference, each of which has its own understanding of information.[35] The most important are:

- The historical dimension (creating, teaching, conceptualizing), which can also be understood as an etymological derivation of the word information. This dimension is made use of when the goal is to trace the supposed roots of the concept of information.
- The colloquial dimension (information understood as: message, news) with all its manifestations in the modern media landscape. One characteristic of this understanding, for instance, is to coin a motto such as "information not entertainment".
- The information technology dimension with its extension to so-called information processing within computer science, up to its use in knowledge databases in the context of big data or artificial intelligence.[36] This dimension has been largely responsible for the quantification of information as well as for ascribing a material value to it and viewing it as a commodity.

---

35 See Capurro: Information, Capurro/Hjørland: The concept of information, Capurro: Was ist Information?, Henrichs: Information, Wenzlaff: Vielfalt der Informationsbegriffe.
36 For an introduction, see Topsøe: Informationstheorie.

- The biological dimension, which understands hereditary material (DNA) as an information carrier and responsible for the development of life[37], or as the immune system with its exchange of information to fight off pathogens.
- The communication dimension in the form of the exchange of information between communication partners (human-human, human-medium, or human-machine).
- The cognitive dimension of human information processing, including the intake of information by the senses and its subsequent processing in the brain.

The consideration of information as a commodity and as an economic good is omitted here.[38] It should nonetheless be added that the gathering and exploitation of information plays a central role in other areas as well, for example in police investigative work or in the world of intelligence services.[39]

When looking at the cognitive dimension of information, it is interesting to note that the term "information", when used without any further given context, always refers to its cognitive understanding, perhaps supplemented by media- and communication-oriented aspects. The concept of information as a whole is in a field of tension between various aspects:

- capability to objectify (data aspect);
- possibility of media storage (substrate aspect);
- linkage to thought processes (cognition aspect);
- linkage to a communication-related consensus and a binding interpretation attached to it (communication aspect).

Our discussion of the dimensions of the concept of information shall be concluded with a small thought experiment, establishing a connection between information, ordered states and an information content related to them: 100 different screws are in a box and it is assumed that there is a common understanding of the information content of this state: screws, different ones, unsorted, in a container (box). If the same screws were well sorted in a screw organizer box, for example sorted by length, thickness, material and head type, this condition would be attributed a significantly higher information content—at least when searching for a specific screw.

---

37 Eigen: Wie entsteht Information?
38 See Pfister: Ware oder öffentliches Gut?, Georgy: Der Wert von Information.
39 Worth mentioning in this context is the thriller *The Inquisitor*, which treats this aspect, albeit in a very specific interpretation. The name of the protagonist's company is "Information Retrieval" (Smith: The inquisitor).

This raises the question: Is there a dependency between the information content and the state of order in which the information is presented? This view is held by many who see information as the antithesis of entropy (a measure of the level of information content). And does even the type of objects matter? Assuming this, would the relationship between state of order and information content also apply to books, for example? Which of the following states of order would then be ascribed a higher or lower information content?

– arrangement by the height of the spine;
– arrangement by color of the cover;
– arrangement by the last name of the (first) author;
– arrangement according to a content-based scheme.

Regardless of the state of sort order, would the book's content play a role in determining the information content, or even the prior knowledge of the person interested?

2.2 Perception and Reality Construction

Cognitive processes serve to engage with the external world. However, before becoming the object of thought processes and cognitive information processing, the external world must first be perceived through our senses. Following the analogy of the pipeline metaphor, there is also a highly simplified model for the process of perception that predominantly focuses on its transportation aspects. According to this model, information from the outside world is passively taken in by the sensory organs and then processed in the brain. Visual perception is thought of as a photographing of reality.

Reasonable doubts about the passivity of perception were raised at the latest with the findings of *Gestalt* psychology. Experiments with visual and optical illusions, like the illusions of hidden faces, impressively demonstrate that the sensory stimuli perceived undergo complex processing in the brain, and that a passive model of information reception cannot explain the perceptual process on its own. On the basis of cognitive processes, the brain arrives at statements about reality that cannot be verified by other (for example, physical) methods of measurement or observation.[40]

---

40 For an impressive compilation of examples, see Hoffman: Visual Intelligence and *Hoffman's* website with animations (Hoffman: Donald D. Hoffman [Website]); see also Lanners: Illusions, Caglioti: Symmetriebrechung und Wahrnehmung, Rock: The logic of perception.

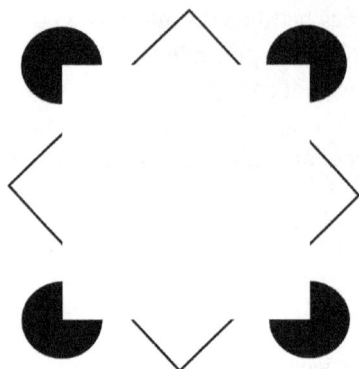

Fig. 2.2: Kanizsa figure.

In Figure 2.2, which is modeled after the well-known *Kanizsa triangle*, you can see a bright quadrilateral resting on underlying patterns. In fact, the edges of the seemingly superimposed quadrilateral are not present; the contours are generated solely by internal cognitive processing. Phenomena like this vividly illustrate that perception cannot be conceived as a passive process.

Information Processing and Interpretation

Because perception is an active process, the nature of information processing should be defined more precisely. There are at least two types of information processing to be distinguished:

1. Cognitive information processing triggered or influenced by sensory perceptions. This process takes place exclusively in our brain. In principle, it is also possible for this type of information processing to occur without being triggered by sensory stimuli, as is the case with dreaming. In both cases, information processing can be described as self-referential.

2. Cognitive information processing situated in a communication context. Here, additional information-processing instances need to be considered, which may add further information and hence possibly influence information processing. A conversational situation in which the aim is to communicate something to each other or to cause an action to be taken can only succeed if there is mutual reference. Information processing in a communication context does not work without feedback.

As a first approximation, the nature of information processing can be conceived as an act of interpretation. Interpretation is often characterized as "subjective" and is thus given a negative connotation, especially in contrast to a model of information processing in information theory which sees itself as objective.[41] What is often overlooked is that interpretation is done (a) as part of a process of understanding and (b) by human beings who, as living beings, are endowed with consciousness and ego comprehension. Subjectivity is indeed an inseparable part of understanding, but is not a mandatory property of the results obtained from processes of understanding.

Following the phenomenological view of *Edmund Husserl*, a parallel can be drawn between data and interpretation with tones and music.[42] Mere tones are not yet music; they are only tones played in succession. Only through the connection made by consciousness, music is created from the individual tones. This way, consciousness, yet listening to the fading sounds, relates the just perceived tones to each other and already anticipates the following tones, and so forth. Reading and listening to text, perceiving visual stimuli, and the interpretation processes that build on them to create meaning can be understood analogously. In all cases, it is the brain's cognitive performance that creates a more structurally complex state. Prerequisite for this is the existence of a temporal or spatial structure in which perceptions can take place. Visual perception, for instance, requires being aware of the own position in relation to the space around you, while the perception of music requires a temporal structure with a sense of "before", "now", and "after".[43]

This kind of interpretation clearly goes beyond the principles of *Gestalt* perception. In order to studying visual perception, *Gestalt* psychology experiments were reduced to comparatively abstract forms serving to isolate the examined *Gestalt* effects. Overloading the experiments with further contexts of meaning would have complicated this study.[44] However, exactly those contexts of meaning do exist and cannot be seen detached from perception. When looking at a coin lying flat on a table, for example, we mentally recognize not only its visible upper side, but also its unseen reverse side, as well as its value as a means of payment, the material, and possibly other attributes as well. *Edmund Husserl* calls this comprehensive interpretation an "intentional analysis", which grasps the core essence of the object:

> Intentional analysis is thus something altogether different from analysis in the ordinary sense. The life of consciousness is neither a mere aggregate of data, nor a heap of psychic atoms, or a whole composed of elements united through gestalt-like qualities [Gestaltqua-

---

41 See Umstätter: Die Skalierung von Information, Wissen und Literatur.
42 Husserl: Husserliana. Bd. 10, p. 23.
43 See Gibson: The perception of the visual world, Gombrich: Art and illusion.
44 See Metzger: Laws of seeing, Arnheim: Art and visual perception.

litäten]. This is true also of pure introspective psychology, as a parallel to transcendental phenomenology. Intentional analysis is the disclosure of the actualities and potentialities in which objects constitute themselves as perceptual units. Furthermore, all perceptual analysis takes place in the transition from real events to the intentional horizons suggested by them.[45]

Recognizing a sequence of tones as music usually does not require a complicated theoretical framework; differentiating music according to style, type of composition, or expressiveness, however, does. The interpretation of data, in contrast, always requires a reference to theory, at least to context. Music seems to appeal more strongly to a deeper layer of cognitive familiarity than it does for data.

Many of the activities of interpretation by cognitive structures that are triggered by perceptions take place in a communication-feedback manner, as people exchange information about their perceptions, for example, when they experience a situation at the same time. In analogy to the distinction between tones and music, a differentiation can be made between the rational notion of cognitive information processing and states of meditating or dreaming. Meditating and dreaming are usually less associated with the goal of communication-driven understanding or knowledge. However, since these are also cognitive processes, they cannot be completely separated from the other cognitive operations. For *Varela*, *Thompson*, and *Rosch*, meditation has the function of transitioning the cognitive system from its uncontrolled, continuous activity to a state of rest that induces relaxation and restores us to the readiness to perform again.[46] It is well known that dreams, which mostly take place without any direct sensory input from the outside world, can have positive effects on our mental performance and emotional processing.

Cognitive Structures and Reality Construction

Information processing, interpretation, or even intentional analysis are processes that depend on the existence of a cognitive structure. Our brains do not store away single pieces of information in isolation, but link them to other associated information. This structuring is important for building our individual realm of experience, from which we draw, amongst others, the ability to remember or to make plans, as well as to act autonomously—all of which properties that are also part of the human strategy for self-preservation.

45 Husserl: The Paris lectures, p. 19.
46 See Varela/Thompson/Rosch: The embodied mind, Emrich: Die Bedeutung des Konstruktivismus für Emotion, Traum und Imagination.

This cognitive structure allows us to actively process information and generate new information. Its purpose is to help us understand and actively participate in the world.

Any cognition-based generation of information is structure-determined; only what is structurally determined is also believed to be recognized and ergo will be recognized. Structural determination is based on the fact that all thought and action processes in the development of a human being leave their individual traces (ontogenesis). The traces overlap with the genetically already existing structures (phylogenesis). These structures are not just abstract memory patterns but the physiological changes in the neurological meshwork of all the neurons involved.[47]

One way of consolidating structural determinacy is through exercises and repetition. A good example of this are action sequences that run "as if on their own" after a certain amount of training, without having to be consciously controlled by the head: Cycling, a slice in tennis, a topspin in table tennis, or shifting gears while driving a car. And, cognitive thought processes also work with this structure-building training effect.

The process of structural determination can be described as open and dynamic, even open to the end. Also, repetitions may be accompanied by small alterations or malfunctions. Structural determination does not mean running a program in a strictly algorithmic way, but rather acting in adaptable structures; once structures have been created, they still can be changed within dynamic limits. This so-called plasticity of the brain also enables changes in its physiological structure.[48] On the one hand, neural plasticity is—to a certain extent—able to compensate for impairments caused by illness or injury; on the other hand, this reorganization also opens the way to the new and unfamiliar without having to give up the orientation provided by structural determinacy. *Humberto Maturana* calls this property "structural drift"[49]:

> Yes, we are structurally determined systems, but we have a plastic structure that is constantly changing. Our plastic structural changes go one way or another depending on how we live. Thus, we are someone else at every moment. We are continuously changing. You are changing right now, I am changing right now. You are changing right now in a way that is conditioned by the interaction between you and me at that particular moment. The same is true for me. But we humans do not live in our physicality, we live in a relational domain. More than that, we not only live in a relational domain, but are human beings with a physicality that

---

47 On the dynamic interrelation between thought and action, mind and physical corporeality, see Calvin: The cerebral symphony, Calvin/Ojemann: Conversations with Neil's brain, Young: Philosophy and the brain.

48 For an introduction, see Schäfers: Gehirn und Lernen – Plastizität.

49 Maturana: Kognition.

dynamically and continuously adapts to our way of life, and our way of life, in turn, changes our physicality. We exist in a continuous dynamic.[50]

Structural determinacy has far-reaching consequences for the possibilities and limitations of cognitively created information. Only what finds its way into the cognitive structure via sensory impressions (perceptual process) and is subsequently processed there in a receptive process can also be recognized. This process of perception takes place all the time and uninterruptedly within every cognitive structure and constructs in us what we regard as reality. Not least, the phenomena studied by *Gestalt* psychology (Figure 2.2) suggest regarding perceptions as hypotheses about the environment arising from a cognitive construction process— perception being a construct:

> Brains fundamentally cannot represent the world; "they must be constructive" both in terms of their functional organization and in terms of their task, which is to create behavior that enables the organism to survive in its environment. The latter guarantees that the constructs generated by the brain are not arbitrary, even if they do not (cannot) represent the world.[51]

When the constructivist and brain physiologist *Gerhard Roth* claims that constructs "are not arbitrary" due to their vital function, this is plausible, but by no means a satisfactory answer to the fundamental epistemological problem of what we can know at all about so-called reality, about the world out there. The question of the degree of correspondence between the external world and the individual inner image must remain open. Figure 2.3 therefore distinguishes between true reality and actual reality.[52]

True reality (the external world) is objective and transphenomenal, that is, it exists independently of us humans and independently of our perception. True reality is withdrawn from perception and can only be postulated ontologically. Examples are all natural phenomena that existed before humanity and will continue to exist in the future. Actual reality is the phenomenal world that directly affects the individual's experience and in which they can act. In other words, actual reality is true reality as being perceived. Actual reality is not directly given, but is the result of a cognitive construction based on sensory impressions. Thus, the knowledge of true reality is the result of a construction of reality, cognitively generated by the individual.

The statements and consequences of this representation of perception and the construction of reality are in clear contradiction to the classical empirical episte-

---

50 Maturana: Neurophilosophie, p. 162 (author's translation).
51 Roth: Das Gehirn und seine Wirklichkeit, p. 21 (author's translation).
52 The presentation leans on Stadler/Kruse: Der radikale Konstruktivismus, p. 97.

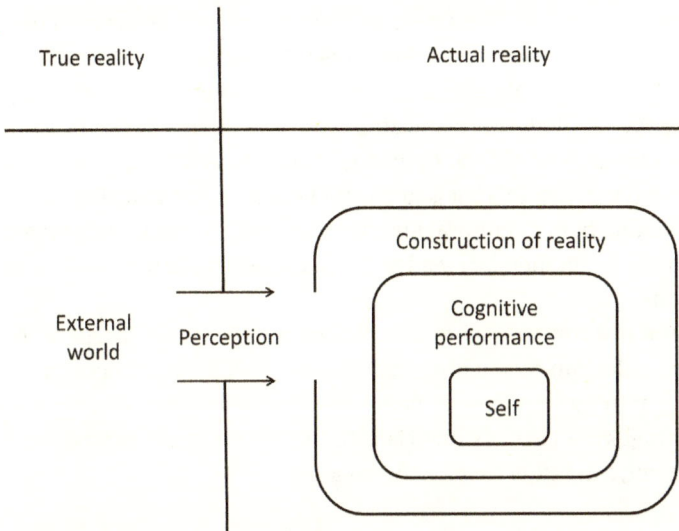

Fig. 2.3: The individual and the world.

mological model, according to which the correctness of a scientific statement can be determined independently of the observer. Statements about the external world are empirically verifiable or at least falsifiable by addressing questions to the real external world. It is often overlooked that an interpretive scheme is essential not only for setting up a theory, but also for formulating questions, planning and conducting an experiment, and especially for analyzing and interpreting its outcome. The history of (natural) sciences is full of examples of such model-dependent statements about the "real" world.

One caveat to the reality construction model is the solipsism objection.[53] In its intensified form, the metaphysical solipsism, it says that the self is the only version of reality existing at all. Nothing outside of our own consciousness exists, not even another consciousness. Other interpretations assume that meaning is determined solely by the individual's states of consciousness (methodological solipsism). However, these inferences are flawed because although the structurally determined construction of reality produces an individual outcome, the conditions for that construction do involve communicative interactions with other people. We observe and learn at the same time and communicate about these perceptions within a social and cultural community. This already prevents us (apart from certain pathological cases) from isolating in a world of our own and from allowing

---

53 See Nüse et al.: Über die Erfindung/en des radikalen Konstruktivismus.

this world to be the only valid. These interactions are precisely the reason why our perceptions may be congruent, even though as individuals we each construct our own reality. Structural coupling through common experience in the same reference domains, together with communication processes, leads to similarity in the structural determinacy of different persons. And if a certain section of the world is collectively perceived, this leads to a similar construction of reality. Different socialization, education, or cultural identification, which entails a divergent structural determinacy, can therefore lead to different constructions of reality for specific perceptions.

The assumptions of constructivism also change the classical concept of the observer. In the classical understanding, the observer is considered neutral, an objective participant in an experiment, who is cognitively mapping what is happening in the external world. In constructivism, the observer can no longer be seen as a passive recipient, but rather as an active creator:

> If one realizes that science in principle cannot explain anything independent of the observer, then assumptions of reality do not play a role anymore; they are even completely superfluous! There is something pleasantly liberating in this, because the superfluous enchants, but does nothing essential, so that one neither needs it nor misses it.[54]

There is no cognitive engagement with the external world without an observer who is also a creator. In the context of radical constructivism, an "internal" observer is distinguished from an "external" observer.[55] Here, the internal observer generates certainty about the existence of the own self together with all own acts of perception and thinking, while the external observer draws conclusions about the environment, its living beings, and their behavior. Internal states are not accessible to the external observer; only the internal observer can distinguish between the self and the environment.

The internal observer thus creates cognitive awareness.[56] This awareness makes it possible to distinguish between those states that were triggered due to sensory perception and those that were generated solely due to internal cognitive processes, such as fantasies, dreams or meditation:

---

54 Maturana/Lippe (eds.): Was ist erkennen, p. 67 (author's translation); on the concept of the observer, see also Maturana: Kognition, pp. 110–112.
55 Schmidt: Der radikale Konstruktivismus, p. 19.
56 On consciousness, see Calvin: The cerebral symphony, Chalmers: The puzzle of conscious experience, Roth: Das Gehirn und seine Wirklichkeit, Changeux/Connes: Conversations on mind, matter, and mathematics.

Consciousness is the brain's "intrinsic signal" for mastering, or having mastered a new problem (whether sensorimotor, motor, or internal-cognitive) and creating new neural networks for it; it is the "characteristic feature" for being able to distinguish these states from others.[57]

2.3 Knowledge and Knowledge Models

Unlike information, knowledge[58] was long considered to be bound to humans, context, and theory, and as something that could only be acquired through cognitive performance. Externalization of knowledge was considered possible in principle, but the reception of externalized knowledge was again said to require cognitive performance. Machine knowledge processing was viewed as a metaphor for the production of data or information intended for subsequent cognitive interpretation. Concepts like the so-called knowledge management and those that succeeded it have led to a changed perspective, favoring the idea of a machine-based knowledge processing. Today, knowledge is understood as a resource that can be manipulated externally, and which includes the idea of knowledge as a quantifiable value.[59]

The relationship between information and knowledge is interpreted differently in different domain contexts. Sometimes, information is seen as a prerequisite for the generation of knowledge, sometimes as the result of knowledge application.

A slogan often used in information science is "information is knowledge in action"[60]. The argumentation presented so far makes it clear that this description cannot be convincing. The slogan suggests that knowledge is something static, something that generates a substance (information). This substance, however, is in turn a prerequisite for a cognitive process in the course of which it undergoes changes so that knowledge can emerge from it.

We use information as a collective term referring to a basic component of all cognitive processes in which knowledge is processed within the context of reality construction. The exchange of information through communication, its fixation and reception by the media, as well as the storage and retrieval of information

---

57 Roth: Das Gehirn und seine Wirklichkeit, p. 213 (author's translation).

58 From the many accounts that typologically characterize the term "knowledge", we pick out Pöppel: Wissen.

59 See Probst/Raub/Romhardt: Managing knowledge, Nonaka: The knowledge-creating company.

60 Kuhlen: Informationsmarkt, p. 34 (author's translation). A *Google* search can easily confirm that the inversion "knowledge is information in action" also has a crowd of followers.

inevitably involve actors. We describe the various procedures that are involved in this as cognitive processes.

An active and multifaceted way of life would be inconceivable without cognitive information processing; more than that, it directly serves the sustainment of life. The process is triggered by internal stimuli or external sensory perceptions and on this basis creates knowledge. Knowledge, in turn, enables us to cope with a wide variety of tasks. The totality of these events constitutes our knowledge of the world (or reality).

A person who wants to gain knowledge can follow several approaches. One would be to take an active role, which first of all requires the presence of interest and curiosity. The person would have to be actively engaged in acquiring the new knowledge, which includes being aware of the responsibility towards the own knowledge. The other possible role is a passive one, in which the person is the addressee to whom something is presented or who wants to consume something worth noting. Here, the acquisition of knowledge is seen from the perspective of entertainment. Characteristic for this case is that the responsibility for the acquisition and the state of knowledge is delegated to another person.

How can the nature of knowledge that exists in the moment be defined more precisely? Is knowledge only existent if something understood has been previously explained or presented? Does it have to be a process that can be repeated at will? Is knowledge lost when I am no longer able to do something but still remember that I once could? Is it sufficient for the existence of knowledge to have known something once and to know about its consequences—even without remembering the underlying hows and whys? Is the knowledge of a fact lost if or because I can no longer represent it? Does it make a difference whether it is scientific knowledge or everyday knowledge?

Knowledge is not static; it is dynamic. It can be extended, corrected, discarded, or otherwise reconstructed, and is dependent on new stimuli. Whether knowledge is "true" or "false" cannot be deduced from any of its inherent features, that is, neither objectivity nor truth are properties of knowledge.

It is generally assumed that people carry knowledge in their heads and that this knowledge can be both communicated to other people and adopted by other people. In addition to direct communication, this can also be done via various forms of media presentation, such as books. Prerequisite for this is the externalization of the knowledge by the person who possesses the knowledge and who, for example, writes a book. The following types of knowledge can be distinguished:
- knowledge in our own mind that is used for all kinds of purposes, like problem solving or taking action;
- knowledge in other people's minds;
- knowledge in externalized form, for example in books.

These types of knowledge each correspond to forms of knowledge acquisition:[61]
- acquiring knowledge through the own cognitive engagement with reality and its objects;
- acquiring knowledge through communicative exchange with other people;
- acquiring knowledge through the reception of sources making externalized knowledge available.

As conclusive as a distinction between types of knowledge and forms of knowledge acquisition seems to be, the character of the process that turns true reality into a cognitive reality still remains unclear. Knowledge is the result of a reality construction. To find out more about the properties of true and actual reality, the Three Worlds theory by *Karl Popper* provides a possible starting point.

Popper's Three Worlds
Popper describes the complexity of reality by assuming three worlds, which he characterizes, here very briefly, as follows:[62]

World 1: "the physical world—the universe of physical entities";
World 2: "the world of mental states, including states of consciousness and psychological dispositions and unconscious states";
World 3: "the world of the contents of thought, and, indeed, of the products of the human mind".

For the externalization and reception of knowledge, World 3 is of particular importance.

By World 3 I mean the world of the products of the human mind, such as stories, explanatory myths, tools, scientific theories (whether true or false), scientific problems, social institutions, and works of art. World 3 objects are of our own making, although they are not always result of planned production by individual men. Many World 3 objects exist in the form of material bodies, and belong in a sense to both World 1 and World 3. Examples are sculptures, paintings, and books, whether devoted to a scientific subject or to literature. A book is a physical object, and it therefore belongs to World 1; but what makes it a significant product of the human mind is its content: that which remains invariant in the various copies and editions. And this content belongs to World 3.[63]

---

61 With this presentation we follow up on earlier work, see Gödert: Aufbereitung und Rezeption von Information, Gödert: Information as a cognitive construction, Gödert/Kübler: Konzepte von Wissensdarstellung und Wissensrezeption medial vermittelter Information.
62 Popper/Eccles: The self and its brain, p. 37.
63 Popper/Eccles: The self and its brain, p. 38.

The model of *Popper's* Three Worlds implies connections or interactions between the worlds that can be principally understood as cognitive interactions, although he has not treated the nature of these interactions in any particular depth.

> Main thesis: our conscious subjective knowledge (world 2 knowledge) depends upon world 3, that is to say on (at least virtually) linguistically formulated theories.[64]

This includes the assumption of inter-subjective objectivity, which allows persons other than the respective originator to take up and further develop his or her ideas. *Popper* introduces two thought experiments on this:

> Experiment 1. All our machines and tools are destroyed, and all our subjective learning, including our subjective knowledge of machines and tools, and how to use them. But libraries and our capacity to learn from them survive. Clearly, after much suffering, our world may get going again.

> Experiment 2. As before, machines and tools are destroyed, and our subjective learning, including our subjective knowledge of machines and tools, and how to use them. But this time, all libraries are destroyed also, so that our capacity to learn from books becomes useless.

> If you think about these two experiments, the reality, significance, and degree of autonomy of the third world (as well as its effects on the second and first worlds) may perhaps become a little clearer to you. For in the second case, there will be no re-emergence of our civilization for many millennia.[65]

The Three World model assigns knowledge to reality. *Popper's* main focus, the explanation of gaining knowledge in the natural sciences, makes intelligible the central importance of scientific theories in his World 3. However, it is questionable whether the idea is suitable to serve as a model for all human dimensions of life, cognition and knowledge.[66] Reception processes for the acquisition of general knowledge cannot be subjected to the same truth claims and falsification principles as is possible for scientific facts and theories.

Only a small part of the externalized knowledge of the World 3 exists as scientific theory, and at the same time the way it is written down is not formally structured. Texts are structureless data whose understanding depends strongly on the context and the time of their creation. Our "capacity to learn from books" might have already suffered so much by the time that consulting such data possibly can

---

64 Popper: Objective knowledge, p. 74.
65 Popper: Objective knowledge, p. 108.
66 See Albinus: Can science cope with more than one world?

no longer initiate a process of understanding at all. Who dares, for example, today to use a technical description from the encyclopedia of *Diderot* and *d'Alembert* to rebuild a mechanical device? It will not be due to the dimensions given in the description, rather the failure will be due to the fact that often there is no longer an idea of the purpose and operation of the device.

Popper argues that the knowledge that continues to exist in his World 3 is available to people for reappropriation, but makes no statements about the nature of this reappropriation or how the knowledge would be made receivable in that case. So what exactly does *Popper* mean when he assumes that our capacity to learn from the knowledge still existing in World 3 will survive?

Popper gives weak evidence for this at best, but acknowledges the difficulty of an explanation when he says:

> [...] that it is easier to understand how we make World 3 objects than it is to understand how we understand them, grasp them, or "see" them. (I will attempt to explain understanding World 3 objects in terms of making or re-making them.)[67]

His model for understanding World 3 objects is based on single problems. It follows the falsification principle by first forming hypotheses and then eliminating detected errors and thus focuses on the searching and researching aspects in learning processes. In his famously straightforward language, *Popper* calls the model the "searchlight theory" of knowledge and contrasts it with the "bucket theory".[68] He assumes the active and evolutionary scheme of trial and error also for cognitive processes, for example, learning, perceiving, and acting:

> In contrast to this [meaning the bucket theory, author's note] I put forward the theory that nothing is "given" to us: that already our sense organs are active adaptations, the result of mutations, thus of precursors of hypotheses; and that all hypotheses are active attempts of adaptation. We are active, creative, inventive, even if our inventions are controlled by natural selection. Thus, the stimulus-response model is replaced by a mutation(=new action)-selection model.[69]

In line with this view, learning from World 3 objects even becomes a creative process:

> According to my view, we may understand the grasping of a World 3 object as an active process. We have to explain it as the making, the re-creation, of that object.[70]

---

67 Popper/Eccles: The self and its brain, p. 44.
68 Popper: The bucket and the searchlight : two theories of knowledge, pp. 341–362.
69 Popper: Die beiden Grundprobleme der Erkenntnistheorie, p. XXXII (author's translation).
70 Popper/Eccles: The self and its brain, p. 44.

The manner of this "making" or "re-creating" is left unclear by *Popper*, but must be in the very center of interest when it comes to the eventuality of externalization and reception of knowledge. Also missing is any kind of description of the interaction between World 2 and World 3, in other words, a model for the acquisition or exchange of knowledge elements.

Collective Knowledge and Institutional Reality

We take the model of individual knowledge reception as a basis to look more closely at the concept of collective knowledge. Knowledge is considered collective when one person or entity is able to make that knowledge available to others. However, with respect to the survivability of knowledge as presented in *Popper's* World 3 the question may be raised: Does collective knowledge still exist also if it is available in externalized form, but no person is left to make sense of it? Or is it lost then? *Popper* would probably affirm the continued existence. With an understanding of knowledge that is oriented toward cognitive processes, the answer would rather be linked to the still or no longer existing capability of reality construction. It is therefore worthwhile looking for further influencing factors on the way to a clear answer to this question.

For this purpose, *Popper's* Three Worlds will be connected by borrowing from the philosophy of consciousness and the account of cognitive processes of knowledge reception. This connection is made by the two concepts "first person ontology" and "third person ontology", which are used in the context of the philosophy of consciousness to describe the reference to reality:[71]

> First person ontology: cognitive states based on the experience of a first person

> Third person ontology: phenomena whose existence is independent of the experiencing subject, thus ontologically objective

The following equation is obvious:

> First person ontology = World 2

> Third person ontology = World 1

Initially, it must remain open which framework conditions may allow for World 3, with its special significance for externalization and reception processes, to be embedded in such an approach of understanding. To establish this framework, we

---

71 See Searle: Mind, pp. 96–99.

extend the concepts of externalization and reception to include a distinction of forms of reality as proposed by *John Searle*. He separates "objective reality" from an "institutional reality". Both realities can be experienced by humans, and an exchange between the two is also possible.[72]

Objective reality includes facts whose existence is independent of human beings, for example the existence of a mountain or the fact that the earth has a certain distance to the sun. As opposed to this, the facts of institutional reality are created by human beings who use linguistic expressions.

The term institutional reality may seem misleading or ambiguous because the concept does not require the existence of an institution in the corporate sense. *Searle* sees in it all the concepts that are created and used by people in social contexts. The use of "institutional" is thus intended to indicate that these aren't concepts used in a more private setting.

Any conventionalization between individuals can solidify into collective rules with an assignment of roles or status functions from which rights and obligations are derived for the members of a social community. Consider, for example, marriage, the roles of the partners involved, and what conditions must be met for the status of being married to be regarded as rightful in the context of a given social community. In a process like this, it becomes clear that numerous agreements have to be reached that make this collective reality a commonly lived reality. At the same time, a pretended marriage may not be accepted by society and, in the worst case, may even imply legal consequences.[73]

In the case of objects that already exist, status functions that are collectively recognized are assigned by speech acts, for example, that something "is money". The starting point here is a material object of physical reality: a piece of metal, a shell, a cut and printed sheet of paper. However, not all these objects have the property of being money; it is a status which can be assigned to objects and also withdrawn from them. A further aspect is added here, namely the belief or conviction that it is money. This belief is not a property of the bill, but the result of collective intentionality.[74] Decisive for the creation of a social fact is the assignment of a collectively accepted status function, in this case the function of "being money", by means of a graded system of speech acts. For more complex concepts,

---

72 Another approach to a social conception of reality, which takes psychological aspects into account, was developed by *Kenneth Gergen*. He calls it "constructionism". An outline of the concept is developed in Gergen: An invitation to social construction; see also Misra/Prakash: Kenneth J. Gergen and social constructionism. For our discussion we prefer to follow *John Searle* because of his closeness to perspectives of communication theory.
73 For a detailed discussion of these relationships, see Searle: The construction of social reality.
74 Searle: The construction of social reality, pp. 23–26.

a shift in thinking is necessary from the initial level of an already created concept ("central bank") to an institutional concept of the next level of thought ("value of money"). Such a process often involves multiple of such conceptual shifts.[75]

The use of language is constitutive for facts of institutional reality and their exchange between people. It is through linguistic expressions that people create objects and facts of institutional reality. A thinking about these objects is always language-bound. This does not mean that language is the basis of all thinking. Objects or entities of thought are related either to a reality whose existence is created by linguistic acts, or to a physical reality.

Objects and facts of objective reality exist independently of human beings. However, they can be perceived by humans and be the cause for actions based on cognitive processes. This form of thinking is not bound to linguistic symbols or structures.

The two statements "Today is Thursday, December 8, 2022" and "Today is the last full moon of 2022" illustrate this. The day to which both statements refer can be conceived as objective reality if the way of thinking is language-independent. The statement itself, however, can only be made and understood with reference to a calendar system whose existence and description involves various linguistic acts. Neither the property of being a "Thursday" nor of being "December 8" can be pre-linguistically founded. Thus, thinking about the calendar system, a fact of institutional reality, is only possible linguistically.[76]

Besides factual references, this expanded conception of externalization and reception includes structural references, cross-references, as well as spatio-temporal contexts. As frameworks, they enable a reception of concepts from the world of scientific knowledge, but also of general facts, in compliance with the necessary conditions of validity or truth, and thus lead to an understanding of externalized contexts.

This allows us to determine the prerequisite for the construction of an individual World 2 from the elements of objective reality. The acting self must be able to direct its attention to something outside itself, and which can be described using third person ontologies. *Searle* calls this presupposition "(individual) intentionality"[77] and means by it:

---

75 See more at Searle: The construction of social reality, pp. 31–37.
76 Searle: The construction of social reality, pp. 64–66.
77 For explanations of the concept, see Searle: Mind, Searle: The rediscovery of the mind, therein: Chapter 6: The structure of consciousness : an introduction, pp. 127–149.

> Intentionality-with-a-t ... is that property of the mind by which it is directed at or about or of objects and states of affairs in the world independent of itself.[78]

Hence, via the cognitive processing of this outwardly directed attention, individual knowledge is generated as the result of a reality construction and can thus be understood as constituent of World 2 (Figure 2.4). Communicative exchange between people or reception from externalized sources of information can refer to either concepts of third person ontology or first person ontology. Here, the concepts of the first person ontology are not formed by reference to real-world objects of physical reality; rather, their existence is based solely on mappings established in the context of speech acts (institutional reality).

Accordingly, the following relations can now be established, which also consider World 3:

Objective reality = World 1

Institutional reality = World 3

The analogy of institutional reality according to *Searle* and World 3 according to *Popper* is not immediately obvious and certainly would not be accepted by either author without contradiction. However, statements can be cited from *Popper* that would suggest such an interpretation:

> Admittedly, of course, theories are the products of human thought (or, if you like, of human behaviour—I will not quarrel about words). Nevertheless, they have a certain degree of autonomy: they may have, objectively, consequences of which nobody so far has thought, and which may be discovered; discovered in the same sense in which an existing but so far unknown plant or animal may be discovered. One may say that World 3 is man-made only in its origin, and that once theories exist, they begin to have a life of their own: they produce previously invisible consequences, they produce new problems.[79]

The concept of intentionality introduced by *Searle* is a suitable basis for a model of knowledge transfer and knowledge acquisition in the context of communication and reception processes of externalized information. Subsequently, and taking into account everyday knowledge, a more accurate model of the transfer processes between World 3 and World 2 can also be derived from this.

In addition to individual intentionality, a second prerequisite is necessary for the communication between people and the subsequent reception of facts from externalized sources of information. What is involved here is a "we-conception",

---

78 Searle: Mind, pp. 174–175.
79 Popper/Eccles: The self and its brain, p. 40.

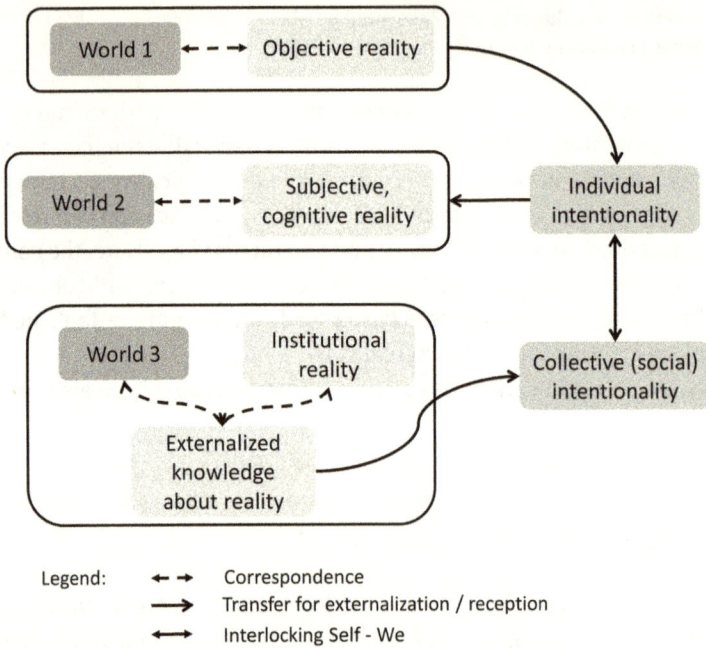

Legend:
←→ Correspondence
→ Transfer for externalization / reception
↔ Interlocking Self - We

Fig. 2.4: Connecting the Theory of mind with the Three Worlds theory.

which contains the following motivation as an imperative element: "I want to acquire (knowledge), I want to understand what another person says or has written down", or even: "I want to build a shared space of knowledge". In the externalization and reception model, this notion is reflected in the mechanisms of structural coupling and consensual parallelization. However, this is not yet sufficient for a comprehensive description of the "we-conception". The description becomes complete only within the framework of a concept that *Searle* calls "collective intentionality".[80]

The statement "We share a common intention" best describes this conception. Collective intentionality seeks in the individual intention (intentionality) the common as a we-intention and understands the own intention as a part of it.

Searle illustrates collective intentionality using the intention of a defense player in a soccer game not to let the opposing striker get a shot on goal. For this particular role, the understanding of an individual intentionality is in fact sufficient. However, it is not sufficient if it is the common goal of the entire team. Only

---

80 Searle: Kollektive Absichten und Handlungen.

in this case does the role of the defense player make sense in the context of the collective intentionality of all players in the soccer game: the own team and not the opponent should win the game. The role of a particular position in playing soccer results from the collective we-action, not from the sum of individual actions.

Collective intentionality is of course also a property of single individuals, whereby there is a direct connection between them. With this, the connection of World 2 and World 3, which has not been given so far, now becomes possible, and it can be explained how reality constructions for the construction of an individual World 2 take place. Figure 2.4 summarizes the relationships discussed.

Consequently, the transfer between World 2 and World 3 can be described as follows: World 3 is to be regarded as reflection and the externalization of those constructs that are created as results of mental activity. Accordingly, these are objects of institutional reality. Through collective intentionality and its natural connection to individual intentionality, these constructs—in the context of a communication or reception process—become the subject of an individual construction of reality. They thus find their way into the cognitive structure of an individual, the equivalent of which is World 2.

2.4 Reference Domains of Knowledge

Individual cognitive information processing is structure-determined, that is, it occurs within frameworks.[81] Depending on the context of expertise, these are referred to as reference domain, context, paradigm, background[82] or, more recently, framing. Figure 2.5 shows these frameworks as reference domains using a simple example.

The first reference domain is called inter-individual validity. Statements within this reference domain claim validity beyond the individual (objectivity); examples are statements about objects in true reality and their properties, for example "gold is a metal".

The second reference domain, the de-individualized validity, is created for all individuals due to many years of socialization in school and education. Here, structures are created that are often seen as so binding that their de-individualized character gives the appearance of being inter-individual. The statement "gold is valuable" depends on the value of gold in a society. This value is not a natural

---

81 Maturana/Varela: Der Baum der Erkenntnis, pp. 105–110.
82 "Background" is meant here in the sense of "giving meaning to", see Searle: The construction of social reality, pp. 129–132.

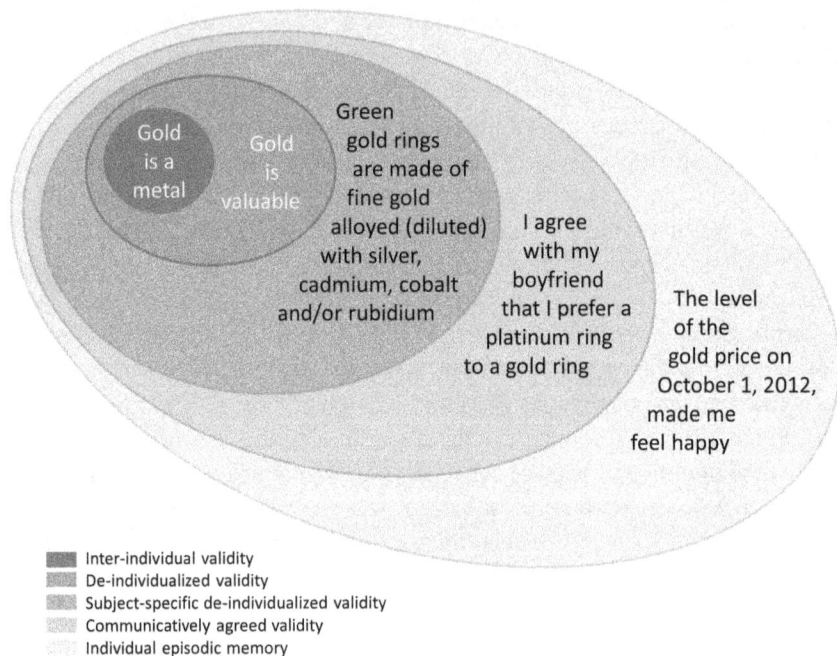

Inter-individual validity
De-individualized validity
Subject-specific de-individualized validity
Communicatively agreed validity
Individual episodic memory

Fig. 2.5: Reference domains of knowledge.

property of gold, but a characteristic assigned by social convention, and that is subject to change.

The third reference domain, called subject-specific de-individualized validity, refers to professional or subject-specific specialization, in contrast to general socialization. The statement "green gold rings are made of fine gold alloyed (diluted) with silver, cadmium, cobalt and/or rubidium" is valid in the professional context of the goldsmith's trade.

The fourth reference domain, the communicatively agreed validity, arises from the diverse social structures of coexistence in societies. The agreed validity includes a limitation related to the communication group, such as to a family, club members or the work environment. The statement "I agree with my boyfriend that I prefer a platinum ring to a gold ring" narrows down the agreed validity to only two individuals.

The reference domain of the individual episodic memory describes knowledge that is not or cannot be shared by others. A statement like "The level of the gold price on October 1, 2012, made me feel happy" seems to completely elude any codification and thus any possibility of media fixation. This category also includes, for example, diary entries or value concepts in people's minds. Nevertheless, every communication process is strongly influenced by this reference domain, as there is a constant connection to the reference domain of agreed validity, which is established through communication processes. Only if a person were to live in complete isolation, the fifth reference domain could attain a predominant role.

The examples lead to the impression that reference domains can be imagined as containers full of isolated entities, which is not the case, since each individual statement, along with the concepts it contains, is embedded in a structure of contexts. Each reference domain is always related to the preceding one, that is, in a current statement the preceding concepts and values are always implied, for example, the understanding that gold is a valuable metal. Thus, the feeling of happiness in the fifth reference domain example is directly related to the attribute "valuable" in the second.

These frameworks, as given here in the form of reference domains, make it clear that structural determination also creates, within its boundaries, some kind of familiarity. It permits to identify and categorize the individual and the specific, but also to derive abstractions on the basis of individual cases. They need not, in fact they cannot, be renegotiated in each act of communication, but they become part of a structurally determined cognitive structure, which facilitates the reception of information exchanged by communication.

2.5 Knowledge Components and Forms of Knowledge

Concepts and their Definitions

Knowledge, as a result of reality construction, can be of different complexity. A common idea is that knowledge is composed of individual parts and that there is a structure in which these individual parts are embedded. There are many attempts to formally capture these conceptual parts. For the purposes of formal knowledge representation, this approach is indispensable; for cognitive representation, however, it usually proves insufficient, or at least conclusive proof of its reliability is yet to be provided. For conceptual knowledge components with a relation to objects of reality, the model of the concept triangle (also: semiotic triangle) has become well established (Figure 2.6).

For the sake of simplicity, the model is limited to illustrating the process of concept formation—including possible abstraction processes—based on objects of objective reality. Later, we will extend the model to the objects of institutional reality, which are created by linguistic acts in a social setting.

The triangle represents the concept formation as a three-valued dependency, in which all vertices are related to each other and from which none of the elements can be removed. The model assumes that concepts are created by making

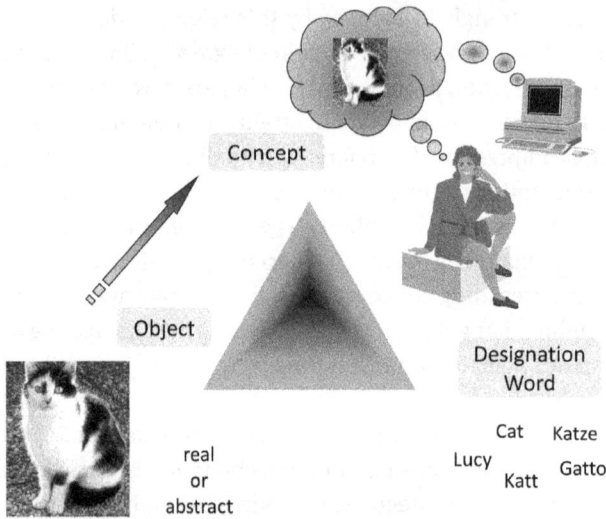

Fig. 2.6: Concept triangle.

statements about real-world or abstract objects, such as by gathering properties or characteristics that are used to define the concept:

A cat is a four-legged animal with fur and a tail; cats have good teeth and sharp claws with which they catch mice and small birds; people value them as pets.

The formation of such statements is secondary to the process of sensory perception and represents an individual cognitive performance. The degree of generality that follows from this performance varies from object to object and is stabilized by acts of communication. The abstraction made consists in the ability to recognize and to apply patterns of knowledge. This transition from the object level to the cognitive representation constitutes the conceptual level, which is fixed intersubjectively by way of designation. The linguistic designation, which is derived from the conceptualization, opens the possibility of communicative exchange with other people. The designation thereby serves as a mediator between communication partners, but does not represent the reality content of the object referred to.

The relations between the object level, the level of concept or meaning, and the designation level, especially in the form of a natural and living language with

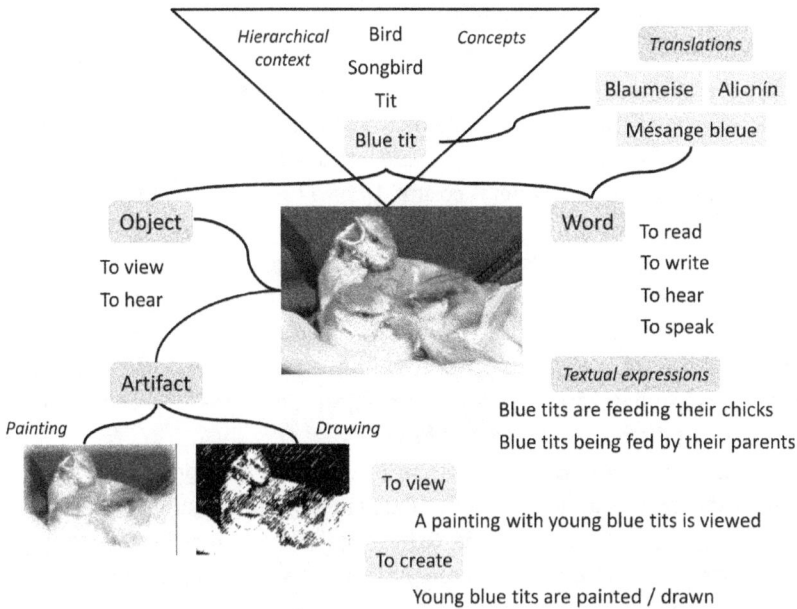

Hierarchical context Bird *Concepts*   *Translations*

Songbird   Blaumeise   Alionín

Tit   Mésange bleue

Blue tit

Object   Word   To read

To view   To write

To hear   To hear

To speak

Artifact   *Textual expressions*

Painting   *Drawing*   Blue tits are feeding their chicks

Blue tits being fed by their parents

To view

A painting with young blue tits is viewed

To create

Young blue tits are painted / drawn

Fig. 2.7: Object – meaning – language.

complex syntax, are manifold.[83] We focus on a few aspects and refer to Figure 2.7, where the language level is explicitly highlighted.

The cognitive representation of an object can be generated or retrieved via various sensory inputs. In Figure 2.7 a photo of blue tits stands for the object layer. By seeing or hearing neural patterns are activated which, with the appropriate preconception, make us recognize something familiar and lead to the assignment of a name (blue tit). Experience shows that this process for each of the sensory stimuli cannot be based only on a singular object presentation, but rather allows for some variability. After all, we recognize in nature not only a particular specimen of a species, but specimens of species in general and this, depending again on experience, also under changing conditions.

Although sensory stimuli lead us to the same designation, they evoke patterns in different neuronal zones in the brain. Despite the same object, whether it is a concrete object or an abstraction of it, neuroimaging techniques for brain mapping show that the neuronal level seems to assume different information contents.[84]

---

83 For the question of how language interacts with the level of meaning, see Hoffmann: Reflexionen über die Sprache, Holenstein: Menschliche Gleichartigkeit.
84 See Bildgebende Verfahren [Sprache und Gehirn].

These imaging techniques have also been used to demonstrate that there is a difference whether pattern generation takes place using texts, sounds or images, or is additionally supported by gestures. In the latter case, a much more complex network in the brain is activated, involving the cerebellum as well as areas in the motor cortex. The linking of stimuli from different sensory modalities is evidenced by increased activity in the parietal cortex. Due to the stronger interconnectedness, we can remember words learned with gestures more easily.[85] This plays a role especially when it comes to objects that are connected to further areas of experience. The concept of blue tit may undergo some transformation if you've ever been pecked in the finger by one.

If the object is an artifact, such as a painting or a drawing as used in our example, the cognitive representation of the object is activated together with the representation of the respective artifact form.

The translations and phrases in Figure 2.7 illustrate phenomena at the level of language. It can be assumed that for foreign language designations (Blaumeise, alionín, mésange bleue) that are known to the cognitive structure (especially those represented by a word of their own), there is also a specific representation in each case, whose relation is also neuronally mapped as a translation.

And if phrases are formed with the term blue tit by the aid of syntax elements, further nuances arise. The following example shows a role change, where the blue tits are once the agent of the action and once the object. In the second statement, moreover, the syntax creates a transfer of meaning: the word "parents" enforces the interpretation that the birds are blue tit fledglings:

> Blue tits are feeding their nestlings.
> Blue tits are fed by their parents.

Conceptual standardization in the form of definitions and the like can be used for linguistic representations, albeit words of any living language are by their nature subject to a constant change in meaning. *Noam Chomsky* characterizes the basic property of language as follows:

> Each language provides an unbounded array of hierarchically structured expressions that receive interpretations at two interfaces, sensorimotor for externalization and conceptual-intentional for mental processes.[86]

This also means that usage of language cannot be thought of as an invariant stream of signals between sender and receiver.

---

85 See Macedonia: Lernen.
86 Chomsky: What kind of creatures are we?, p. 4.

In addition to the principal meaning, there are secondary meanings in the conceptual-intentional interpretation of language elements, which, as can be seen in the following examples, are activated or discarded in a concrete speech act situation:

I am completely in the dark about his plans.
Flying planes can be dangerous.

Several mental processes are involved in fully understanding the example sentences: The first example requires knowledge of the different meanings of "in the dark". In the other example, additionally, either the context must be known, or the one that contributes most to the understanding of the sentence must be chosen from possible suitable contexts, while other options must be discarded.

In addition to concepts with a reference to objects of physical reality, there are those that are created by linguistic acts.[87] Language is then directly involved in the formation of meaning and thereby also creates reality. *Ludwig Wittgenstein* has referred to this interaction:

Is meaning then really only the use of a word? Isn't it the way this use meshes with our life?[88]

The concept of institutional reality addresses the ability of language to create reality. Properties of objects in reality can be determined independently of the observer and in a repeatable way. Designations of objects in this sense have a purely declarative or communication-related function.

This is different when it comes to concepts of collective or institutional reality. Here, language itself creates reality. The concepts are created by speech acts in the context of social conventionalizations and are not created by reference to objects of physical reality. They cannot be determined by intensional definition because they do not have stable intrinsic characteristics that are independent of the assignment of meanings by humans. In many cases, a context must be considered to determine their meaning.

Concepts of social reality do not acquire their definition by the specification of properties. Rather, their understanding is consolidated by their use being permanently under test of validity and truth. For a concept to be used appropriately in a given context, there must be different imaginable scenarios to choose from. Conversely, all of these scenarios must refer to the one concept. Using the example

---

87 For the background of this approach, see Searle: The construction of social reality, Chapters 4 and 5.
88 Wittgenstein/Rhees/Kenny: Philosophical grammar, p. 65.

of "money", *Searle* makes clear that this mental setting does not only stand for an arbitrary attitude, but more the confidence, secured by rules, in the justification of the action undertaken:

> The word "money" marks one node in a whole network of practices, the practices of owing, buying, selling, earning, paying for services, paying off debts, etc. [...] The word "money" functions as a placeholder for the linguistic articulation of all these practices. To believe that something is money, one does not actually need the word "money". It is sufficient that one believes that the entities in question are media of exchange, repositories of value, payment for debts, salaries for services rendered, etc.[89]

That is, different types of concepts correspond to different methods leading to their definition. Concepts of social reality even seem to resist any definability. A prime example of this is the concept of "consciousness", for which there does not even exist an approximate definitional approach.

Concept Schemes and Conceptual Structures

The relationships between entities, meanings, and linguistic representations are increasingly discussed in terms of their modeling in artificial intelligence systems. These systems are designed to be learning-capable and are meanwhile able to take over almost all subtasks from the fields of perception and representation. The different functions of the sensory organs (seeing, hearing, feeling, smelling, tasting) can be translated by programs which perform tasks that are usually created and optimized independently of each other. But it is yet another case, if several or all of the functions are to be connected with each other. As self-evident as neuronal interaction is in the processing of various tasks, this interaction is not self-evident in information technology contexts.

Further discussion will be based on a model of elementary knowledge and will refrain from considering higher levels of terminological complexity.[90] This approach does not allow all cases to be discussed; however, it does allow the principles to be clarified.

To make the interconnections between knowledge components describable, relationships are used that can be characterized by different relationship types. (abstraction, partition, association). The diversity of these relationships can be partially typified and formalized. In addition, the individual elements can be connected by syntactic rules to form assertions resulting in a higher level of complexity.

---

89 Searle: The construction of social reality, p. 52.
90 See the fuller discussion in Gödert/Hubrich/Nagelschmidt: Semantic knowledge representation for information retrieval, Chapters 6 and 8.

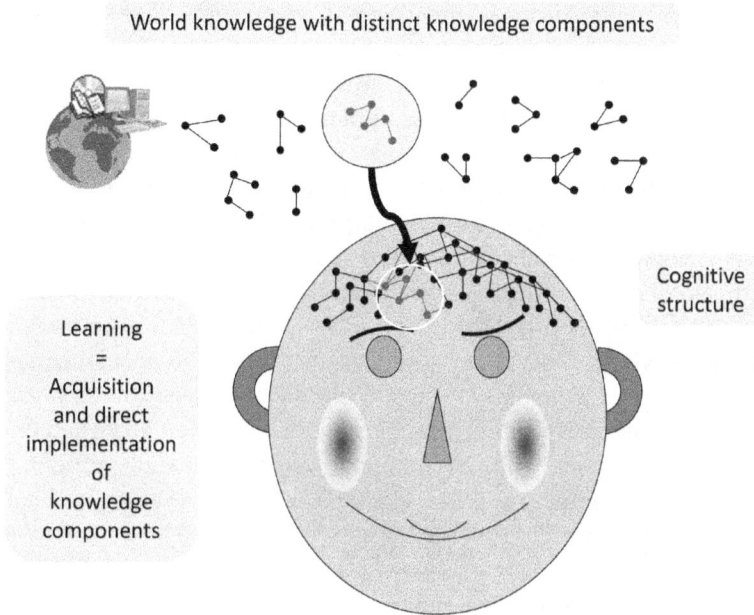

Fig. 2.8: Knowledge acquisition from externalized knowledge (1).

The sum of all relationships and rules forms a structure that must be processed cognitively if knowledge is to be acquired from it. For the sake of simplicity, the name structural knowledge will be used here for the knowledge characterized in this way.

Many ideas of learning processes—from the *Nuremberg funnel* to *Popper's* bucket theory to the pipeline metaphor based on information technology—paint a very simple picture of the adoption of knowledge from externalized information sources (Figure 2.8). These models of knowledge acquisition assume that nonexistent knowledge can be identified and located, for example, in externalized form, in order to integrate it into a cognitive structure. It is assumed that this process can take place even without any adjustment in the cognitive structure. People like to orient themselves by looking up dates, current temperatures, the length of a river or the amount of a country's gross national product, etc., while overlooking the fact that data in particular can only be understood with reference to a theoretical framework. In this context, it is argued that once the cognitive structure is sufficiently developed, knowledge growth becomes a rather additive process allowing us to incorporate new knowledge almost on the fly.

It is more likely, however, that before knowledge can be "added", the structure must undergo a change, which may well be the result of an elaborate learning process. And if—for whatever reason—learning of this kind cannot be done (anymore), there may be situations in which this structural change is not possible either. Conversely, a change in structure can also mean the dissolution of connections due to lack of training—and consequently the loss of knowledge components.

Another form of knowledge to mention is action-based knowledge or procedural knowledge, which is needed for the performance of movement sequences—like riding a bike or using the clutch in a car. Passing on this form of knowledge is as difficult as describing or formalizing it.

Since the second half of the 20th century, new ways of describing human thought and action have emerged that have had a significant impact on our understanding of knowledge. With the development of computer-based information processing and its inroads first into the world of work and then into the whole of social life, the relationship between people and the tools they create and use has changed fundamentally.[91] Initially, computer-based information processing was seen as a tool to improve or facilitate work. As part of the history of technology, they were thus in the tradition of serving as a compensation for non-existent human capabilities.[92]

However, this period lasted only about twenty years, roughly from 1965 to 1985. In the relatively short time since then, we have seen the advent of large-capacity mainframes, the triumph of the personal computer, distributed data storage, the Internet, and cloud computing. New fields of application emerged with performances that were not even considered possible before. The "victories" of computers against humans in typical "intelligence situations" such as chess and Go, have marked a new turning point: With the beginning of the 21st century, the computer metaphor was seen as an explanatory model that could be used to describe cognitive processes.

But even without reference to this metaphor, humans have already achieved intellectual feats, which were even responsible for the fact that this analogy could be thought of as a concept at all.

Forms of Knowledge

For an overview of different forms of knowledge that are relevant for understanding externalization and reception, we first specify the distinction between factual knowledge and structural knowledge.[93] Making the distinction seems obvious,

---

91 See for example Steinbuch: Masslos informiert, Steinbuch: Die informierte Gesellschaft.

92 This view is attributed to *Arnold Gehlen*; see Rapp: Fortschritt.

93 Descriptions of knowledge typologies can be found in Böhme-Dürr (ed.): Wissensveränderung durch Medien, Luft: Zur begrifflichen Unterscheidung von ‚Wissen‘, ‚Information‘ und ‚Daten‘,

yet it also contains some fuzziness. For one thing, it is not clear whether factual knowledge is only present when there is no context at all, either communicated or followed in thoughts. Nor is it known how much context is required to qualify as structural knowledge. Intuitively, the assumption seems to be plausible that the acquisition of factual knowledge presupposes the existence of structural knowledge. But conversely, is structural knowledge even possible without factual knowledge? Reducing the understanding of knowledge to the accumulation and possible retrieval of facts falls short in any case.[94]

Under the influence of the computer metaphor, there seems to have been a shift in this understanding. Factual or data knowledge is given increasing importance over analytical, descriptive or experiential knowledge. Identical events, for instance, can be temporally classified with completely different information, for example by:

- a date (for example, in the Gregorian or Julian calendar system);
- a point in time in a codified knowledge system (for example, in a historical observational calendar, the day before the third full moon after Easter);[95]
- a general or personal event taking place at the same time (for example, "two days after I witnessed in the stadium how Germany became soccer world champion for the fourth time").

Despite the theoretical equivalence, it is difficult to imagine in our culture that, for example, a boxing fan is allowed to state his date of birth in an official form by means of a transcription (13 days after *Cassius Clay* became Olympic light heavyweight champion) instead of stating the date September 7, 1960. Thus, the codification system gets to influence what we do and do not recognize as knowledge within a given social community. In other words, knowledge is subject to social evaluation and acceptance.

With the help of the reference domain of de-individualized validity, a distinction of knowledge into individual or experiential knowledge and codified knowledge can be made, such as is acquired in learning within an organized educational system.

Luft: ‚Wissen' und ‚Information', Scheidgen (ed.): Information ist noch kein Wissen, Piekara: Wie idiosynkratisch ist Wissen? Spies: Unsicheres Wissen, Wersig: Inhaltsanalyse, Wille: Begriffliche Datensysteme als Werkzeuge der Wissenskommunikation.

94 See Hentig: Die Flucht aus dem Denken ins Wissen.

95 The distinction between these first two possibilities is somewhat artificial, since a calendar is of course a codified knowledge system. Today's lack of bias in giving a date already clearly shows the acceptance of "this" codified knowledge system.

In order to determine how viable a model of knowledge acquisition from externalized sources can be and what conditions must be met, it is worthwhile to look at various situations that are characterized by non-knowledge. In doing so, it is common to distinguish between knowledge that is externalized by a person for him/herself and externalized knowledge as based on *Popper's* World 3.

Personal records, for example, are knowledge externalized for oneself. Personal records document the result of an acquisition of knowledge in a form adapted to the individual's cognitive structure. Normally, it will then also be possible for the person to fit his or her own recording back into the individual cognitive structure at a later point in time. This process, however, does not always run smoothly. Thinking back to school math lessons makes it easy to understand how difficult it can be to recapitulate what you once knew from notes you made yourself.

More interesting is the second process—the externalization in the sense of *Popper's* World 3. In this case, own non-knowledge is to be replaced by objectified externalized knowledge. Although other persons have medially fixed the result of a cognitive or knowledge acquisition process according to their cognitive structural determination, we presume that we can also make this result usable for our own cognitive structure.

The following examples are limited to forms of knowledge that are not to be understood as action-oriented or procedural and serve to examine the conditions of knowledge and non-knowledge for each case.

Unknown facts:
- What is the postal code of Gatlinburg, TN?
- What is the fare of a train connection from X to Y in August on day Z in class K?
- Which Spanish painters lived at the time of the French Revolution?
- How many protons does a gold atom contain?

In all these cases, it is reasonable to assume that, given sufficient structural knowledge, getting the exact answer (from a reference book, for example) in terms of factual knowledge is all it takes to close the knowledge gap. Nevertheless, the presence of a certain educational or socialization knowledge could also be required in each of these cases. Indeed, even from these simple examples of phenomena of non-knowledge, it must be expected that prior acquisition of additional structural knowledge will be necessary to have these questions answered successfully.

The second example uses expressions of a specialized language, which should be read as if they were unknown.

Unknown technical terms:
- tower crane;

- hypoelliptic differential operator;
- coextensive representation of document content in a syntactic indexing language.

In these cases, the presence of a more or less well-developed structural knowledge (usually from the reference domain of "subject-specific de-individualized validity") is mandatory to close the knowledge gap. A description of the respective terminological expression accepted by "experts" may be possible here. However, these descriptions will not be sufficient to close the existing knowledge gaps for everyone else with no such expert knowledge.

Or, the knowledge is in principle existent, but the name of a bird, a plant, a piece of music or a person does not come to mind. Often it is then possible to give descriptions that indicate that the knowledge is actually available, but even access to all the characteristics of a concept (e.g., through a definition) is not sufficient to access the name as well.

Unknown definitions:
- fluctuations in economic data within a cycle (period comprising an economic upswing and downswing);
- fluctuations in the degree of utilization of an economy's production potential;
- long-term, fixed-interest bond issued by land credit institutions; secured by mortgages and marketable; callable only by the mortgage bank.

It remains open when a concept formation is complete and when additional features of a concept system outside the concept to be named are to be considered.

Unknown connotations:
- leaf peeper (regional term for nature lovers who visit areas for their colorful fall foliage);
- mean machine (slang term for fast vehicles);
- being in the hot seat (expression used for being in a high-pressure situation).

The understanding of terms may also fail because connotations are not known or not fully known. In the mentioned cases, the binding of the knowledge gap to a historically, culturally, geographically or otherwise determined sphere of life becomes clear, which at the same time also constitutes the preconditions for its elimination.

What all the above examples have in common is that, on the one hand, they consist of concepts to be considered in isolation, but on the other hand, they form a transition to the more difficult cases of not knowing the concept scheme or the theory behind, which require disproportionately more structural knowledge:

- game, set, match;
- milk (raw material, product, economic good, food, metaphor, etc.);

- yard gate, rolling gate, garden gate, sluice gate;
- knowledge, understanding, comprehension, recognition, cognition, truth, certainty, memory, information.

Without any knowledge of the appropriate context, one will not be able to pigeonhole the examples. Usually, concepts are defined by characteristics and these characteristics are also considered as the basis for the relationships between the concepts. How can this fully work for the "milk" example? Can all required characteristics be specified for all examples? The basic ambiguity of the individual terms makes an assignment even more difficult. Only the addition of further concepts provides context. Can the question be answered at what point elements constitute a concept scheme and when such a concept scheme is to be regarded as completed and consequently as complete? How is it decided whether concepts are still missing for the scheme to be considered complete? More specifically, this leads to the following questions:

- Is it possible to specify a terminated set of properties for each concept?
- Is it necessary to also specify properties (including other concepts) that do not apply? And if so, how many?
- Referring to a single concept, is the formation of concepts a process that can reach a completed state?
- Is it possible to understand each property as an element of a single property space (aspect)?
- Do all properties of a property space automatically lead to a concept scheme?

Concepts or terms of institutional reality cannot be determined solely by specifying properties, as they are also subject to changing conditions of validity within the social environment. For this reason, concept formation and understanding have a temporal component as well. So it is by no means certain that a concept will retain its meaning over time. Numerous examples from our daily lives can testify to this.

By and large, people seem to do well in adapting their language use to changes in conceptual understanding. It is much more difficult to find solutions for a time-bound externalized representation of concepts and their structures—especially for concepts of institutional reality.[96] A conceptual determination, which is made via the context, cannot be represented so easily in a formal system.

In summary, lack of completeness of conceptualizing features, lack of context, and lack of temporal dimension all are factors contributing to phenomena

---

[96] See the proposals to use a semiotic tetrahedron instead of the semiotic triangle for conceptual modeling, which also addresses the pragmatic dimension of the use of concepts (Hesse: Information).

related to non-knowledge. Ignorance of the rules of logical reasoning, incorrect logical conclusions, the lack of ability to perform combinatorial processes and misinterpretation of statistical phenomena are equally part of the problem.

Information and Knowledge

Information and knowledge are two concepts that are not always easy to distinguish. The first difficulty already lies in the question, which entity category can be assigned to the concept of "information". In externalized form, information is bound to a physical (material) carrier without itself possessing any materiality. However, it is not a property of the physical carrier that could be lifted or read out in an extraction process. Rather, information is part of a complex cognitive process and, in this context, is described as the result of interactions of the neural networks in the brain. In this respect, information is to be placed before the knowledge resulting from it, but can itself be extended and changed by knowledge.

Perhaps the most important difference between information and knowledge is the relation of knowledge to a reality problem shared by others. Knowledge, in this sense, is a social phenomenon. Information, in contrast, does not have to be related to reality and must not necessarily be shared by other people. Examples include dreams or individual fictional fantasies as parts of information processing that do not require direct reference to the external world.

Information, understood as a cognitive event, is not quantifiable and therefore cannot be described by conservation laws, such as the physical quantity "energy", which is often used as a comparison. The quantification of information by bits of the binary system, which is often done by following the approaches of information theory, is a purely data-technical approach without any relation to cognitive processing.

As a central description and possible differentiation of both concepts it can be stated: Knowledge has reference to a reality problem that is shared by other people. Knowledge is created on the basis of information. The cognitive process required for the transformation is processing the information and thereby generates knowledge. Information becomes the object of cognitive processing through sensory perception of the external world or interaction with other people, but can also be the object of a purely self-referential process.

Information and Informational

For a characterization of informational, the reference to a model for human information processing events tied to data and signal transmission falls short. Events of cognitive information processing can only be described by interpretation within the framework of interpretation schemes. Here, an indispensable position is taken by the concept of "context". Data can be thought of as entities with or without context, whereas information can only be thought of with context.

The sequence of digits "314159" can be seen as a pure sequence of six randomly chosen digits or as a number:

$3 \times 10^5 + 1 \times 10^4 + 4 \times 10^3 + 1 \times 10^2 + 5 \times 10^1 + 9$

The second interpretation requires cognitive abstracting by knowledge of the decimal positional notation system. A third, even more challenging interpretation recognizes the first digits of the circular number π, which is facilitated by a separator: 3.14159.

The example shows that human information processing always takes place in consideration of a context.[97] Hence, it is individual and requires communicative action, not least for the purpose of comparison with the performance of others. In an interview, Austrian computer pioneer *Heinz Zemanek* gave the following answer to the question "Can information be measured?":

> You can count letters, but information cannot be understood by measurement alone; it is not physical by its nature and requires representation and interpretation beyond what can be measured by physics and technology.[98]

The *Turing machine*, as the purest form of an information processing system in the sense of information technology, does not know such a context nor a context-related communication. It is therefore universal because it is invariant to all contexts.

As a cognitive state, information has no substance character. It can be exchanged with others, represented and externalized with the help of appropriate structuring. In doing so, it is not bound to a single representational scheme. It exists outside of cognitive structures, but accessing it mentally requires cognitive processing. Information is needed for the cognitive processes to take place, once from the outside, via sensory perceptions, and as part of the self-referential processes of an autopoietic system[99] as an internal basis for cognitive processes. In connection with a reality construction, information generates knowledge. The totality of these information-creating and information-accessing processes is characterized here as informational.

---

97 Even the understanding of digits presupposes a certain theory, which in turn demands a cultural bond based on historical developments.
98 Karner: Mailüfterl, Al Chorezmi und Künstliche Intelligenz (author's translation).
99 See Maturana/Varela: Der Baum der Erkenntnis.

2.6 Autonomy and Informational Autonomy

Autonomy

Autonomy can be described as a state of self-determination and self-reliance. For it, different reference levels can be distinguished.

The first level is exclusively related to the individual. It comprises all physiological processes involved in sustaining life and include sensory perception, neural processing, comparison with existing patterns and the formation of new patterns, as well as the resulting actions and their control. This level can be considered the basal level, which has autonomy even when no other level is present.

The second level is described by forms of cognitive information processing as used in problem solving, especially rational problem solving. At this level, an informational process can take place detached from sensory perceptions or other interactions with the environment. In practice, there will still be interaction with the environment, since the problem originates in the environment and the result of a problem solving should in turn have an impact on the environment. Therefore, the first level must be included.

The first and second level together constitute the prerequisite for what is called cognitive autonomy. As a result, eliminating the autonomy of the processes at any of these levels is not possible. Only for certain second-level problems external factors have the potential to control the processing or to discard achieved solutions as useless.

The third level of reference is defined as the level of human interactions in social and institutionalized structures. Here, too, aspects of autonomy must be considered. Examples include legal, political or economic autonomy of individuals, groups, social communities as well as of companies, organizations or even states. Here, the influences acting on the individual from the outside are much stronger compared to the other two levels.[100]

Autonomy as a personality trait is not only seen in a positive light and is not unreservedly deemed desirable. Autonomy is polarizing, with proponents and opponents balancing each other out. A particular field of conflict is the one between autonomy and authority. Since we are mainly concerned with the individual in the context of informational questions and processes, we see cognitive autonomy as an indispensable basic property of human action. We characterize this position as informational autonomy.

---

100 See Pauen/Welzer: Autonomie, Schmidt: Kognitive Autonomie und soziale Orientierung.

Informational Autonomy

Informational autonomy is the ability to cognitively process information of states that are self-initiated or triggered by sensory perception or the associated reception of externalized information. In both cases it is bound to the structual determination of the cognitive system and cannot be described by a sender-receiver model. There is no data stream that would be readable in any character code. Nor is there any way to predict the outcome someone will produce cognitively based on the sensory perceptions received. It is merely neural signals in complex network structures being compared to existing patterns for the purpose of cognitive processing.

The result of human information processing is therefore individual. The probability that a result will differ from that of another person increases depending on the subjective influencing factors involved, such as experiences or feelings. If testing against similarities shows congruent results for different persons, this is not only due to the same input signals, but also to similar general conditions. Examples of this are the social and cultural context, comparable educational paths or the regulation of behavior through sanctions, if the result of informational autonomy was not accepted or even condemned by the social setting. Whether these sanctions were justified or unjustified does not necessarily cause a change in the individual's attitude toward his or her informational autonomy.

In addition, the cognitive processes are performed consciously or unconsciously, depending on the physiological operations they are assigned to. In particular, the processes associated with life support cannot be influenced at will, or only to a very limited extent.

Suspension of the cognitive processes assigned to consciousness is possible; a definitive cessation is inhuman, taking "brain washing" as an example. This means, conversely, that current conceptions of being human imply continuous and ongoing cognitive information processing, one that can be considered a higher-order function and whose performance involves multiple individual decisions, as in the following examples: "Am I going to the movies today? "What am I going to wear?" "Do I ask person xy to come?" "Are we going to eat something beforehand?" "Where?" "Are we going to have a drink afterwards?" "Where?".

Cognitive information processing is under the premise of autonomy until, for example, informational paternalism or regulations determine when informational autonomy is permissible and when it is not. The result then is informational dependence. The basic prerequisite for an individual to be able to notice the transition from informational autonomy to informational dependence is the presence of consciousness.

2.7 Informational Autonomy and Consciousness

The subject of consciousness[101] is relevant to our context of discussion for several reasons. One is that there is a relationship between consciousness and autonomy; the other is that endowing artificial systems with consciousness is seen as a key factor in the development of "human-like" artificial intelligence, known as *Artificial General Intelligence* (AGI).[102]

Consciousness can be described as a physiological state with the ability to generate sensations, gather experiences, and share them with others. It is at the same time subject and object of one and the same process and is thus subject to the principle limitations of its complete cognition—as is the case for all formally closed systems.

Consciousness is furthermore considered a basic mental state that controls selective attention. This includes the ability to make a spontaneous and autonomous decision about the selection of the area to which this attention should be given.[103] The attribute "spontaneous" means that the decision may turn out differently in a comparable situation at a different time, i.e., it is not predefined or dependent on characteristics that are different in the situations. The key is to base it on the individual's past history and current intentions with respect to the future.

Conscious actions can thus be related to attention and intention. Both, in turn, are related to selective perception and the choice of areas to pay or not to pay attention to. For example, when listening to a radio program in which traffic information, the weather forecast, and the lottery numbers are presented as part of the news, not all listeners will pay the same attention to all the messages. Knowledge about a situation is the result of cognitive processing, which is based on selectively acquired information. It is an individual construction of reality because a single individual cannot carry out simultaneously the sum of all reality constructions of all other individuals also present.

If cognitive processing and decision-making is not to be seen as externally controlled, it must be understood as autonomous. It is not possible to describe an autonomous and conscious participation in life without presupposing actively controlled and selective processes. A consciousness with equal attention to all en-

---

101 For an introduction, see Searle: Mind, Calvin: The cerebral symphony, Edelman/Tononi: A universe of consciousness, Edelman: Bright air, brilliant fire, Edelman/Gally/Baars: Biology of consciousness.
102 Also known as "Strong AI" oder "Full AI". For an introduction and overview of the different positions, see Blackmore: Consciousness, Blackmore: Conversations on consciousness.
103 See Searle: The rediscovery of the mind, Chapter 6, Searle: Putting consciousness back in the brain.

vironmental stimuli is not consistent with current models of cognitive information processing.

In summary, this means that assuming a human or a machine to have consciousness, the following properties would also have to be present:

- temporal experience with past stored as memory;
- developing a sense of self in conjunction with a continuous perception of time;
- independence in decisions and actions;
- intentions for future actions that are subject to review after they have been realized;
- sensory perception, communication and interaction with the environment;
- ability to distinguish which actions are in response to external stimuli and which are self-induced (association with instinctive actions);
- ability to select which actions should not take place;
- no determination by the environment;
- ability to associate with feelings, sensations, preferences, desires.

Informational Dependence

In assessing the presence of information dependence, it is important to consider whether a person's information processing is self-initiated or externally initiated; especially if the input of sensory perceptions or data is decided upon by an entity other than the person using that input for a cognitive information process. This case occurs, for example, in teaching and learning situations and is usually considered appropriate for accelerating the achievement of a result. The decisive factor here is whether the person who is the target of the external stimulation is given the opportunity to stop or change the process by making their own decision.

Adherence to general principles (laws, rules, traditions, or customs) or ethical norms, such as those intended to protect oneself or others, has less influence on information processing, but may have a great deal of influence on its outcome.

With the increasing acceptance of the computer metaphor as a guiding principle for cognitive performance, combined with the expanding orientation toward parameter-driven processes for decision-making, it may be assumed that cognitive performance will be measured more and more by the results of algorithmically achieved outcomes. If people lose the skills they have acquired over long periods of time and increasingly subordinate themselves to what is produced by algorithmic methods, this gives rise to informational dependence or reinforces it where it already exists.

Interestingly, in the context of artificial intelligence, there are efforts to exempt robots from strictly following predefined algorithms if doing so would harm them and if no one else would be harmed by not following the programmed instructions.

In a model discussed by the literature, an experiment is described in which a robot has to learn to trust a human when the human tells the robot not to hesitate to jump off the tabletop, since the human will surely catch it.[104] This is commented by the authors as follows:

> [...] the main problem is the fallibility of the robots' human creators and masters. Humans make mistakes. They might give faulty or confused instructions, be inattentive or deliberately try to deceive a robot for their own questionable ends. Because of our own flaws, we need to teach our robotic assistants and smart machines when and how to say "No".[105]

2.8 Informational Literacy

On the basis of the preceding descriptions, our understanding of informational literacy can now be defined in more detail. We have chosen this very specific designation exactly because we are not interested in claiming the interpretational sovereignty of the term information literacy.[106] The differences between informational literacy and information literacy will become clearer in the course of our discussion.

Information literacy is an imprecise concept that is often used in arbitrary contexts, as shown by the German *Wikipedia* article:

> Information literacy is the ability to deal with any information in a self-determined, competent, responsible and purposeful manner. For the individual, ethical and conscentious as well as economic, efficient and effective use of information are therefore considered to be its basic principles.[107]

This characterization could be read as expressing the broad meaning of the concept. In our opinion, this rather shows a kind of powerlessness in the face of a temporary phenomenon and we see the statement of the second sentence as contradictory. As a programmatic statement, this view may be useful, but it would then also have to be substantiated with criteria.[108]

---

104 See also Rojas: Die Tugend des Roboters.
105 Briggs/Scheutz: Why robots must learn to tell us "No".
106 See e.g., Deutscher Bibliotheksverband e.V.: Informationskompetenz, especially "Standards and positions".
107 Informationskompetenz [Wikipedia] (author's translation).
108 An impression of the state of discussion of the concept in library and information science is provided by: Sühl-Strohmenger/Barbian: Informationskompetenz, Weisel: Ten years after, Dreisiebner/Beutelspacher/Henkel: Informationskompetenz.

Such a criterion could be seen, for example, in the appropriate use of information products. At a minimum, information literacy means being aware of the temporal boundedness related to a product's respective functions in order to know which functions require which type of use. This would be primarily a matter of instrumental skills, which would have to take into account not only the temporal aspect but also the familiarity aspect that the use of information products entails over a certain period of time.

Knowledge of this kind can either be based on personal experience or be the subject of learning in an educational system. In this context, it would be desirable for the possibilities and framework conditions of the educational system to be designed in such a way that practicing information literacy can be adapted to the respective cognitive capacity of the individual. Less desirable would be the subordination of social aspirations to the interests of economic exploitation. It would be even better to incorporate such considerations at the time of product development and to factor them into the setting of standards.

Information literacy represents the human quality of being able to bridge a deficit with adequate means and, even more, to achieve a desired state of purpose from it. Being competent in this sense today is primarily about knowing or recognizing what actions and efforts are required to get to the desired target state for a data or information-related problem. This also includes being able to assess which measures are not appropriate for dealing with the problem. Described in this way, the abilities that constitute information literacy would be open to scaling, that is, to numerical indications of their increase or decrease.

Also playing a role is the notion that being competent to do something is generally associated with doing the right thing. The "right thing" always goes back to a value system, which can be based on logical, instrumental or ethical-moral principles. Generally, these value systems are independent of each other. Thus, an action induced by information literacy may be highly logical, or at the same time morally reprehensible. Thanks to our rational abilities, humans are able to act efficiently and logically, even if their intentions are morally questionable. So there is no one and only right way to proceed, and information literacy is no exception. Fact is that any competence aiming at ethical-moral evaluations requires insight based on consciousness.

Informational literacy is to be distinguished from digital literacy. Digital literacy focuses on a concrete medial form of externalization and therefore leads to a narrowed discussion of the concept of literacy. Therefore, cognitive information processing and information processing based on information technology aspects without any medial limitations will serve as a frame of reference for addressing the concept of informational literacy. This perspective is of particular interest when searching for time- and media-independent invariants of informational literacy, which make it possible to discriminate between new developments that merely represent short-lived trends and those that form the basis for a cultural technique that is becoming established in the long run.

Our understanding of informational literacy is inextricably linked to the concept of informational autonomy. As a first characterization, it can be stated: Informational literacy is the ability to process information for the purpose of self-determined action or knowledge acquisition. It can be understood as the sum of a set of inalienable basic cognitive functions that are consistently present over long periods of time. Together they form the potential for processing specific informational tasks. We conclude: Informational literacy is lived informational autonomy.

Informational literacy is a prerequisite for the development of information literacy. On the other hand, information literacy is a component of informational literacy which is based on criteria and parameters. Informational literacy consists of abilities and competencies that allow, if necessary, a transfer from already known to new factual situations. It is the sum of these abilities and competencies that makes it possible to deal effectively with time-bound informational tasks.

Time Constraints and Invariants of Informational Literacy

The common understanding of information literacy is often associated with current media, hardware, and software products and the skills to use them. This promotes the tendency to downgrade the preceding generations of a certain media or technology. As opposed to this, we consider informational literacy as a time-independent phenomenon.

An example from the historical development of media types shall illustrate the difference. Knowing how to use the index of a printed bibliography or how to look up a person's phone number in a printed telephone directory is not associated with information literacy in the internet age. However, both actions require no less informational literacy than the proper use of a search engine. The fact that bibliographies and telephone directories are considered historically outdated media should be of minor importance. Isn't it precisely this spectrum of media types growing over time—and being able to use them appropriately—that should be considered the basis for determining competence? Whereas the narrowing to the respective contemporary type of media, which can be replaced by a new one tomorrow, cannot be seen as a proof of information literacy.

Informational literacy is characterized by precisely these invariants: It persists even if the technical framework changes. This applies to a whole range of cultural techniques, such as mastering the alphabet or the place value system of numbers, which enable us to make sense of accordingly ordered environments. This includes the ability to combine letters into words and individual digits into numbers; an ability that is in danger of being lost through the operation of information technology devices via keyboard, touch display, or voice control. Developments show that children are already increasingly expressing words through the sequential pronunciation of letters and numbers through the sequential enumeration of digits.

Basically, the invariants of informational literacy are characterized by their ability to handle an informational problem competently in any technological environment, new or old. Not every new development and the mastering of the tools that go with it is per se associated with a higher level of competence, especially not if this may even result in the loss of knowledge about the connections between the levels of progress and how problems were solved at an earlier stage. This understanding of progress includes knowing the old ways and the new, and being able to make appropriate, problem-oriented decisions about which way to go for in order to accomplish a specific task. If the familiar approach cannot be applied (such as in the case of a defective parking assistant) and one has to switch (perhaps even in an emergency situation) to another approach originating from an earlier time, the relevance of this understanding of progress becomes very clear.

3 Externalization and Reception of Information

It is theory which decides what we can observe.

Albert Einstein[109]

3.1 Constructivist Model of Communication

Based on the model of perception introduced earlier, we will now develop a constructivist model for the communication between cognitive structures. This will also be used to describe knowledge acquisition from external information sources. Overall, this sets out a step-by-step model:
1. Information acquisition through sensory perception (Chapter 2.2);
2. Information acquisition through acts of communication;
3. Externalization of information through different types of media;
4. Reception of information from different types of media.

Potential and Actual Information
Externalization of information into, for example, a written form converts information within a cognitive structure into information outside that structure. To distinguish these two types of information, we introduce the concepts of potential information and actual information.

Potential information exists in medially externalized form and can be made available for later reception through a structurally determined cognitive structure. Potential information has already been subject to cognitive information processing and thereby is bound to a certain reference domain. Here, cognitive information processing can be triggered by a direct act of communication or by the reception of externalized information. In this case, we can speak of potential information whose full reception (that is, the reactivation of the meaning that the externalizing cognitive structure had associated with it) is tied to certain conditions, such as the specified reference domains.

Not all externalized information, and certainly not all data, is potential information. If there is no longer any possibility of structural coupling with a recipient (e.g., if the reference domain has disappeared), externalized information can no longer be incorporated into cognitive structures. Applied to the libraries in *Popper's* thought experiment, this would mean that their sense and their entire knowl-

---

109 Cited by Heisenberg: Physics and beyond, p. 63.

https://doi.org/10.1515/9783110693744-003

edge would be lost. The reception of information fixed in medial memory always requires a recipient with a cognitive structure.

Actual information can be described as the cognitive processing pattern of a structurally determined system that occurs at the moment when reality construction or the direct exchange of information between two cognitive structures takes place. It is generated by self-referential cognitive processes, but also in the course of any direct act of communication. In the first case, it serves to generate reality; in the second case, it serves to exchange information through communication between two cognitive structures. Actual information becomes conscious either through self-initiated cognitive reactivation or through information processing triggered by external sensory perception. To convert potential information into actual information, the structural components of a reference domain are required.

Information processing in technical information systems always refers to data, at most to potential information. For a cognitive structure, processing mere data is not sufficient to generate actual information. In the case of processing potential information, this depends on which reference domain is referred to with regard to subsequent reception.

It is therefore not self-evident that potential information is transformed into the same actual information by different people (at different times, in different places). After all, this would only work on the assumption that the reference domains were identical. In times when communication was only verbal, knowledge externalization was almost impossible. Only the combination of language as text or symbols with the physical means of preserving it gave us the idea of storing information in such a way that it can be passed on at any later time.

Information Transfer through Communication

To begin with, we consider a situation of direct communication between two persons (Figure 3.1).[110] Both persons shall be conceived as individual cognitive structures whose respective information processing and the related ways to store knowledge takes place within a cohesive self-referential system.

When interacting with other people, communication takes place via various sensory channels, the communication mechanisms of which must be acquired over time. Communication functions as a corrective to self-referential information processing in an autopoietic system and depends on the ability of the communication partners involved to take into account the recipient role of the other. Here,

---

[110] This model was first introduced in Gödert/Kübler: Konzepte von Wissensdarstellung und Wissensrezeption medial vermittelter Information.

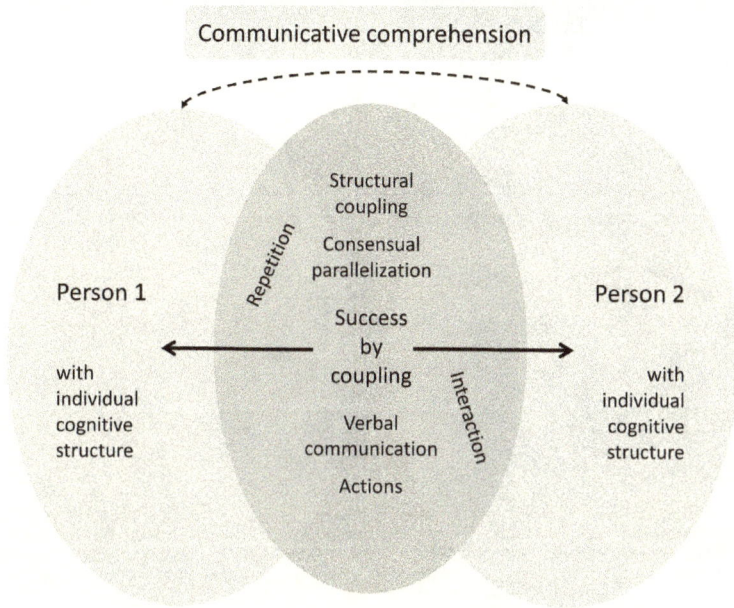

Fig. 3.1: Knowledge acquisition through communication (1).

verbal communication is conditioned on the semantic representation of concepts in the cognitive structures.

A simple case of such communication consists in referring to a real-world object that is familiar to both communication partners and for which a conceptualization has already preceded. Even if the same designation is not shared—for example, if the communicating partners speak different languages—a common understanding can be achieved by direct reference to the object. Conceptualization is then made possible via feedback references, thus ensuring the success of the communication (Figure 3.2).

The situation becomes more difficult when abstract concepts are involved (Figure 3.3). The degree of complexity even increases with unknown real-world objects, unknown abstract objects, lack of conceptualizations, and unknown designations.

3.2 Communication and Feedback

Communication takes place through the exchange of signals (sounds, language, gestures) between cognitive structures, for example between two persons. These sensory impressions are compared with existing knowledge structures within the

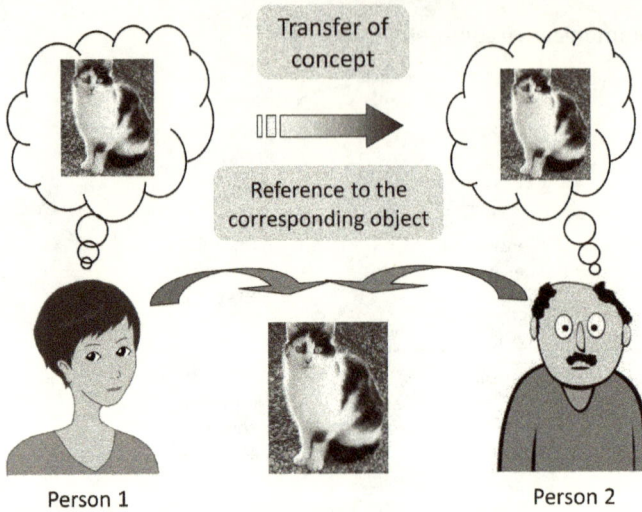

Fig. 3.2: Knowledge acquisition through communication (2).

respective self-referential information processing and adapted or built up into new knowledge structures (Figure 3.1).

Successful communication requires a structural coupling of both communication partners, ensuring that the message sent and received is not just something uttered, but that common knowledge structures are present through which an exchange on that utterance can take place in an act of communication.[111] By taking on the role of a mutual observer, it is possible to sound out and verify that the act of communication is based on a common consensus, so that it can succeed and any missing preconditions can be compensated for.

As long as there is a consensual parallelization for both partners, such as by access to a common domain or a domain that is equally familiar to both, there is a greater chance of structural coupling for the concrete act of communication. Comparable structures and mutually familiar domains are created through shared participation in events and knowledge, as well as through any communicative exchange about them. However, consensual parallelization is not a necessary prerequisite, since both partners can achieve structural coupling via the mutual observer role.

What other conditions can contribute to a successful communication (in the sense of information transfer from one cognitive structure to another) or be con-

---

111 For an explanation of the concept of structural coupling, see Maturana: Kognition.

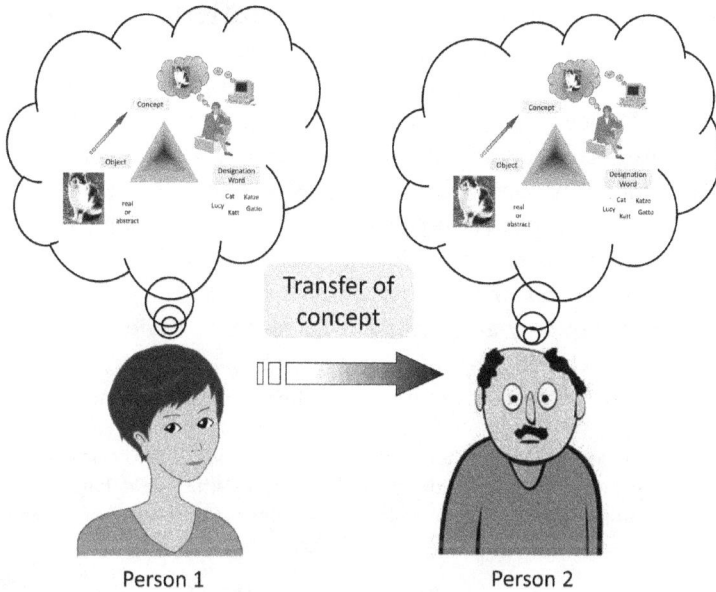

Fig. 3.3: Knowledge acquisition through communication (3).

sidered as its preconditions? For a verbally initiated act of communication, both cognitive structures must have, in addition to conceptualization, an equal understanding of the words used as carriers of conceptual meaning. In an act of communication, no context-free concepts are exchanged, but syntactically formed phrases in a concrete situation. This includes mutual knowledge of the syntactic structures used, but also of possible connotations. Therefore, communication problems can occur due to divergent individual memories, differences in situational or emotional memory, or personal animosities. Even a scientific dialogue can be hindered by affective components.

Not all acts of communication are successful. This is only natural, since hardly any two individuals undergo the same ontogenetic development. That there is still a good chance of mutual understanding is also due to neural plasticity, which allows our brains to constantly review, adapt, and change our cognitive structures (Chapter 1.3).

Is there a test criterion for success in communication that can also serve as a criterion for the equality of information between the communication partners involved? It seems most plausible to not only tie the success to a unilateral speech act, but to test it again via feedback. The simplest form of feedback is the verification of an action initiated by the act of communication. When asked "Pass me the salt shaker, please", the success or failure of the verbal exchange is directly verifiable. This type of feedback can be practiced and learned. It is noteworthy that the majority of successful situations are not remembered in detail, but the experience of success leads to an increased degree of confidence, which in turn results in a skilled use of concepts and their designations in any future act of communication. Also, action situations themselves can lead to conceptualization and thus to the formation of concepts. These concepts are communicated in contexts, which further clarifies what is meant. In this way, concepts can be successfully communicated even in a context that is detached from actions.

Language, then, is not only an instrument for mapping reality, but can—according to *Terry Winograd* and *Fernando Flores*—also be part of and a means of expression for a constructive process of understanding related to action:

> Knowledge and understanding (in both the cognitive and linguistic senses) do not result from formal operations on mental representations of an objectively existing world. Rather, they arise from the individual's committed participation in mutually oriented patterns of behavior that are embedded in a socially shared background of concerns, actions, and beliefs.[112]

If, in such a dialogue, language is given the role of expressing directives for an action, the correct execution of this action presupposes, in addition to an understanding of the concepts used, an insight into complex interrelations of effects. For example, actions can be placed in a conditional context: "When the milk starts to boil, the pot must be taken off the stove top."

The next level up is that the contexts are components of larger "scripts"[113]. In addition to the previously mentioned action sequence for preparing breakfast (Chapter 1.3), these can be, for example, scripts for crossing a busy street, checking in at the airport, or going to a concert. All these situations are characterized by the fact that they consist of complex processes that are designed according to self-defined rules or rules set by others. Familiarity with sequences of actions grows with experience, but communication about the concepts and contexts describing them increases the confidence to navigate within such complex scripts. The greater the confidence becomes, the less the use of the concept is tied to verification by an action.

Consequently, understanding and the correct use of concepts is the continuation of a communication situation that builds on elementary actions and the

---

112 Winograd/Flores: Understanding computers and cognition, p. 78.
113 It is quite intended to associate with the use of this word the language use of artificial intelligence, as introduced by *Roger Schank* (Schank/Childers: The cognitive computer, Schank: Computer, elementare Aktionen und linguistische Theorien).

verification of their success.[114] A concept is demonstrably understood when it can be used meaningfully (correctly) and this is confirmed by others. There are two ways to describe this condition:

1. I can perform a meaningful action related to the concept or underlying object. It is not necessary for this to give anything like a definition of the concept. I can eat soup with a spoon without knowing a definition for "spoon".
2. I can use an abstract concept in a defined environment according to the rules that prevail in that environment and evaluate the reaction of other members of that group. This is often the case when a new concept is introduced that does not yet have an established paradigm usage. But also standard learning situations in all fields of knowledge proceed in this way. The action-related test in these cases is replaced by the use of linguistic means.

Humans develop extensive experience for understanding and correctly using concepts throughout their lives. The following description of a learning game for children shows how conceptualizations are cognitively triggered and accompanied by actions. The game consists of a wooden board with cutouts (Figure 3.4). The cutouts have different outline shapes and in some games contain the designations of the objects to be inserted. Exactly one of the objects (puzzle pieces) fits into each cutout. In our example, each puzzle piece shows a motif of a farm, like an animal, a tree, or a farm building. Once you have taken all the pieces out of the wooden board, the goal is to put them back in. We all know lift-out puzzles from our own childhood or from watching children playing this game.

Dealing with this task involves different levels of conceptualization. First, there is the option of just trying, i.e., trying one of the pieces until it fits into one of the cutouts. This will at first only promote a familiarity with the concept of contour and the specific outline of the object as seen from one viewing direction. If an abstract idea of this already exists, comparing the outline with the contour of a cutout can lead to faster success than is possible by pure trial and error.

If the cutouts are additionally labeled and the corresponding designations are known, on the one hand the design of the puzzle piece can trigger a hunch about the motif depicted and on the other hand the notion of the label aside the cutout can lead to an attempt to insert it. This is confirmed or rejected simply by whether the puzzle piece fits in the cutout or not. If these conditions are met, it is also possible to establish a previously unknown connection between appearance and designation.

---

114 We recall the view of knowledge by *Karl Popper*, who understands the grasping or comprehension of a concept as an active process in which the associated concept is replicated or recreated.

Fig. 3.4: Lift-out puzzle.

Adults observing the game pronounce the names of the depicted motifs aloud in the event of both success and failure. Thus, the child has no choice but to associate the illustration with a linguistic statement; even if it cannot yet speak the name itself. It is very likely that such a game will be played not only once, but again and again. This results in strong repetition and correction effects, whereby even the simple possibility of pure trial and error can be followed by conceptualization processes involving the memorization of verbal naming.

The formalized educational structures established in social communities along with their elaborate procedures for knowledge transfer and knowledge acquisition lead to the formation of shared cognitive structures. We can convince ourselves every day in our immediate environment or by observing the conditions in other cultural groups of how great the measure of commonality is—but how great nevertheless also the measure of diversity can be.

In summary, successful communication is tied to a structural coupling of the communication partners (as structurally determined cognitive structures). Structural coupling is ensured via reference domains of knowledge (now meant as the sum of used concepts, contexts and scripts of action and communication environments). Using the same words or committing to using the same concepts is nevertheless no guarantee for an act of communication to be completely congruent at the level of meaning.

3.3 Reception of Externalized Information

Knowledge acquisition through potential information from externalized sources is to compensate for non-existing knowledge (non-knowledge). A simple model of knowledge acquisition in terms of the unmodified, "additive" incorporation of externalized components into a cognitive structure, has already been presented and rejected. Acquiring new knowledge always involves more than a mere transmission in the sense of a one-to-one hand-over of information. This becomes especially clear by the difference between factual and structural knowledge and leads to the question how complete the coordinated facts and structures have to be in order to be considered as external representations. Structural knowledge is considered superior to factual knowledge in this respect, since numerous examples demonstrate the human ability to deal structurally with a conceptual system, even if not all facts are known.[115]

The incorporation of a new piece of knowledge into a cognitive structure usually alters the preexisting structure by creating new connections or extending, degrading, or reinforcing already existing connections.[116] Figure 3.5 visualizes this process in a highly simplified way. The hierarchical layering and clustering into neuronal substructures, as well as the complex variety of recursive influences on neuronal cells for situation-specific attenuation or amplification, cannot be visualized within the scope of this representation. However, it is essential not to associate neuronal knowledge expansion with the generation of new neurons; the illustration should be interpreted more in terms of activating existing cells and reorganizing existing structures with their circuitry.

Also, the cognitive structure is different from person to person. Changes due to external incentives as well as consuming the same external knowledge components lead to individual cognitive structures. The extent of the rebuild and the effort that is to be put into it are proving to be unpredictable, which is confirmed by scientific observations of learning effort and learning success. Of course, there are cases in which a change in the cognitive structure is no longer possible, and neither learning nor knowledge growth can occur.

If an externalized knowledge component has already been built into the cognitive structure and belongs in principle to the knowledge of a person, a new reception will nevertheless not remain without changes in the existing structure. The process of reception and integration is fundamentally connected with comparison

---

115 See Hentig: Die Flucht aus dem Denken ins Wissen.
116 See Lehmann: Neues vom Gehirn, Strohschneider: Wissenserwerb und Handlungsregulation, Bauer et al.: Selbstorganisierende neuronale Karten.

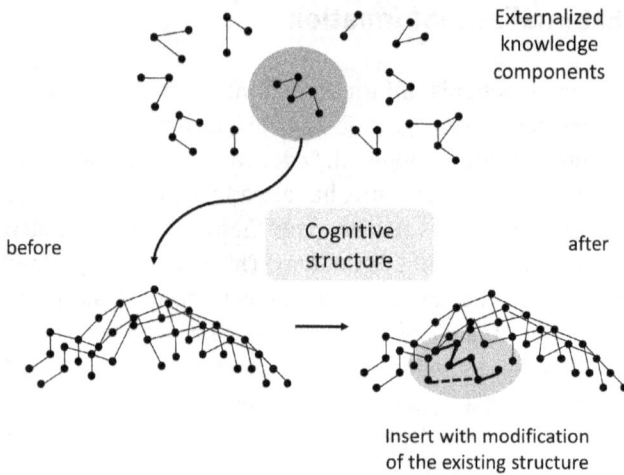

Fig. 3.5: Knowledge acquisition from externalized knowledge (2).

and change, both for what is already known and for what is new. Existing connections are dissolved, degraded or reinforced, new connections are established. It is in line with general experience that looking at a familiar object again or repeating a thought process that has already been carried out produces altered associations and thus indicates altered cognitive structures. The cognitive structure is not a storehouse of knowledge with static conditions, but is constantly rebuilding itself.

At this point it is useful to distinguish between subjective experiential knowledge and the assignment of this knowledge to different intersubjectively shaped reference domains (Chapter 2.4).

In intersubjectively shaped reference domains (understood as the sum of concepts, contexts, and scripts), individual success within the system is determined much more strongly by participation in agreements than is the case in the domain of individual experience(s). Compared to direct interpersonal communication, phenomena of non-understanding are then also found more frequently in such areas. When representatives of different disciplines want to engage in a dialog, they enter the terrain of true interdisciplinarity. Here it is advantageous, if not a prerequisite, to be aware of each other's knowledge structures (often apostrophized as scientific socialization). When this is lacking, often only an exchange of factual entities is possible, which is accompanied by a multitude of phenomena of non-knowledge and consequently of non-understanding.

In general, building structural knowledge is perceived as not only more superior but also more difficult than incorporating a datum into an existing structure. The building of new structural knowledge—roughly comparable to the process of abstracting—is accompanied by a subjective feeling of effort. The repetitive inclusion of facts in an already existing structure, by contrast, is rather experienced as tiring. For example, reading a second novel in which only the names of the characters, places, etc. have been changed from the first novel, but not its basic structure, may still be considered enjoyable, but further novels in the same style may be felt as boring. In such a case, an arc of tension can be useful for the reception of structural or factual knowledge, which resembles a mixture of symmetry and non-symmetry, and which, together with the individually correct mixture of structural and factual knowledge, creates a sense of aesthetic well-being.[117]

3.4 Theory Binding of Knowledge Elements

Theory binding plays an important role for knowledge acquisition from externalized information sources. Following on from the topic of contextualizing concepts and statements and assigning them to intersubjectively shaped domains of reference, we will now examine more closely the extent to which it is justified to distinguish between the acquisition of factual and structural knowledge.[118]

Data and facts are generally considered the simplest forms of knowledge elements. They are liked to be thought of as context-free, presumably because the context is so obvious. People experience data primarily in an associated experiential context, in a factual context, or in connection with theoretical modeling.

Events in space and time first shape us through our own physiological processes and their spatio-temporal relationships before an abstract understanding of space and time is developed from this. The never resting cognitive process of abstracting any current event may be impaired by physiological ailments, but rarely completely paralyzed. Humans are constantly active and always integrate previous experiences and existing (previously cognitively represented) knowledge. And neither consists of data alone. The process of abstraction leads from a concrete event to an abstract context. The ongoing abstraction processes lead to the formation of a cognitive structure, and this becomes the framework for integrating data and facts. This framework is not static, but can be changed by new integration processes.

Data can be completely meaningless without context. For example, the number "42" can only be interpreted through a corresponding frame of reference: as

---

117 For a representation related to the field of language, see Holenstein: Symmetrie und Symmetriebruch in der Sprache.

118 Hübner: Die Wahrheit des Mythos, pp. 239–290, Hübner: Critique of the scientific reason.

an amount of money in Euro or US Dollar, as a temperature indicator in Celsius or Fahrenheit, as a length in the metric or Anglo-American system of measurement, or even as a universal answer in *Douglas Adams' The Hitchhiker's Guide to the Galaxy*. This kind of context binding of data—and thus their theory binding—is more readily accessible when used within the scientific world with its abundance of artificial conceptual creations. Perhaps this has also contributed to the bland flavor associated with the commitment to theory. Nevertheless, it cannot be denied that theory binding is omnipresent and that our life would not be possible at all without theory binding.

An example will explain this in more detail. Nowadays, we are used to opening files on a computer by double-clicking on the file icon. In doing so, we sometimes forget that a suitable program must first be linked to the file in order to present its content in the correct manner. This link is usually made via the operating system's default settings. For unknown file extensions, the attempt to open the file is followed by a request to the user asking which application program should be launched. You can easily get your own impression of this by renaming a *.jpg* file to a *.txt* file. Double-clicking the renamed file will produce something other than the expected image display.

Such examples show that data, as long as they are not just context-free digits or coded character sequences, have a higher state of aggregation than, for example, cognitively interpretable sensory impressions. Data are sensory impressions put into a processable form or results of theory-guided processes. The fact that machine processing is tied to data is no contradiction to this. Machine data processing can only produce useful results if it is based on theory, reference domains, and the resulting interpretability of the data.

But it is not only data that is theory-bound. Ambiguous terms (homonyms) are examples of theory binding even at the level of concepts. Gestures (like shaking the head as a way of negating or affirming), symbols (like the varied design of a cross), advertising messages (like a washing machine standing next to a deer in the woods), or other forms of culturally shaped artifacts demonstrate the importance of context for correct interpretation on the social level as well.

In summary, it can be stated that there is no direct empirical access to facts of actual reality, but that all knowledge (thus, in particular, also the factual) can and must be acquired only via theory-guided models and by addressing questions to actual reality. The assumption that there is an increase in complexity from data to information to knowledge to wisdom (*DIKW* pyramid) is also challenged by this. Based on the argumentation made here, corrections to this view are necessary.[119]

3.5 Knowledge Representation in Artificial Intelligence

One ambition of artificial intelligence is to master the most challenging approaches to formal knowledge representation, including the assumptions already discussed about theory-bound data and forms of knowledge. We will now revisit this aspect and examine the conditions under which externalization of knowledge can occur in order to approximate performance capacities as encountered in cognitive externalization and reception processes.

Artificial intelligence methods are used, for example, in knowledge bases and expert or diagnostic systems to model data, concepts, and assertions as entities and relationships in order to derive conclusions using formal inference mechanisms. These systems gain special value through the compilation of content, which is often thought of as the sum of the knowledge of a larger group of people ("expert system"). Conclusions can thus be drawn on a basis that goes beyond the capabilities of individuals. The application of such systems, often used as assistance systems in diagnostic settings, has become well established.[120]

However, one consideration is overlooked here: a diagnostic system must allow for case distinctions and, to that end, provide mandatory standards that can be used for queries. Any form of standardization—even if it involves compiling the experiences of as many individuals as possible—requires that the experiences gained be brought into line with the schemes of standardization. It is therefore likely that this will leave out cases which will then not be considered in the subsequent support provided by the diagnostic system. This would be unremarkable, because in the context of human diagnosis, it would not matter. However, once people have become accustomed to viewing the diagnostic system as the yardstick of analysis, they will not pay as much attention to new or changed phenomena. The supposed completeness of the diagnosis can then lead not only to facts being overlooked, but also—and more importantly—to skills being lost.

Some have long seen in such systems for knowledge representation a benefit for human knowledge processing, up to memory extension or even its replacement.

---

119 This view is taken especially in the context of information economics, organizational theory, and knowledge management, see Knowledge [Wikipedia]; for a critique of the model, see Frické: The knowledge pyramid.
120 See Rötzer: Chinesischer Roboter.

This position becomes even clearer when referring to the potential of virtual worlds with their multimedia representation possibilities:

> Virtual worlds technology may provide a key to assimilating complex information stored in databases. Instead of displaying the results of a database on a screen, we may be able to step "through the looking glass" and immerse ourselves in the data. This presentation of data could take advantage of all our senses.[121]

At least the replacement of the human memory is not yet demanded here. However, it is already being looked at ways to use neuroimplants to compensate for lost brain functions to expand memory.[122]

The hopes for the effect of the *Nuremberg funnel* have not been fulfilled. In modern times, these hopes have instead morphed into expectations for the use of information technology in teaching and learning. In the technology euphoria of the 1960s, information databases were predicted to replace encyclopedias, which would allow for short-term updating and which could be easily queried.

One of the most recent candidates of IT-based educational efforts, the *Massive Open Online Course (MOOC)*, is seeking success with multimedia online courses, offering access to the curricula of elite educational institutions and advertising with the advantage of anytime access and no need to meet physically.[123]

It is a constantly recurring pattern of argumentation: the use of technology and automation in education are supposed to create free space for learning and creativity. Well, giving examples to justify this pattern is not easy. Rather, it seems difficult to avoid the impression that the use of modern technologies creates new obligations on top, which must also be managed through increased administrative efforts. It is beyond dispute that the multimedia representation of externalized knowledge can increase the potential for acquiring knowledge. Whether or not this actually happens, and even leads to increased or improved knowledge on the part of the individual, is by no means certain. If so, shouldn't the data being surveyed to determine educational success show a steady upward trend?

Much greater challenges arise with respect to creating systems that are intended to represent all knowledge types of human information processing in addition to specialized knowledge. Modeling everyday knowledge with relationships and inferences requires the consideration of numerous entities with no domain-specific restrictions and with an even larger number of relationships between these entities.

---

121 Miller: Virtual reality and online databases.
122 For an overview, see Mensch – Maschine – Visionen [Spektrum].
123 See for example Röthler: Lehrautomaten.

There is a fundamental difficulty for each modeling, as shown by the following example: The attempt to characterize all birds as vertebrates that can fly is disproved by penguins. In formal modeling, exclusion clauses are therefore needed to avoid erroneous inferences.[124] Moreover, the exclusion clauses must be associated with the correct entities in the hierarchical structure of the represented knowledge. This in turn leads to the consequential problem that even drawing inferences about represented relations between concepts must not lead to false conclusions.

Tables 3.1 to 3.5 compare characteristics of information processing respectively referring to humans, animals, "ordinary" personal computers and autonomous computers using artificial intelligence methods. These comparisons show the differences in the externalization of knowledge between machine systems and human cognitive processes.

Basically, there are different approaches for the representation of knowledge in externalized form. Formal knowledge representation (ontologies) is based on characteristics, attributes and properties of the entities to be represented. From this data, relationships between entities are established using various inference rules and prepared for machine processing. These relationships or correlations may or may not correspond to those of cognitive interpretation.

The meanwhile classical concept-oriented structures (classification systems, thesauri) requires users to have a prior comprehension of the concepts that are represented in a structured way by means of relations. It is not common to specify the entire set of characteristics for each represented concept. In most cases, not even the characteristic that is decisive for structuring is explicitly identified.

Hybrid knowledge representation systems that incorporate properties from both worlds in the same way have been rare so far.[125]

The future way of how we understand knowledge will be influenced by what is known as semantic technologies.[126] Here, available knowledge is formally mapped to three-part entities, so-called triples, each of which form a statement:

A blue tit is a bird.
A bird has wings.
A blue tit is singing on a branch.
Blue tits eat insects.

---

124 Bibel/Hölldobler/Schaub: Wissensrepräsentation und Inferenz, pp. 58–60.
125 See Gödert/Hubrich/Nagelschmidt: Semantic knowledge representation for information retrieval.
126 For a synoptic view, see Dengel (ed.): Semantische Technologien.

The large number of available concepts and formalized statements are an ideal basis for deep learning methods. The deep learning approach originally sought to replicate the deeply layered architecture of the human brain for the purpose of machine learning. Meanwhile, the simulation of the human capacity to comprehend and explain has long since been superseded as a goal by successes in the analysis of huge data sets (big data).[127] The guiding idea behind big data is: By analyzing a sufficiently large number of cases (represented by data in suitable data models), fewer of the cases that occur in reality will be overlooked than if the previously known cases were systematized on the basis of a predefined schema and made available for analysis. In short, no knowledge model can better represent the diversity of real-world phenomena than a complete data image of those phenomena.

The success of machine translation systems such as *DeepL* is precisely not based on the fact that they have learned the extensive linguistic skills of human translators. What they know about correct translations and the grammatically and syntactically correct use of the language, they learn from very large amounts of previously translated data. Machine learning performance critically depends on training data, which must be available in sufficient quantity and quality. Whether it is machine translation or face recognition, it is impossible to do without the human skills needed to produce the training data.[128]

Against the backdrop of such approaches, it is easy to imagine that knowledge in the future will no longer be oriented toward understanding and explaining, but will be seen as a fragment of data derived from big data that has proven successful in a particular context.

---

[127] For an introduction, see Jones: Deep Learning.
[128] Entire business areas have emerged from this necessity, see Schmidt: Crowdproduktion von Trainingsdaten.

Tab. 3.1: Signal perception and stimulus perception.

	source	process	result
human	sensory stimuli	neural processing	internal pattern
animal	sensory stimuli	neural processing	internal pattern
computer	sensors	algorithmic processing	data in structured form
autonomous computer	sensors	algorithmic processing	data in structured form

Tab. 3.2: Self-induced information processing.

	source	process	result
human	neural patterns	neural processing, structure building, abstraction, assessment	inner pattern
animal	unclear	?	?
computer	not known	?	?
autonomous computer	desire? feasibility?	algorithmic processing, assessment	data in structured form

Tab. 3.3: Communication.

	source	process	result
human	language, sounds, symbols, gestures	neural processing, structure building, abstraction, assessment, feedback	internal pattern, actions
animal	speech, sounds	reflex, neural processing	actions
computer	data in structured form	algorithmic processing	data in modified structure
autonomous computer	language, sounds, symbols, gestures, data in structured form	algorithmic processing, assessment	data in structured form, actions

Tab. 3.4: Externalization.

	source	process	result
human	neural patterns	neural processing, structure building	language, sounds, symbols, actions, texts, medial forms
animal	neural patterns	neuronal processing	sounds, actions
computer	data in structured form	algorithmic processing	data in modified structure
autonomous computer	desire? feasibility?	?	?

Tab. 3.5: Reception.

	source	process	result
human	texts, medial forms	neural processing, structure buildung	inner pattern
animal	not known	?	?
computer	not known	?	?
autonomous computer	desire? feasibility?	algorithmic processing, structure building	data in structured form

4 Elements of Informational Literacy

There's no longer a whole man confronting a whole world, only a human something moving about in a general culture-medium.

Robert Musil[129]

Information processing serves humans to assess, decide, and act, whereby there is no fundamental distinction to be made between the rational and emotional parts of information literacy. Information has a dual function here. It is the source for initiating and carrying out information processing and at the same time it is a part of the process that changes it and leads to a result. All in all, this is an extremely complex process, which we will now discuss in more detail. The focus here will be on rational processing.

It is often argued that assessing and deciding is dependent on the completeness of the information known about a given situation or problem. This completeness, however, can only be assessed if one knows the extent of what is not known, which is usually not possible. Referring to the completeness of available information gives the impression that non-availability has something to do with an insufficient "amount" in the sense of a quantity. Yet this falls short, because the context of the available information and the prior knowledge of the individual are of considerable importance for the usability of this information. For each of the following scenarios, imagine that you are an observer who is provided with all the information about the situation in the same way as the actual actor:

- an examiner who must grade an examination;
- a doctor who must make a diagnosis;
- an entrepreneur who needs to make an investment decision.

All of the above examples have one thing in common: the observing layperson may have the same information about the situation, but cannot make any assessment or a decision because assessments and decisions require their own context, which is linked to knowledge and experience in addition to the situational information.[130]

Thus, there must be other factors that serve as basic functions of cognitive information processing, independent of knowledge and situational information, and which enable people to act competently. To this end, we first propose the

---

129 Musil: The man without qualities, p. 234.
130 There are situations in which one may not know everything at all in order to be able to act, or in which complete knowledge may even result in the prohibition of acting, such as the prohibition of insider trading in stock exchange transactions.

https://doi.org/10.1515/9783110693744-004

concepts of context, contextualization, abstraction, inferring, analogy, intuition, and plausibility as cognitive prerequisites for informational literacy. In the context of cognitive science, they are related to the concept of so-called cognitive operators.[131] In Table 4.1, cognitive operators and cognitive prerequisites of informational literacy are juxtaposed.

Tab. 4.1: Cognitive operators and cognitive prerequisites for informational literacy.

Cognitive operators	Cognitive prerequisites
the holistic operator	to contextualize
the reductionist operator	to instantiate, to specify
the abstracting operator	to abstract
the quantitative operator	to infer
the causal operator	intuition, plausibility
the binary operator	–
the existential operator	–
the operator for emotional evaluation	to assess and to decide

4.1 Contextualizing

The presence of context is so familiar to us that we usually do not consciously think about it. We are always moving within a certain time and a certain space. We each have our own experiences and meet other people with their own experiences. Some of these experiences are shaped by a socio-cultural environment and thus are shared by many people. Others may first need to be exchanged and brought into congruence for a common understanding. The concept of contextualization is used for these processes. By this we mean the assignment of a context to a concept or statement within a communication or reception process in order to express or grasp the specific meaning. This is a basic technique, without which communication is not possible.

The manifestations of context are very diverse, and so is the task of contextualizing. For example, it may be a matter of clarifying the meaning or usage of concepts in different subject fields, everyday contexts, or factual situations. Any linguistic ambiguity gives rise to contextualization. Below the level of linguistic ambiguity of nouns or adjectives, verbs provide good examples of the need for con-

---

131 Newberg/D'Aquili/Rause: Why god won't go away, pp. 46–53.

textualization, which, however, is carried out largely unnoticed due to the great familiarity we have with their usage. A verb like "to cut" does not change its meaning by itself, but has to be contextualized differently in statements like "I cut the hair", "I cut the cake" or "I cut the grass", which is of importance at the latest when choosing the tool for the respective activity.[132]

Personal contexts also play a role, which are shaped by individual relationships and experiences over and above the general contexts, or by reference domains of knowledge (Chapter 2.4). Some (many?) experiences are even bound to individual interests that are not meant to be shared at all and accordingly make communication difficult. This case must remain outside our discussion. The only situation we can point to is one that has mutual understanding as its goal.

An example of a disambiguation task can be provided by the concept "milk". If this concept comes up in the context of an everyday discussion, there will hardly be any doubt about its meaning. However, a closer look reveals a variety of reference systems with different statistical significance related to the context. Milk can be raw material and product, economic good and food, and it can come from different animals or plants. The word can also be used to characterize a particular appearance, as in "coconut milk", "glacier milk" or even "milk glass". The distancing of the context of milk coming from an animal producer has since led to a legal dispute as to whether soy milk should be designated as milk at all.[133]

4.2 Abstracting, Specifying, Instantiating

The abilities to abstract, to specify, and to instantiate are keystones of human cognition and communication and an indispensable basic competence for many other cultural techniques.[134]

Abstracting means that in a variety of appearances the common is recognized and summarized to a concept, which includes the single appearance as an example, but goes beyond it in its meaning. Abstracting is the ability to recognize and apply patterns of knowledge. Specifying or instantiating means the reverse, namely the transfer of knowledge patterns to more specific concepts or individual objects. Specifying and instantiating are not always sharply distinguished in their meaning. The concept of instantiation is to be used here for the lowest level of a

---

132 See the remarks on the concept of "background" in Searle: The construction of social reality, pp. 129–137.

133 The *European Court of Justice* ruled on June 14, 2017, that milk as a food is tied to an animal producer (Court of Justice of the European Union: Press Release No 63/17).

134 For the philosophical background of the concepts, see Axelos et al.: Allgemeines/Besonderes.

specification process, which is usually expressed linguistically by an individual name.

Tab. 4.2: Specification – Instantiation.

Concept	Specification	Instantiation
landform	mountain	Mount Everest
tower	wrought-iron lattice tower	Eiffel Tower
ship	passenger ship	Titanic

Recognizing the common from a multitude of phenomena requires the ability to assign the individual to a whole. This also includes, for example, the interpretation of a sequence of digits as a number in the decimal place value system. We recall the sequence of digits "314159" that we used earlier when discussing data and information, the latter of which can only be thought of within a context (Chapter 2.5).

Alarmingly, observations reported from elementary schools indicate that children have problems deriving words from sequences of letters even for simple everyday words. Analogously, the same can be said for interpreting numbers from sequences of digits.[135] It can be surmised that without mastery of these two basic techniques, it will be very difficult to learn the abstraction techniques that build upon them.

Abstracting and specifying or instantiating, each viewed from a different angle, are involved in an interplay between the general and the particular (or specific). Together, they typically come into play when different hierarchical levels meet in semantic contexts. Although this happens quite often, it is not always presented in a transparent manner. An example will illustrate this: a "Media Package Birds of Europe" can be understood to include:

– voices of the most famous songbirds in Germany;
– an illustrated book of the feathered winter guests in the Lower Rhine Region;
– video footage of bird migration over Spain.

On the one hand, the three subjects are characterized by a combination of several aspects (type of media, animal, place, action); on the other hand, the aspects

---

135 The potentially associated longer-term consequences are among the subjects of the *IGLU* studies, most recently in 2017 (Stabile Ergebnisse bei zunehmenden Herausforderungen [BMBF]).

are also differently general or specific in each case. While the complexity of this interaction is not an issue for understanding, describing it is more difficult.

Much of our language-related cognitive ability is expressed in concrete speech acts through this switching between the general and the particular. Why do people tend to give different answers to the questions "Can you hold growth in your hand?" and "Can you hold birds in your hand?" It is because "growth" and "birds" are both abstract concepts. And abstract concepts—even those derived from real objects—cannot in principle be held in the hand. The two questions differ, however, in that "birds" is abstracted from a large number of object-based concepts of the real world and is thought to be cognitively connected to them as instances. Individual birds can be held in the hand, and this property is transferred to the abstracted conceptuality. "Growth", by contrast, is an abstract concept (and an ambiguous one at that) to be assigned to institutional reality. In principle, you cannot hold such a concept in your hand.

The distinction made here has found expression in literary form in *Umberto Eco's The Name of the Rose*:

> "All the same," I said, "when you read the prints in the snow and the evidence of the branches, you did not yet know Brunellus. In a certain sense those prints spoke of all horses, or at least all horses of that breed. Mustn't we say, then, that the book of nature speaks to us only of essences, as many distinguished theologians teach?" "Not entirely, dear Adso," my master replied. "True, that kind of print expressed to me, if you like, the idea of 'horse', the verbum mentis, and would have expressed the same to me wherever I might have found it. But the print in that place and at that hour of the day told me that at least one of all possible horses had passed that way. So I found myself halfway between the perception of the concept 'horse' and the knowledge of an individual horse. And in any case, what I knew of the universal horse had been given me by those traces, which were singular. I could say I was caught at that moment between the singularity of the traces and my ignorance, which assumed the quite diaphanous form of a universal idea. If you see something from a distance, and you do not understand what it is, you will be content with defining it as a body of some dimension. When you come closer, you will then define it as an animal, even if you do not yet know whether it is a horse or an ass. And finally, when it is still closer, you will be able to say it is a horse even if you do not yet know whether it is Brunellus or Niger. And only when you are at the proper distance will you see that it is Brunellus (or, rather, that horse and not another, however you decide to call it). And that will be full knowledge, the learning of the singular. So an hour ago I could expect all horses, but not because of the vastness of my intellect, but because of the paucity of my deduction. And my intellect's hunger was sated only when I saw the single horse that the monks were leading by the halter. Only then did I truly know that my previous reasoning had brought me close to the truth. And so the ideas, which I was using earlier to imagine a horse I had not yet seen, were pure signs, as the hoofprints in the

snow were signs of the idea of 'horse'; and signs and the signs of signs are used only when we are lacking things."[136]

We understand abstraction as the ability to assign a place to the individual in a context which is suitable for it. This view does not imply any claim to universality or to the creation of a normative plan for all phenomena in the world. Abstraction is rather seen as an open development with a dynamic flow of additions and changes. It thus holds a place between the disordered diversity of the world and the plan of a normative order of the world.

The relationship that a citizen of a civil society has with laws is a good illustration of the relationship between a single normative rule, its context, and the need for abstraction. Laws are particularly committed to a context and a theoretical modeling of society, without which their meaning often cannot be inferred. If we presuppose that an individual is willing in principle to obey the laws, this is practically possible only if the laws have already been enacted with reference to a corresponding regulatory fact.

However, dynamic developments in a complex society keep generating contexts so new that they cannot yet have been regulated by legal provisions. Current examples include the internet economy and copyright law for digital media. The tradition of Roman legal interpretation—less so the Anglo-American practice with its case-based jurisprudence—offers as a way out legal action by derivation from superordinate rules, by making analogies, and by reference to the idea or spirit of pre-existing legal norms. This, too, is a typical abstraction performance. The better the individual succeeds in this task of abstraction, the fewer disputes the institutionalized justice system will have to deal with. In whose interest would this be? Is it surprising that in a time when ideas and spirit are no longer highly valued, even the making of analogies to judge legally correct behavior rarely receives natural approval? Is it not logical, then, that many problems should rather be decided by recourse to legal action?

The ability to abstract is not exclusively an intellectual, rational function; rather, it is part of the basic set of survival functions that have been developed through evolution. The ability to abstract can also be observed in many animal species. For example, some European songbird species choose peanuts as their preferred food, regardless of whether the choice of food offered is with or without a surrounding shell. Since the birds could not have come into contact with this food source in their natural environment, they must have some sensorium enabling them to rate this particular food as being especially palatable or high in energy

---

136 Eco: The name of the rose, pp. 30–31.

(presumably the fat content plays a role in this). Such a process of recognition can only be interpreted as a performance of abstraction.

Another important function of our ability to abstract relates to processes of remembering and memory itself. Remembering must not be understood as accessing a non-erasable memory, because the idea of human memory as an inactive depot for retrieving information from the past is increasingly proving to be untrue. *Hannah Monyer* and *Martin Gessmann* demonstrate the importance of memory in shaping the future.[137] What is particularly impressive in our context is that facts can be "remembered" individually, even if they were never known to the individual. This process, which at first seems ghostly, is based on our capacity for abstraction and plausibility combined with the capabilities of collective memory. Unknown details are thereby constructed by matching them with analogous life situations or by drawing on what can be described as life wisdom. This view is confirmed by the assumptions that developers of autonomous learning systems base their work on:

> Our brains are constantly trying to predict the future—and updating their expectations to match reality.[138]

> Our minds are prediction machines, using prior experience and knowledge to make sense of the deluge of information coming from our surroundings. Many neuroscientists and psychologists believe that nearly everything we do—perception, action and learning—relies on making and updating expectations.[139]

Abstraction makes it possible to predict events for phenomena not yet known, to test them against reality, and to integrate them into our own realm of experience.

There is a close relationship between the concept of abstraction and the concepts of paradigm and transcendence, both of which we will introduce in Chapters 5.3 and 6.5.

4.3 Hierarchy, Association, Facets, Semantic Environment

The ability to abstract is connected with two types of relationships distinguishable between concepts: hierarchy and association. Collectively, their different manifestations result in the semantic environment of a concept and thus generate its context.

---

137 Monyer/Gessmann: Das geniale Gedächtnis, pp. 231–232, Korte: Gedächtnis.
138 Kwon: Intelligent machines that learn like children, p. 28.
139 Kwon: Intelligent machines that learn like children, p. 30.

The example of the concept "birds" has shown how relations between concepts can be used to generate assertions that can refer to a varying number of concepts in a concept field. Such correlations can only be established by creating semantic hierarchies for the concepts contained in each of the facets involved. Facets can be regarded as aspects under which instances of the same type appear as specifications. It must be possible to place these in a hierarchy with strict inheritability of the properties. In a taxonomic consideration, one property is added from level to level, so that all assertions with the following structure are correct: "A blue tit is x, x from {titmouse, songbird, bird}". For the above example, this results in the following hierarchy:

Bird → Songbird → Titmouse → Blue tit

Errors occur when more than one facet is used to create the hierarchy:

Bird → Migrant bird → Songbird → Titmouse → Blue tit

Not all songbirds are migratory, and not all migrant birds are songbirds; thus, the two concepts do not show a hierarchical relationship. The assertion "A blue tit is an x, x from {titmouse, songbird, migrant bird, bird}" is no longer true in every case, since a blue tit is not a migrant bird. The characterization as a migrant bird results from another aspect—the bird's migratory behavior—rather than taxonomic features that specify the concept "songbirds".

Our ability to distinguish these facts is the result of a long learning process in which the abstract is repeatedly associated with its instances. If the learning process has been successful, the results can be retrieved without effort. Switching between hierarchy levels, between abstraction and instances, is then easily possible. This explains, for example, that the question "Would you please pass me the salt?" is not met with incomprehension or rejection, although the question actually refers to the salt shaker. It is consistent with the plausibility of everyday life that a salt shaker usually contains salt. If we had to check all the preconditions for plausibility in every situation in life, and if we could not apply the abstracted results of the instances we have already learned to the basis of our actions, we would simply be lost in everyday life. We are not even aware of all the criteria and decision-making ramifications involved in such a process. Examples like these color our daily lives and manifest themselves in many ways.

The second type of relation that contributes to build the semantic environment for a concept is association. Associative relationships are markedly diverse and their boundaries difficult to define. Starting with the concept "blue tit", for instance, other animal species could be associated, but also concepts such as "feeding" or "bird watching"; from the animal "beetle" you can easily get to a German cult car, and so on. There are almost no limits to the creation of such chains of associations, because they are the result of a cognitive performance that does not follow standardized paths. For this reason, the formal representation of associative relationships is difficult, for which the definition of boundaries and a typification of the relationships is required.[140]

From the above examples, it is easy to see why modeling everyday knowledge in expert systems is much more difficult than modeling specialized knowledge in diagnostic systems. Diagnoses are based on criteria even when performed cognitively, and can be comparatively well algorithmized in decision trees—a form of hierarchical context—that underlie the subsequent diagnosis as a flow guide. For the design of the algorithms, the collection of criteria from many people can trigger an additional positive effect. However, whether a newly occurring noise in a passenger car is already a cause for concern is a typical associative viewpoint. If the readout of all stored measurement data shows no abnormalities, an experienced automotive technician who has already been confronted with many different situations will be able to assess this better than any data-based diagnostic system. And this experience-based association is not so easy to model formally, even by collating the experiences of many.

The use and understanding of associations as well as the handling of conceptual hierarchies constitute in their entirety the ability to orient or navigate conceptually in semantic environments. Moreover, the ability to switch between hierarchical levels is an important cultural technique. Wisdoms of life such as "Think globally—act locally" or "Think outside the box" are vivid examples of this.

4.4 Intuition, Heuristics, Hypotheses, Creativity

Closely related to the ability to abstract is the ability to intuition. It also has clear parallels to association, but is more focused on a goal. In our context, intuition can be understood as the ability to recognize new correlations and gain insights. It is often used to solve a task or problem in a new or different way. If intuition is not to miss the target of a task, it must be accompanied by the basic techniques of checking and matching; especially if one wants to approach a target step by step. Intuition is based on preconditions that are difficult to describe and that are

---

140 See for example Gödert/Hubrich/Nagelschmidt: Semantic knowledge representation for information retrieval, Chapter 8.

strongly tied to individual personality development rather than to formal pathways within a codified educational system. While it requires the aforementioned capabilities, it still goes beyond them and cannot simply be turned on or off.

Intuition is of particular importance in decision-making situations. *Gerd Gigerenzer* also sees a close connection with informational tasks:

> The lesson is to trust your intuition when thinking about things that are difficult to predict and when there is little information.[141]

Abstracting and instantiating, contextualizing and building a semantic environment can be trained, but this does not apply so much to intuition. Intuition is more closely associated with spontaneous inspiration. In addition, success in solving a problem through intuition is more strongly associated with well-being. This gives it a positively connoted special position in the group of human abilities.

Nevertheless, intuition does not have to remain completely without preparatory support. The use of heuristics as well as analogy forming can be seen as helpful techniques for its unfolding. Heuristics allow responding to situations where quick decisions need to be made. Their application does not require an extensive rational argumentation sequence or calculation. They are, as it were, preformed instant responses to complex problems, mostly acquired on the basis of success-dependent experience. Without the use of heuristics and their function for the formation of intuition, we could hardly succeed in everyday life. Many everyday decisions have to be made within narrow time frames that do not allow for an extensive analysis of all parameters that can be considered for a rational decision. When craftsmen spontaneously estimate prices for more extensive projects, this indicates the use of a heuristic. In this case, a connection between heuristics and plausibility as a control or correction instrument often becomes apparent.

The use of heuristics is an example of cognitive performance that does not follow rational rules at the moment of its application, but is therefore not irrational. Its genetic and experience-based foundation, its constant review for success or failure, and its principle rational transparency give it the status of a suitable technique for a wide variety of tasks in coping with life.

There are examples that rationality is not always a better guarantor of success in parameter-driven processes than is intuition. A study using a computer simulation to control the output of a factory plant demonstrated that as the complexity of

---

141 Gigerenzer: Gut feelings, p. 151.

the procedure increased, the subjects who optimized intuitively performed better than those who believed they had the optimization algorithm figured out.[142]

People have learned and applied many such heuristics throughout history. They have thereby ensured the survival and development of their species. With increasing consideration of rational factors for decision making, the use of heuristics has probably not declined, but possibly their appreciation has.

Heuristics and intuition are closely related to hypotheses. Hypotheses are assertions whose validity is considered possible under fixed and reproducible conditions, but which have not yet been proven or verified. The world of science is inconceivable without the formation of hypotheses. Hypotheses often stand at the beginning of the formulation of theories from which predictions for real-world events are to be derived. A hypothesis must be testable by its inferences, and depending on the result, it can be either proved or verified, or disproved or falsified. The analysis of successful heuristics and the identification of their rationally flexible components are often at the beginning of hypothesizing.

Intuition and creativity can be combined with each other. Creativity is perhaps the highest feat of intelligence ever achieved by humans. Without these two abilities, the continued development of human societies would hardly be conceivable.

Creativity is usually considered a special ability of an individual and is often associated with giftedness. However, creativity manifests itself in many ways, and all people have the potential to be creative, it is not a phenomenon of only the great geniuses. Creativity is also evident in details, but is often not perceived as such out of exaggerated respect for the achievements of creative giants.

It is beyond dispute that cognitive processes are involved in creative performance; likewise, it is regarded as being part of the human self-image and has a close connection to the emotional level. In the context of artificial intelligence, creativity is now also being attributed to adaptive algorithms. Here, human creativity is utilized as a basis so that algorithms can be designed accordingly. Whether this enables algorithms to enhance or replace human creativity is a matter of heated debate. Abstracting, contextualizing, analogizing, and inferring are essential prerequisites for creativity. And this requires knowledge about previous developments and an understanding of them.

Another topic of heated discussion is the existence and usefulness of swarm intelligence in the data sphere and the derived role of social media for science.[143] Might there even be creativity in the collective data sphere? If swarm intelligence

---

142 Berry/Broadbent: On the relationship between task performance and associated verbalizable knowledge.
143 König/Nentwich: Soziale Medien in der Wissenschaft.

means the united effort of individuals to solve a clearly defined problem, it still remains a process that is tied to human individual creativity and cognitive capacity. Proponents of swarm intelligence base their assumption of anonymous intelligence performance on experiments like the "jelly beans in a jar" experiment, where a number of individuals are guessing how many jelly beans are contained in a jar, and the collective guesstimation is very close to the exact number.[144] However, such phenomena can also be explained by statistical distributive laws and do not yet justify any form of collective creativity being possible without autonomously acting individuals. The extent to which the involvement of individuals in a collective process can be imagined, and the extent to which the creative individual wants to step back behind the collective, depends not least on which reward mechanisms come into play for the individual or the collective.

In summary, creativity and autonomous information processing are mutually dependent and play a significant role in cognitive performance. Both are closely linked to the image of the individual and their role in social communities. If informational autonomy is the basis for all deeper processes of cognitive information processing, creativity is naturally based on it as well.

4.5 Analogy Making and Plausibility

Not all situations and not all facts are so new that one has no clue at all how to evaluate them or how to deal with them. In many cases, they differ only slightly and we have experienced or thought through similar things before.

In the scientific context, making analogies is a standard method of gaining new knowledge and is often accompanied by intuition. Nevertheless, not every assertion made by analogy is immediately true. Its confirmation (or disconfirmation) must be done by other methods. Making analogies is an important tool in everyday life. The criteria used here for confirming or refuting everyday statements are not so much the truth content but rather the reliability or coherence of the statement.

In order not to derive speculative or fictional results from the processes of abstracting and instantiating, making analogies, applying heuristics, or unfolding intuition, it is helpful to have criteria for the coherence of the results available. Here, the criterion of plausibility comes into play. Plausibility does not imply a general claim to truth, but first of all only the subjective impression of coherence. Plausibility serves as a kind of filter that evokes attention or doubt and thus gives rise to closer scrutiny. The result of considering plausibility may or may not be con-

---

144 See Wisdom of the crowd [Wikipedia], Keen: The cult of the amateur.

firmed interpersonally through acts of communication. It is always the preliminary stage of a truth statement. Applying plausibility considerations does not serve to complete an assessment process, but only supports its execution. However, if a binding statement is to be made about the truth content, verification on the basis of further criteria is required.

The following task combines intuitive notions of orders of magnitude and scaling and can be easily verified by calculations after a first plausibility assessment: How often do you have to fold a sheet of paper (printing paper with 100 g paper weight and 0,01 mm thickness) to reach the mean distance from the earth to the sun? And how much larger is this number than the inverse probability of having six matching numbers out of 49 in a lottery?

The answer to the first question is: For a mean distance of 150,000,000 km, you have to fold the sheet 54 times.[145] Compared to the 13,983,816 possibilities for the result of a lottery drawing with six correct numbers, the number of folds is 259,000 times smaller.

Special emphasis is put on plausibility in the interpretation of visually processed data. Visualization claims to be able to make faster and simpler statements based on data analysis. This is done on the basis of comparisons, averaging, data progress, trends, etc. As a general rule, visualization must not distort or even falsify the original data. Nevertheless, this principle is often violated, in particular when special attention is to be drawn to a specific circumstance or fact. Popular techniques for corrupting or biasing data by means of visualization include disproportionately displaying increases, truncating axis scales, and masking out temporal segments.

An example: The development of the amount of household waste per capita of the population in Germany has changed only minimally within the years 1996 to 2000 (Table 4.3).[146] This is what the visualization of the data in Figure 4.1 shows at first glance. However, if one were to care about the statement that the amount of waste has decreased significantly in the period from 1996 to 2000 (which would not correspond to the facts), exactly this impression could be created by the biased representation in Figure 4.2.[147] The fact that this misleading effect is achieved by

---

145 A formula for calculating this is: $2^n \times 0.01 = 1,500,000,000$, corresponding to: $n = \log_2(1,500,000,000,000)$.

146 Source of figures: Haushaltsabfälle je Einwohner in Deutschland bis 2016 [statista].

147 The original can be found at Balzli et al.: SPD.

leaving out part of the scale and the resulting distortion can only be seen on closer study.[148]

Tab. 4.3: Household waste amount per capita in Germany 1996–2000.

Year	Quantity
1996	429
1997	443
1998	437
1999	431
2000	425

Edward Tufte coined the terms graphical integrity and graphical excellence and with them proposed design principles for data visualization. For this purpose, he has compiled numerous criteria that make violations of data integrity caused by graphical visualization detectable.[149]

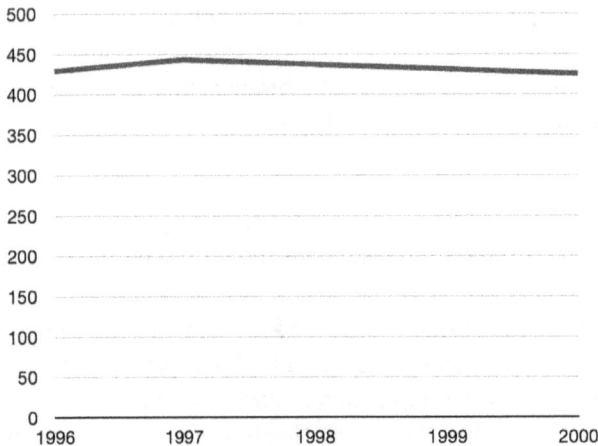

Fig. 4.1: Graphical integrity (1).

---

148 Even more subtle are visualizations that use logarithmic scales. If they are displayed appropriately, the risk of bias lies in the viewer's ability to interpret them. If they are not displayed, it is simply a case of data falsification.

149 See Tufte: Envisioning information, Tufte: The visual display of quantitative information.

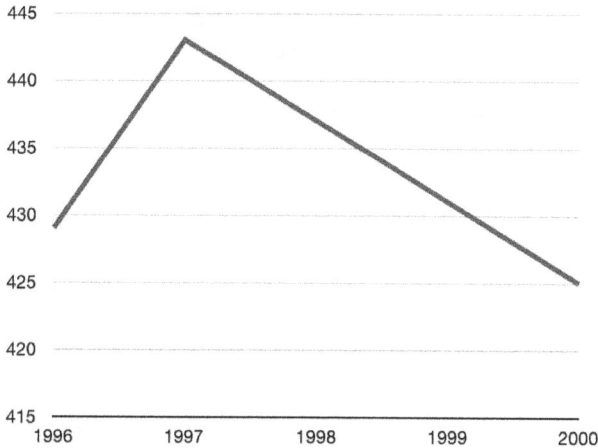

Fig. 4.2: Graphical integrity (2).

The particular benefit of plausibility in our context can be seen in the fact that it leads to critical attention and thus encourages further scrutiny. In addition, it can also help to identify contradictions. Immediate and definitive verification of a statement or fact is not always possible. In such situations, plausibility considerations can prevent erroneous assessments and premature judgments. Still, they cannot prevent the possible power- or interest-driven objectives behind data manipulation; at best, they can expose them.

4.6 Inferring

Making analogies and checking plausibility are the preliminary stages of making inferences. Inference serves in a special way to verify the truth content of complex statements. Here, rules are used which allow the truth content of complex assertions to be determined from the combination of simple true assertions. Although we often talk about a statement being logical or illogical, the rules of reasoning and the conditions for identifying the formal or logical truth content of an assertion are hardly known.[150] Even the distinction between a formal and a substantive truth content often causes difficulties. Many assertions that are given the attribute "logical" in everyday life are more likely to belong to plausibility. This does not automatically mean that an assertion must be "illogical", but neither are they

---

150 See Tetens: Philosophisches Argumentieren.

based on the strict requirements for determining logical truth. Some examples will illustrate the neglect of the logical background in everyday life:

> Forming truth values for compound statements:
> "I go to work, and when I'm sick, I stay home."
> "I'll go to work or I'll stay home if I'm sick."

> Distinguish conjunctions and *Boolean operators* links:
> "I'm going to buy apples and pears."
> "I'm going to buy apples or pears."
> "I'm going to buy apples ∨ pears."[151]

> Distinguish causal and temporal causes:
> "If it rains, the earth will get wet."
> "When it rains, the earth gets wet."
> "The earth will be wet if it rains."
> "The earth gets wet when it rains."

> Distinguishing between necessary and sufficient conditions:
> "Is rain necessary or sufficient for the street to become wet?"

> Use of permissible and impermissible universal quantifiers:
> What difference does it make whether a Chicago resident says: "All Bostoners are hardworking" or whether a Boston resident says this?

> Using colloquial and logical negations for statements:
> What is the correct negation of "All x are/have y."?
> "No x is/has y."
> "There is an x that is not/has not y."

Due to its special significance, the distinction between "necessary" and "sufficient" will be considered in more detail.

A necessary condition is a condition without which an event does not occur. A necessary condition must be imperatively fulfilled. If it is not fulfilled, the corresponding situation cannot occur. Nevertheless, a fact may also not be true if the necessary condition would be fulfilled. For example, being unmarried is considered a condition for being a bachelor. However, not all unmarried men are necessarily bachelors (cf. a surviving spouse).

A sufficient condition is a condition, which, if fulfilled, necessarily causes an event to occur. In other words, if the sufficient condition occurs, the corresponding event must also occur. Here again, this does not mean that the situation cannot

---

[151] The symbol "∨" is used to represent the logical operator "or".

occur even if the sufficient condition is not met. A proven and sanctioned speeding is sufficient for a fine notice. However, speeding is not a necessity, because other traffic violations also result in fines.

As a rule of thumb, it is generally more difficult to formulate necessary conditions than to specify sufficient ones.

For the question "Is rain necessary or sufficient for the street to become wet?", it can now be stated: Rain is not necessary for the street to become wet, since there are many other reasons possible for a street to become wet. So is rain perhaps sufficient for a wet street? Further analysis reveals that rain is not sufficient either because the street (or a part of it relevant to the determination) may actually be located in a tunnel or under a bridge. As to what are sufficient or necessary conditions for a resulting wetness of a street, consequently requires a more precise description, because confusion of the two conditions entails misunderstandings and wrong conclusions:

> Statement 1: "After it has rained, the street in front of my house is wet."
> Statement 2: "There was no rain, so the street in front of my house is not wet."

The second statement is a fallacy. As described before, rain is not a necessary condition for a street to become wet.

> Statement 1: "After it has rained, the street in front of my house is wet."
> Statement 2: "The street in front of my house is wet, so it has been raining."

Again, the second statement is a fallacy, as it is sufficient for the street to be wet if the neighbor sprayed water on the street with a garden hose.

One particular field of inference-based assessment affects the relationship between correlation and causation. Humans are not very good at estimating the probability of an event to happen, as can be seen from the widespread hope of winning a lottery. The unexpected meeting with a person not seen for many years during a vacation abroad is considered "a great coincidence" because the probability of this event is considered very low. However, if all known factors for this event were taken into account—respective motivations for the trip, common interests and preferences, predetermined vacation times, etc.—, an encounter might not be so improbable anymore. This separation of correlation and causality is not trivial when drawing conclusions and also affects the interpretation and significance of statistics. The correlation between the values measured there and those brought into relation is often all too quickly mistaken for causality. Whether there is a correlation or a causal relationship between sick leave and the average water consumption of a four-person household in 2015 depends on numerous conditions and is not easily assessed.

If our ability to think is to be related to the design and operation of algorithms whose logic is based on reasoning under conditions, then it is strongly advised that we develop and foster the ability to make factual inferences as a familiar competency.

4.7 Ordering and Structuring

The abilities described so far form the basis for the more general cognitive ability of ordering and structuring, or, in a broader sense, systematizing. This ability allows us to recognize correlations, patterns, or order.[152] Thus, this function essentially supports cognitive processes about the objects and phenomena of the world. Structuring and selecting enable us to distinguish the important from the unimportant in a given situation. Without this central ability, learning would not be possible, and finding our way in the world almost inconceivable. Ordering and structuring are also very important tools for the externalization of knowledge as potential information, and its reception. The recognition of correlations, patterns and orders creates the prerequisite for organizing objects or facts. This makes it possible to implement concrete requirements, for example, when objects are to be arranged in a specific order.

According to the common understanding of information literacy, the issues involved are considered solved and manageable—at least in its professional context. This is a misconception that we believe makes the topic particularly interesting for determining informational literacy.

Some examples: Existing orders always require the integration of new subject or knowledge areas into the already developed systematic structure. You don't even have to think about professional facilities like warehouses, libraries or archives. The domestic environment alone offers enough everyday situations in which a new object must be brought into line with an existing systematic order. One usually hopes for an incremental inclusion without having to change anything in the established order. Unfortunately, this is not always possible. For example, organizing systems at home are already disturbed when a newly purchased cooking pot cannot find a place in its intended location because, for example, there is not enough space between the shelf boards. You won't want to buy a new kitchen to fix the problem. Instead, you will seek compromises that, however, may be disadvantageous to the existing organizational structure: Maybe you will find another place away from the other cooking pots, but then the new pot will be outside the existing

---

152 Bowker/Star: Sorting things out, Weinberger: Everything is miscellaneous.

order. This illustrates how easily the attempt to maintain a certain organizational structure can be disrupted.

The same applies to all kinds of physical but also digital collections. Efforts to create uniform classification systems are further challenged when dealing with objects that have changed their media carrier over time, as is the case with sound recordings, photographs, and even books. A well-organized collection of physical sound carriers, records of all sizes, CDs, DVDs is inadequate for storing digital music files; traditional photo albums cannot be supplemented with digital photos; bookshelves are not suitable for storing e-books. Such ruptures, like those created by fundamentally different types of media, hinder us to create a unified organizational framework outside of our own heads.

In addition to the possible formal disruptive factors in creating stable orders, there are problems related to their actual content. Sooner or later, in the effort to maintain a stable order, an object will emerge that expands the range of ordering criteria used up to that point, thereby calling into question the entire organizational structure. The system applied to a photo collection of portraits will no longer work if the collector's interest shifts to architectural photography. Adding new objects, new concepts, and new topics usually also involves a new look at the overall structure underlying the entities being systematized. Different interests or unpredictable technical developments may have an impact on the criteria used to date or even fundamentally question them. This may even lead to wanting to reorganize the entire collection according to a more advanced criteria scheme. Usually, such a reorganization, which takes place cognitively at first, can be better imagined than implemented in practice at the end.

These transformative processes are taking place on both a small and a large scale. For example, the classification of animals and plants as developed by *Carl von Linné* is perceived as a long familiar scheme. The classification was based on the criterion of which species are capable of producing offspring. Even today, new species are still being discovered and consequently integrated into this existing structure. A completely different systematic approach has been developed by genetic research, which may lead to the evolution of fundamentally different ideas about animal and plant relationships in the future.[153]

To date, there is no known methodical procedure for how to accomplish such a change of perspective while preserving the existing order. A solution is probably only offered by complete reorganization, which is seen as an unpopular approach because it involves a great deal of effort. Therefore, systematic structures are considered vulnerable to obsolescence processes, and people tend to seek refuge in an

---

153 For an introduction to the topic, see Taxonomy [Wikipedia].

alphabet-based order instead. However, dynamically adapting verbal concept representations in alphabetical sorts is not a fundamentally easier task. If one accepts the linguistic development as it happens, and this is the current model of popular search engines, a linguistic label always finds only a temporal snapshot of the content it represents. This can be beneficial, but it can also lead to the loss of relevant material. In any case, the possibility for a successful comprehensive search decreases with the size of the time window. Cross-temporal representation by linguistic expressions with simultaneous representation of conceptual correlations cannot be achieved without a systematizing approach. Here, too, the difficulties just described remain.

5 Informational Literacy in Action

Regaining our confidence in our own ability to think and dream is necessary to (re?)establish a multi-dimensional view of humanity.

Joseph Weizenbaum[154]

5.1 Abstraction and Plausible Inference

As discussed in the previous chapters, the cognitive prerequisites for informational literacy cannot be considered in isolation from each other. In fact, they are interconnected in many ways. Moreover, they are usually activated not in simple and schematic situations, but in life contexts of varying complexity. The ability to abstract and to make plausible inferences, for example, is often needed when critically dealing with topics of general importance.

For several years now, there has been a heated debate about "fake news" and "alternative facts". One of the reasons for this is that posts circulating rapidly on social media are increasingly competing with the traditional media industry, especially when it comes to representations and opinions on current world events.[155] In part, the debate seems to be characterized by a collective loss of the ability to make conclusions by means of plausibility. A less resentful and more empowering way to deal with fake news would be to strengthen the individual's ability to judge—through informational literacy as lived informational autonomy—rather than lamenting the loss of importance of the own branch.[156]

Some argue that complete knowledge of all the facts would be sufficient to identify fake news. But even supposedly complete facts can be manipulated if power- and interest-driven motives are at play. Since it has become possible to use fake news specifically to pursue personal interests, its use and the extent to which it can be deliberately manipulated has reached a next level.

Just as alarming is the habituation effect that has set in almost unnoticed, and which is affecting even the established quality media. Today, for example, it is common practice to use the same image material for different media posts, which is particularly problematic when the visual material is taken out of its original

---

154 Weizenbaum: Computermacht und Gesellschaft, p. 43 (author's translation).
155 See Nguyen-Kim: Die kleinste gemeinsame Wirklichkeit, Quattrociocchi: Internet, Russ-Mohl: Die informierte Gesellschaft und ihre Feinde, Hauff-Hartig: Fehl-, Falsch- und Desinformation aus dem Blickwinkel der Informationswissenschaften.
156 See Bredemeier: Was sagt uns die Debatte zu ‚Fake News'.

https://doi.org/10.1515/9783110693744-005

context and alienating contexts or evaluations are created by re-commenting the story. The line to manipulation can so be all too easily touched or even crossed.

Potential for improvement is mainly seen in control mechanisms to prevent the spread of hate speech and misinformation.

However, it is not fake news per se that is the problem, but the way we all deal with it, which gives it the potential to go from a minority to a majority phenomenon. And on the recipient side, even more than on the producer side, this is primarily a problem of informational literacy.

It is well known that strengthening intellectual skills helps identify misinformation and biased narratives, and that this is the right way to go. Still, algorithms are the first choice to tackle this task, although it is clear that they become ineffective after a certain time.

Even media fakes today considered classic—recall *Orson Wells'* radio play *War of the Worlds*, a hoax broadcasted in 1938—could only work out because a sufficiently large number of people believed the fictional content to be possible in reality.

Science and fake news should not really have anything in common. After all, the scientific publication system of peer reviewing was created to guarantee quality control before publication. And yet, even journalistic uncoverings such as the *Sokal affair*[157], which took place more than twenty years ago, do not prevent grotesque articles from continuing to appear in renowned journals and newspapers.[158]

Of course, it is legitimate to expect reputable sources not to spread any falsehoods. Yet there is a wide range of fake news, from blatant misreporting to small manipulations that are difficult to detect. Most often, its dissemination serves the pursuit of goals that are not being disclosed. Outsmarting the poor quality control in the scientific publication process with a falsified study at least serves to highlight the existence of a problem. In contrast, it is unlikely that political actors pursue noble goals when using fake news. If fake news is to be a tool for manipulation, it will try to hide its true character. A principle applies here that *Elmar Holenstein* formulated as follows:

> Even more dangerous than clumsy and plain falsehoods are half-truths.[159]

---

157 Sokal affair [Wikipedia].
158 Boghossian/Lindsay: The conceptual penis as a social construct.
159 Holenstein: Kulturphilosophische Perspektiven, p. 300 (author's translation).

A study conducted by the *Columbia University*[160] demonstrates that people who are in the company of other people are less inclined to check information and assertions for their truthfulness or for coherence. In contrast, people who are alone use information more critically. This is true even if there is no direct social interaction, and other people are merely present as contacts in social networks.

Additional control mechanisms will not make our own ability to assess information expendable—on the contrary, with all the new technical possibilities, it will have to be promoted even more strongly. The ability to abstract and to check facts for plausibility are an important basis for this. Strengthening these abilities by means of suitable programs would be more promising than the use of so-called fact checkers.

5.2 Searching and Finding

Thanks to internet search engines, searching in information environments has become an everyday process and has long since ceased to be the domain of subject specialists. Regardless of all improvements and facilitations made so far with respect to the search and find processes, there is still a fundamental problem: It is not possible to determine the extent of what has not been found. To date, only professional test environments have been able to identify corresponding factors that can be taken into account for improving search and find functions.[161] The results of these studies show that the proportion of what is not found in a search result is always greater than zero; in other words, there are always documents or information that are not found for a search. Apparently, we have to live with this uncertainty. The assumption "I have access to an information system that provides me with everything relevant to my question" is thus pure fiction. And the current state of research does not indicate that this situation is likely to change in the near future.

Completeness-oriented searches require an extremely elaborate approach. It consists of many individual steps and, in addition to the machine processing of complex algorithms, also requires specifications from the seeker, which presuppose profound background and practical knowledge. The estimation of what is not found can only be done step by step by means of plausibility considerations, the application of alternative strategies or the use of further aids.

---

160 Jun/Meng/Johar: Perceived social presence reduces fact-checking.
161 For the results of the *TREC* studies and the pooling method used for them, see Text retrieval conference (TREC) [Website]; an overview is given by Voorhees/Harman: TREC.

There are many reasons for the principle incompleteness of search results. Even if the information system contained all of the relevant material, the search result would still be incomplete. For example, it only takes a quick test to see that entering "French Art Nouveau interior" in *Google* will return many hits. The extent of completeness, however, cannot be determined; neither can the criteria for compiling the set of hits. The only thing that is clear is that the selection of "one" specific search query simultaneously excludes many others. Other search terms could be synonyms, (generic) broader or narrower terms, or associations with different semantic proximity. Considering them all in one search is simply not possible.

Assistance in the formulation of search queries could be offered by semantic data modeling of conceptual correlations in an appropriate manner. This, however, requires an elaborate procedure, which does not correspond to current trends. Rather, today's search engines provide good examples of how intellectual approaches are being replaced by word-based automated analyses. The approach that is primarily employed here is to derive conceptual correlations from statistical analyses of co-occurrence. The general buzzword in this context is big data, coming with the idea that differentiated analyses of huge volumes of data produce quality. Yet it is far from proven that the undeniable successes of big data can also be transferred to fields with rich semantic content. At the same time, there are still no studies available proving that intellectual procedures are soon becoming obsolete. Therefore, it cannot yet be ruled out that, by abandoning intellectual modeling, the number of errors will increase and one day no longer be tolerable.

Basically, the incompleteness of searches in search engines is not a defined error, but part of the overall system. Even the statistical analyses of document properties or words used in search queries applied by search engines cannot compensate for this incompleteness. What matters most to search engine providers is that users rate what they have found as successful and are happy with it—an attitude that is generally widespread. A critical look is taken only when the result sets for searches on the same topic with the same query vary at different times or on different computers, or when results are known but not found or presented. Since a *Google* search—*Google* is used here as a paradigmatic example for search engines—is in principle algorithm-based, but the parameters applied are individualized and known only to *Google*, the search results remain inconsistent and intransparent to the user. The extent to which this is considered annoying or disadvantageous certainly varies from person to person. As long as that is the situation, the only way to deal with it is to rely on our own judgment and use our ability to establish plausibility.

Evaluating the Search Results

As an alternative to searching for all available results, the goal may be to find the best ones or the ones that are most appropriate for the user. To determine only the best, however, requires that everything has been found beforehand. Otherwise, it can be only the best among what has been found. If one had access to the actual entire set of results of a search query, one could determine the best by oneself. If this access is not available, the determination of the best is left to the algorithm of the search engine. Thus, there can be no satisfactory answer to the search for the best result delivered by a search engine, but only the relatively best of what competing search engines offer. In any case, an algorithm can only determine what is individually most fitting if it has defaults through parameters that characterize a personal preference.

Searchers often start from the requirement that the documents they find should be "relevant", in the sense that they are likely to answer a particular question or contribute to the solution of a problem. However, these requirements are not the same for all searchers, but depend, for example, on the respective previous knowledge or situation that gave rise to the search. The concept of relevance, which is central for the evaluation of results, is not easy to characterize.[162] For algorithms, it can only be considered in an objectified sense, for humans it will always have a subjective dimension as well. This is clearly evident in the case of fee-based information services, such as specialized databases: No matter how relevant a hit may be—if the information is already known, and the user is nevertheless asked to pay for it, the subjective displeasure quickly outweighs the objective dimension. In professional contexts, this kind of subjective evaluation is also called "pertinence"[163], a concept that is often not sharply distinguished from the concept of "relevance".

The objective evaluability of relevance is usually determined by the formal correspondence of document parameters—including content-describing metadata if applicable—with query parameters. This is done, for example, by querying for matches of an expression present in the text—whether it is a word, a phrase, or a particular character string—regardless of how well or poorly the expression corresponds to the document's content. This evaluation can be in conflict with subjective interpretation: The presence of an expression does not necessarily allow reliable conclusions to be drawn about a content match with the entire document.

---

162 See Bookstein: Relevance, Meadow: Relevance?, Schamber: Relevance and information behavior.

163 For a more detailed presentation of the concept, see Howard: Pertinence as reflected in personal constructs.

An important tool for the presentation of search results is the so-called relevance ranking. The method uses algorithms that perform a relevance calculation for each document found in order to output the search results in a sorted way. Thereby, the most relevant documents are to be displayed first. The various ranking algorithms rely on objective relevance interpretation for generating the result order, which is then supplemented by other parameters. These do not have to be part of the document, but can also originate from the integration of the document into the network's link topology, as happens, for example, when citation links are evaluated by the *Google* algorithm. The gain from relevance ranking in finding the supposedly best results at the top of the list is at the expense of uncertainty about what is at the bottom of the list.[164] Initially, this may be thought of as a problem where the user must weigh the need for a complete overview against personal convenience. However, it becomes problematic if the complete search result is no longer displayed at all, but only the beginning of the list sorted according to more or less known criteria, as is common practice in web search engines today.[165]

There is no doubt that with *PageRank*, *Larry Page* and *Sergej Brin* have developed and refined an algorithm for *Google* that has set new standards in the field of search engines.[166] Today, its basic functioning is no longer a secret.[167] More or less unknown is still the number of its parameters, how it takes into account data from search profiles and how it adjusts them in personalized settings when used for the search engine *Google*.[168]

Ranking algorithms as used for sorting search results are good examples of the application of plausibility aspects. When it comes to the maximum pertinence of a search result for a search query in the context of specific subjective interests, even the best algorithm cannot help. It is striking that the distinction between objective and subjective factors for evaluating a search result has not become generally accepted and that for both concepts largely only the term relevance is used, although their difference is obvious.

---

164 See Schaer et al.: How relevant is the long tail?

165 *Google* does display the usually very high total number of all hits found, but allows a view of hit pages only for a much smaller portion of these hits. An example: Searching for "indexing" returns "About 801.000.000 results (0,50 seconds)" with 210 results displayed on 21 hit pages; the function "repeat the search with the omitted results included" yields "About 771.000.000 results (0,51 seconds)" with 414 hits on 42 pages displayed (search performed on 2022-11-24).

166 Brin/Page: The anatomy of a large-scale hypertextual web search engine.

167 Berry/Browne: Understanding search engines, Langville/Meyer: Google's PageRank and beyond.

168 See Fiorelli: Hummingbird unleashed, Haynes: Your Google algorithm cheat sheet.

Relevance Feedback

When evaluating search results, there is often a desire to adjust the search query in order to further increase the pertinence of the result. Insufficient individual skills in formulating search queries should ideally be compensated for by the options of the search system. This is what relevance feedback is all about.[169] A typical relevance feedback procedure enables an individual evaluation and marking of the displayed hits as relevant or not relevant. This evaluation is then used by the system for a new search. The new hit list based on the feedback then contains such documents that are similar to those previously rated as relevant. Relevance feedback enables successive approximation of the actual desired search result without the user's knowledge of how the system works. Yet, the major search engines do not leverage the potential of relevance feedback. Individual attempts have so far not been able to prevail against the algorithm-based result ranking.

The methodological approach of relevance ranking is to focus on objectifiable and generally binding parameters promising to improve the overall relevance. Subjective factors are not considered in this approach. To design such procedures, a first step could be to hand over control mechanisms to the end-user side, instead of performing the parameterization exclusively and intransparently on the providers' servers.[170] Whether this could develop user-controlled pertinence feedback is nevertheless questionable. Even if this were methodically and technologically feasible, it would remain a balancing act between the possible benefits resulting from the specification of personal preferences to get optimized search results and the potential harm to users that would result from the exploitation of their data by system providers. Previous experience from the field of social networks, their users and providers rather suggests that trends towards non-disclosure of procedures on the one hand and convenience in use on the other hand will continue to prevail over transparency and user control.

The mechanisms of relevance feedback make it clear that plausibility is an important factor in the evaluation of search results. Plausibility cannot be replaced by relevance ranking methods or big data analyses.

---

169 Manning/Raghavan/Schütze: Introduction to information retrieval, pp. 162–177.
170 Schaat: Von der automatisierten Manipulation zur Manipulation der Automatisierung.

5.3 Medialization of Knowledge

Externalization and Reception of Form and Content

Medialization of content is a special form of externalization of knowledge.[171] This also inevitably affects essential areas of social life, since social practices and cultural sense-making today are inextricably interwoven with the use of media. In Chapter 3, the role of interpersonal communication in the reception of information has already been discussed in detail. The concepts of content transfer discussed there—consensual parallelization and structural coupling—cannot be transferred to the dialog between a human being and a machine (information system) or any other carrier of medialized information (for example, a video). Here, other mechanisms must enable the reception of medially externalized information.

Information systems—especially those that are intended to support learning processes in their role as knowledge repositories—must make use of an externalization of cognitive knowledge in a form that is suitable for the user's subsequent cognitive reception. Unfortunately, up to now, information is too often presented without context and, even more so, with a weak structure, and it is then left to the recipient's structural knowledge to successfully generate new knowledge. There have been quite attempts to develop and offer alternative models. Examples include the *Brockhaus Enzyklopädie*[172] in various digital versions and with its associative knowledge graphs, or the *Project Krünitz*[173] with the digitization of the *Oekonomische Encyklopädie* by *Johann Georg Krünitz*, which was intended to make historical contexts transparent in a special way. So far, however, such attempts have failed to attract sufficient attention from the general public and have not been able to establish themselves on the market.

The medialization of content is often seen as a fundamental advantage for reception processes, especially for learning processes. The topic has played a role recently in the education policy discussion on promoting digitization. The motivation for the initiative is the belief in improved learning outcomes through digitization. It is still unclear how learning from purely digital resources will evolve as opposed to learning from paper sources or other learning strategies such as auditory, visual, or haptic learning. What impact does digital typing have on so-called hand knowledge, which is shaped by handwriting? Will learning in virtual reality environments (propagated as "immersive learning") be able to compensate or even replace forms of learning that are considered outdated? The fact that medi-

---

171 See Hug: On the medialization of knowledge in the digital age.
172 Bibliographisches Institut: Brockhaus Enzyklopädie Digital.
173 Oeconomische Encyclopädie online [Krünitz].

alization creates better conditions for learning processes than conventional forms of representation has not yet been conclusively substantiated.

One factor is that the transformation of a text to another media representation is often a purely formal redesign. The *PDF* file of a textbook or the one-to-one conversion of an encyclopedia into an e-book do not convey different (or even less) impressions than the respective original. The structural properties of the source file, for example the outline, references or the associated index, are often not transferred to the new media form. And only rarely are they edited with regard to the target medium's specific possibilities of expression. If medialization is to provide enhanced cognitive stimulation, it must do so with enriched content features, while at the same time not having to sacrifice the structural representation of classical media forms.

Every media form—and this includes the book and texts in general—has a specific materiality. This materiality can be the object of pure contemplation, but it can also influence the process of reception. Since a (cognitive) exchange of information takes place between the creator of a medially fixed piece of information and the recipient of this information, its mechanisms are to be described in more detail, taking into account different media forms.

Here, too, the principle of consensual parallelization and structural coupling should come into play as conditions for successful direct communication (Figure 3.1). In this case, however, the concept of consensual parallelization cannot be applied to the reception of externalized information because there are no two partners who could actively establish consensus. This means, an equivalent replacement must be created for the structural coupling. A task not trivial. What is the role of the carrier medium in an act of communication? This question must be raised again. To make matters worse, in a dialog between humans and media-fixed information, feedback to check for alignment is not possible. What substitutes can be given on the information systems side for the various factors that normally guarantee the success of interpersonal communication? Are there any at all? Is there, for communication, any equivalent as corrective to the self-referentiality of cognitive information processing?

As a possible condition for a suitable simulation of the communication situation, the reference domains can be used, which are possessed by every individual who is capable of acquiring knowledge. This would mean that not only informational units are medially fixed, but also structural components of a reference domain have to be implemented in the course of externalization. Only in this way can a structural coupling between the information externalized in a medium—and thus the medium itself—and a human communication partner come about, which is necessary for the reception of the knowledge fixed in the medium (Figure 5.1).

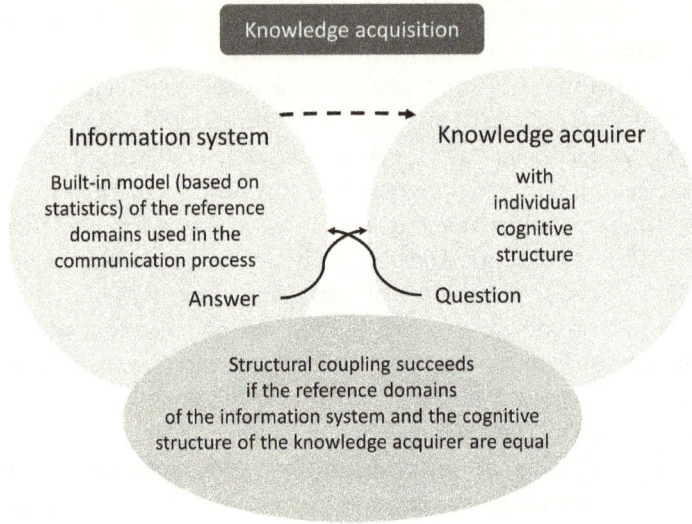

Fig. 5.1: Knowledge acquisition from externalized knowledge (3) – Coupling.

Not all individual cognitive structures can be met in an information system that contains medially offered knowledge. Only a statistical model of the reference domains, usually a time-dependent and time-bound model, can be incorporated to support the reception of the externalized information and thus the acquisition of knowledge. In order to provide the intended benefits in the long term, the reference structures would also have to be continuously adapted to developments. Special problems are encountered here in the medial fixation of the reference domains of communicatively agreed validity and individual episodic memory as introduced in Chapter 2.4. These two domains are most affected by change. A system that is supposed to support learning will therefore never be able to meet all individual requirements in the same way.

The limitations of considering structural properties of reference domains can be examined on specialized or general encyclopedias. The latter explicitly address a general audience and have found a variety of forms to enrich the facts to be presented via different forms of media presentation. Nevertheless, according to general experience, articles on specific topics cannot be comprehended without appropriate background knowledge. For example, an article on *Heisenberg's uncertainty relation* in a modern general encyclopedia will remind an expert of the essence of the assertion—here the article does not miss its target. For a layperson, however, the article is usually less comprehensible than an introduction to the topic in a physics textbook. The encyclopedia article presupposes the structural background for its understanding, in this case a professional reference domain.

With their encyclopedia, *Diderot* and *d'Alembert* presented the knowledge of the world for the first time in a systematic and structured form made for reception by the enlightened and educated public.[174] Later, there was an increasing tendency to subdivide related subjects by means of an alphabetical order of the articles. Although the principle of alphabetical ordering supports rapid access to matching informational units, it makes them difficult to understand if the recipient does not have the associated structural knowledge as a context. Acquisition of the underlying structural knowledge is hardly possible from today's encyclopedia types.

New reference structures have to be built for each form of medial externalization. If the potential information present in the medial externalization is to be transformed into actual information suitable for the recipient, analogy and plausibility considerations are necessary. For the integration into suitable reference structures, cognitive information processing needs to be triggered in order to build up the necessary, but possibly not yet existing, structural knowledge.

Along with the new possibilities for externalization, the number and variety of reference domains required in the cognitive structure are equally increasing. As is well known, the reception of a new type of media does not succeed from the outset, but instead must first be learned.

This circumstance probably also marks the limits of the medial externalization of information. Even when analogy and plausibility procedures are used to identify commonalities and construct abstract patterns, there are limits to the number of structures that can be rooted for reception. Structural determination occurs both phylogenetically and ontogenetically, first and foremost via sensory impressions on the basis of the confrontation with the living world: Knowledge is the result of a construction of reality.

Moreover, in the context of cognitive plasticity, the "distance" between an externalized structure and a recipient's primary cognitive structure limits the possibility to manage ever further receptive processes. From these conditions, criteria for the quality of medially externalized information can be derived, as seen, for instance, by externalizations in multimedia form.[175]

---

174 See d'Alembert: Preliminary discourse to the Encyclopedia of Diderot.
175 Reliable indicators still require empirical confirmation. The ones presented in literature so far are inconsistent and do not allow for a conclusive assessment, see Large et al.: Multimedia and comprehension [1994], Large et al.: Multimedia and comprehension [1995], Nix/Spiro (eds.): Cognition, education, and multimedia.

These are, after all, fundamental conditions that apply to any media externalization, and which, given the large number of products used in this context, place high demands on the individual. Having to deal with too many of these demands and meeting all of them equally can lead to a state of mental overload, today commonly designated as "cognitive overload".

And there were great expectations for the possibilities of multimedia to show information embedded in its structural contexts. Instead, the new electronic forms of encyclopedias continued the trend toward structural flattening by following the imperative to present information in screen-friendly snippets.[176] An impressive example is provided by the first CD-ROM edition of the *Encyclopædia Britannica*. This edition has the full textual content of the print version, but compared to other electronic general encyclopedias, the media presentation can only be described as inadequate.[177] The new packaging does not offer possibilities for the reception of the content that are adapted to the medium.

Compared to ambitious products with structural quality enrichment, like the aforementioned *Brockhaus Enzyklopädie*, resources that are only available online and are furthermore created collaboratively by a large community tend to show a flattening of the structural depth of their content. The most prominent example of this is *Wikipedia*.[178] The market's preference for freely available offerings has so far led to the dominance of products with little structure over those with structural quality enrichment. It remains to be seen if and when this state could one day be perceived as a deficiency.

The consideration of reference domains for the reception process from externalized sources leads to an extended understanding of potential information. Potential information is externalized information that is supplemented by structural information for the purposes of reception, taking into account reference domains. The result obtained from this is then the actual information within a cognitive structure. Actual information is the cognitive processing pattern of a structurally determined system that builds at the moment when reality construction or the direct exchange of information between two cognitive structures takes place (i.e., in the course of any direct act of communication). Actual information becomes conscious at a certain point in time by way of self-induced cognitive reactivation or information processing triggered by external sensory perception.

In direct communication, for example, its success can be demonstrated by an action ("Pass me the salt shaker, please"). As for the reception from externalized

---

176 See Gödert: Multimedia-Enzyklopädien auf CD-ROM.
177 Segal: The Britannica and its dongle, Hoffert: The encyclopedia wars.
178 Holze: Digitales Wissen, p. 191.

sources, this is not immediately possible. A criterion is needed that allows testing the equality level of the externalized (potential) information and the received (actual) information. Such a test is based on subjective assessments or judgments of third parties, depending in turn on the individual's internal fulfillment conditions, which must be met beforehand.[179]

The concept of fulfillment conditions can be explained by the example of an everyday statement like "Peter drinks a glass of milk", which should not cause any problems of understanding. Nevertheless, to achieve actual understanding, some conditions must be met:

–   it is necessary to know that there is a person—a boy, a man—whose name is Peter;
–   it is necessary to know what kind of glass it is, what it looks like, what function it has—after all, it is not the glass that is drunk, but what the glass is filled with;
–   it is necessary to know what milk is, what it looks like, what it is good for, what substance properties it has;
–   it is necessary to have an idea of the process of drinking;
–   it is necessary to have some knowledge of grammar to interpret the sequence of the words as a sentence that has a meaning.

Each of these conditions in turn depends on other preconditions, and all of them must be represented cognitively. Only then can they, as in the example, be examined and confirmed in order to assign truthfulness to the given statement. It is easy to estimate how far the analytical verification of the conditions may go in the case of complex statements. We are so routinized in our daily tasks that we rarely consciously recognize them as a success. Most of the time, we only notice conditions that have not been met.

It becomes even more difficult when the fulfillment conditions are not properties of objective reality, but the result of an individual construction of reality.

Two examples will illustrate the mechanisms of the test for information equality. Here it is assumed that information is received from an externalized source. In the first example, a practical action is to take place on this basis; in the second, an examination of an abstract task takes place.

Case 1. *IKEA* shelf assembly:
There is an instruction (externalized information) that must be received for an action (building the shelf). The test is to check the stability of the shelf. If this succeeds immediately, that's good. The reception was successful and no confirmation is needed (or the mounted

---

179 For the concept, see Searle: Mind, pp. 185–192.

shelf is the confirmation). If difficulties are encountered in understanding the instructions, you can try until you might succeed. If a knowledgeable communication partner is at hand, feedback communication can compensate for the deficits.

Case 2. Handling an exercise for a written exam:
In this case, the reception does not result in an action, but initially remains in the mind of the recipient and accordingly cannot be directly verified by another person. If there is a sample solution for the exercise, this is not even necessary because the test can then be done as a comparison between your own solution and the sample solution itself. If there are communication partners, for example teachers, further possibilities arise. The recipient's approaches to the own reception, which may or may not be correct, can then be judged by the communication partner, who could either just give some assistance in interpreting the task, but could also give direct hints for finding the solution.

In summary, information equality for externalized information exists if the result of an actual information cognitively generated by the act of reception is equal to the information preceding the externalization act. This means that the medially externalized information and the result of the cognitive reception can be thought of as the result of a structural coupling in the same reference domain.

Individual characteristics and experiences determine the character of an externalization and influence the success of a subsequent reception process. In own records, such as a journal or transcript, these characteristics and experiences can be well integrated and—at least within a certain temporal proximity—received again. Otherwise, recipients are only able to do this to a limited extent. Here, information referring to the reference domains must then be added to the externalization in the most possible transparent way. Externalized information therefore always involves social, cultural or scientific frameworks—a kind of "Zeitgeist" in the bottle of structural information. A timely reception under comparable "Zeitgeist" conditions is thus in principle quite possible. However, the more time passes between externalization and reception, the less chance there is for easy reception.

Thus, there must be an understanding of informational literacy that incorporates development over time, and that takes into account the reference domains underlying the medial externalization and their changes. Media representation alone does not ensure permanence for later reception (Chapter 2.3). This also means that digitization, as a special case of the medialization of content, is no guarantee for the preservation of content.

Direct communication, with all its verbal and non-verbal possibilities for interactive and feedback communication, is always aimed at understanding and continuing, and not at rejecting. And this is true even when the act of communication involves unknowns or deviations from the known. Cognitive plasticity not only accepts what is already known, but actively searches the boundary of the unknown for patterns that open paths to the known. Problems as they arise in communication situations can usually be solved by this and by the opportunity for direct feedback—in analogy to cognitive plasticity, communication plasticity emerges. Reception from externalized sources must do without these positive effects.

Shift from Content to Form

The digital media transformation currently underway should actually help to make content easier to grasp through a different formal design. With the growing technical possibilities of digital offerings, however, attention has shifted more and more from content to form. A particularly striking example is the change in the design of websites, especially the way they are presented and the enormous effort required to create and maintain them, which is nevertheless perceived as contemporary.

When the creation of—mostly static—websites was still a quick and easy exercise using the modular web builder kits, there were many sites with excellent content offerings that were created and maintained by the professionals responsible for the content.[180] For a while, it seemed that a way had been found to fulfill the promise of the web as an open and high-quality repository of knowledge. Remnants of this belief and design customs have survived in the *Wikipedia* context.

With the advent of more sophisticated tools for designing dynamic or interactive web pages that required more effort to address all formal aspects, many of these professionals ceased their web activities. In the more fortunate case, those websites were transferred to institutional care with the support of an online editorial team. Often, however, these pages live on without being further maintained, or they are entirely removed from the web.

Something similar happened with e-mail messages. In the early days, it was only possible to download messages from the e-mail server through a client application on the computer, which were then displayed as plain text. Rapid data transfer and new preferences for convenience and aesthetics have led to formatted and media-enriched message forms that are increasingly read, edited, and sent via cloud-based web clients. Messenger services, social networks and smartphones further fuel this development. Anyone who still considers e-mail to be an adequate form of correspondence is considered backward, and someone who prefers reading e-mail via a local client in text-only mode is considered to have fallen out of time. The fact that this form of use also has advantages, such as the avoidance of tracking, reduction of dangers from "contaminated" links, etc., appears at best in theoretical presentations by those with safety concerns.

---

180 See *Fauna in the Garden* (Fauna im Garten [Website]).

Humans are not capable of an algorithmic evaluation of digitized data. Digital data, however, opens up entirely new ways of analyzing data, such as the analysis of so-called big data. It cannot be ruled out that the possibilities offered by algorithmic processing of digital data sets will shift the general understanding of knowledge in the direction of algorithmically generated correlations. We have already discussed that big data has changed notions of knowledge representation and reality experience (Chapter 3.5). It is thus only natural that content, and perhaps even knowledge, become understood as the result of an algorithmic evaluation of medialized data rather than as the result of human cognitive performance.

And this despite the fact that human perception is multimedia anyway due to the simultaneous addressing of all sensory organs. Multimedia forms of medialization are special only because they attempt to re-create by technical means something that is deeply familiar to human beings. In the beginning, the focus was on picturing real segments of the world, but now multimedia tools are being used to (more or less) inventively create a virtual reality of its own.

In view of the large spectrum of human perception, the externalization of cognitive information as implemented to date—predominantly texts, possibly enriched by images and other media elements—actually represents a significant reduction compared to the sensory perception humans are capable of. That is, externalization influences and, moreover, reduces the original cognitive information.

The common belief is that we may have survived the previous disruptions without any damage. Whether this will also be true for future changes, given the ever faster development cycles, cannot be said with certainty. The losses caused by such disruptions have been comparatively well researched in the case of the transition from the spoken to the written tradition. Even in the late 20th century, there were examples that allowed the characteristics of both traditions to be studied together. Perhaps it is justified to consider losses that have occurred so far to be bearable in the face of the new challenges. With regard to the changes arising from digital medialization, it is not yet possible to reliably say whether and to what extent losses will occur. By creating so-called immersive experiences in virtual reality environments, perceptual spaces will be expanded again. The effects of this reality shift will probably not be fully understood for at least 50 years.

The form of media externalization has undergone a process of development. If, for the sake of simplicity, we mark its beginning with text documents, the next stages are marked by image, audio and video, which together form the range of multimedia documents. The current stage is reached with electronic or digital media. This stage is also characterized by a change in quality, since it allows the simultaneous fixation of previously separate media elements, and the medium itself—that is, the computer as a media storage and processing system—is ascribed information processing properties.

This is further intensified by network structures serving as storage locations and the dissolution of the closed document character by means of virtualization and dynamically distributed data storage. At this level, a document has no materiality of its own, nor can it be described as an entity. The reference object is created by combining distributed components at the very moment of viewing. As a product of this genesis, it can be frozen and materialized. Whether repeating the process will result in the identical product depends on circumstances beyond the control of the viewer. Compared to all previous stages in the historical development of the externalization of media information, this is a completely new quality that is given its own reality.

With the possibilities of information technology and especially through the developments in the field of virtual reality, it is possible to create simulations of real-world experiences.

Different forms of media representation have different imaginative effects.[181] For example, it is relevant for the effect whether a work of fiction is received as a text or as a film adaptation. This is shown for instance by the embodiment of fictional novel characters in a corresponding movie; the literary character of *Harry Potter*, for example, is firmly linked to the imagination of the actor *Daniel Radcliffe*. Despite casting a role with different actors, the imaginary coinage by one of them prevails, for example the role of *James Bond* played by *Sean Connery*. And even in the case of real historical figures of whom there exists known portrait material, the impression created by the film prevails, as in the case of the *Empress Elisabeth* (*Sisi*) and the actress *Romy Schneider*.

So far best studied are the processes of text comprehension.[182] An equally good understanding of the reception of other forms of media externalization (and even more so for the digitized variants) has yet to be developed. Similarly, more detailed knowledge is needed of the bridges of comprehension required when switching from one form of externalization to another.

Despite some euphoric expectations, it remains to be said that most advanced externalizations using multimedia or virtual reality can only ever be seen as snapshots. A real-world perception of the same situation will always take place slightly altered by different conditions. Even repetition does not happen without changes, no matter how small. These changes are an important corrective for cognitive categorization, recognition, and adaptation. For cognitive information processing, repetition in no way means only redundancy, but rather serves to sharpen a con-

---

181 See on this topic Hasebrook (ed.): Multimedia-Psychologie.
182 See Boehm/Gesellschaft für Angewandte Informationswissenschaft (eds.): Texte verstehen, Hasebrook (ed.): Multimedia-Psychologie.

cept and the understanding gained about it. In the context of cognitive plasticity, repetitions enable the subsequent recognition of similar phenomena and thus make an essential contribution to the formation of cognitive structures.

The multimedia design of information products has led to new presentation and interaction interfaces that not only provide support in the reception process, but also require attention themselves. The form of the media interface and the conditions of its operation overlay the representation of the content, so that the support originally intended becomes a new requirement instead. Information literacy, in its most trivial interpretation, is readily understood as merely the skill of operating the latest generation of devices. Informational literacy, on the other hand, includes the ability to distinguish between form and content, between representation and the represented. Informational literacy requires constant practice in the interplay of instance and abstraction, of objects and their conception.

Reference Domains and Cognitive Overload

The so-called cognitive load theory assumes that learning is associated with cognitive load.[183] It describes what can facilitate or impede learning. In this context, working memory is considered to play an important role in problem solving, information processing, and knowledge acquisition. It is assumed that the capacity of working memory is limited and only a certain amount of information can be activated at the same time. Another assumption is that people use so-called "schemas" to store their knowledge. These schemas are not rigid, but change dynamically. During learning processes, new schemata are constructed as well as new knowledge is linked to already existing schemata. For the processes of schema comparison and construction, the working memory must have sufficient capacity and must not be cognitively overloaded.

There is a relation between the theory of cognitive overload and the model of reception of externalized information presented here (Figure 5.1). The schemata can be seen as corresponding to the reference domains referring to externalization and reception. The adaptation of schemata corresponds to cognitive or neural plasticity.

The cognitive load theory has consequences for the engagement with information offerings in digital media forms. The form of presentation itself always demands a certain amount of attention, which, with the given limited capacity, influences how we engage with content. This cognitive load caused by the media form and its operating requirements surely varies from system to system and prod-

---

183 See Plass/Moreno/Brünken (eds.): Cognitive load theory, Sweller/Ayres/Kalyuga: Cognitive load theory.

uct to product. But it is certainly alarming when dealing with the question of how to handle the technology becomes an end in itself, and hardly any capacity is left for dealing with the content itself.

Our ability to pay attention is influenced by environmental factors today more than ever, as we are distracted by media everywhere we go. We are so used to picking up our smartphone to consume short snippets of news or text, then putting it away, only to pick it up again an hour later and repeat this behavior. We constantly feel like we don't want to miss anything and need to be available 24/7. Usually this happens when we are actually doing something else, such as at work, when focusing on a statistic or preparing a presentation. Switching our attention from the actual activity to the smartphone and back to the actual task entails a measurable effort for our brain, which leads to a limitation of our ability to focus over a longer period of time and to faster mental exhaustion. There is evidence of a link between frequent smartphone exposure and waning attention, decreased learning, and mental exhaustion.[184]

Another factor of cognitive load is the need to adjust to a growing number of reference domains for the externalization and reception of such media-represented information. The reference domains used for information externalization can be so diverse that they may even have the character of a paradigm shift.[185] A paradigm shift here is not substitution by forgetting, but a replacement of a less good solution by a better one, which can be justified at any time by comparing the performance of both approaches. Also the old view had provided knowledge and skills for problem solving. Accordingly, there can be a successful coexistence of different paradigms.

In science it is common practice to see paradigms as the ranges of validity for the respective theoretical approaches and to learn the techniques that lead to results within a certain range of validity. What this teaches us in particular is not to misjudge the boundaries of such validity ranges and not to apply techniques or procedures of one validity range to the problems of the other.

Comparable problems also exist in everyday life, for instance, when actions have to be performed in familiar and less familiar environments, like shopping in different supermarkets, using public transport in different cities, etc. For these, too, there are important framework conditions in each case that should not be disregarded for action decisions. The more self-evident it is to think in terms of contexts, ranges of validity, paradigms, or the fulfillment conditions already presented, and the more specific requirements are observed, the easier it is to avoid misjudgments and erroneous conclusions or actions.

---

184 Hari: Your attention didn't collapse.
185 See Kuhn: The structure of scientific revolutions.

Paradigm shifts lead to significant requirements for information externalization. Here, unlike when concepts are tied to different contexts, there are no smooth transitions and no gray areas of evaluation. Statements are not only modified or relativized. In the case of a paradigm shift, the foundations of a theory are exchanged so that statements that were considered true under the old paradigm are considered false under the new. This is the reason for the difficulties that arise when the use of information systems requires consideration of changed reference domains caused by paradigm shifts.

Transparency in Externalization Models

Externalized structural knowledge can only ever be an average representation and can never be tailored to individual needs. At best, it is possible to become familiar with a larger number of externalization models over time, based on experience. The limits to this are marked by cognitive overload.

It cannot be taken for granted that the recipient of externalized information is aware of the structural knowledge on which the externalization is based. This awareness, however, could lead to a deeper analysis and thus also contribute to the strengthening of informational autonomy. Such an analysis would yet require dealing with an additional issue: thinking about reference domains of externalization; an issue that goes far beyond the original reason for consulting the information resource.

A contradiction could be seen between a storage of structural knowledge in externalized sources and the demand for informational autonomy, because it is a commonplace that any form of externalization can at the same time be an interference with the informational autonomy of the individual recipient. This contradiction can hardly be avoided. It should be clear, though, that not modeling structural knowledge can by no means be seen as a better solution. This would bypass individual needs and would unnecessarily increase reception barriers. Modeling and storing structural knowledge, if necessary by use of different approaches, and especially the transparent disclosure of the applied methods are the only recommendable solution here.

The resulting task for the design of information systems is to use suitable modeling to ensure the transparency of the framework conditions for any subsequent reception. After all, the relationship of pure data to theories, to the context set by the reference domain or to the paradigm with their respective ranges of validity, can only be recognized if these relationships are also indicated.

5.4 Creating or Configuring Information Systems

So far, we have discussed informational autonomy predominantly from the perspective of the user of an information environment or the recipient of externalized information. Creating information systems is usually reserved for professionals. However, we all have to deal with the organization and archiving of objects in our private lives, too, when the goal is the later retrieval and reception of stored documents or otherwise captured knowledge.

A type of object that makes an excellent example here is photography. While in earlier times there was a way of dealing with a comparatively small number of paper prints (in photo albums, cigar boxes or shoe boxes) that was learned or handed down over generations, the era of photography through digital cameras and mobile devices has created a completely new situation. First, the number of photos has skyrocketed; 10,000 in two years is not uncommon. Second, there is no traditional or generally established procedure of organizing and storing the photos. The rapid change in technology even ensures that no permanent procedure can be established. Operating systems, file formats, and storage media are subject to continuous change, creating multiple incompatibilities.

Basically, two solutions have emerged: Either do it yourself or leave it to unknown forces in the cloud. No need to say that the second solution is the more convenient and faster, and meets with a high level of initial satisfaction among many users. Leaving aside all arguments that have anything to do with copyrights, privacy or data protection, the two approaches can also be compared purely on the basis of cost and revenue considerations.

The effort to be calculated quickly grows into unreasonable dimensions if the set of objects is to be processed manually (an actually trivial argument that is still too often ignored at first). If a time of 30 seconds is taken as a basis for processing an object, a workload of 83.3 hours is reached for 10,000 objects.[186] And the same effort must in principle be estimated for any reorganization.

Therefore, if you still want to find a solution for your own procedure, such estimates of effort will not get you anywhere. Another well-known experience is that these initial efforts are usually abandoned again as the collection continues to grow, so that in the end the virtually only aid for searching in this confusing data situation is your own memory. Scalability of the method used does not help

---

[186] We refrain from carrying out a differentiated analysis of the time required for individual sub-activities. Assigning a single tag or keyword to characterize the content of a photo usually takes less than 30 seconds, while a comprehensive formal and topical description takes far more. A more detailed overview is given in Chapter 2 of Gödert/Lepsky/Nagelschmidt: Informationserschließung und Automatisches Indexieren.

Tab. 5.1: Effort required to create a collection-based information system.

Objects	Seconds	Minutes	Hours	Workdays
100	3,000	50	0.8	
1,000	30,000	500	8.3	
10,000	300,000	5,000	83.3	10.4

either, because a method that is suitable on a small scale rarely translates well to a larger scale.

In addition to the aspects of effort, there is the aspect of keeping the overview. 10 objects can be captured at a glance and evaluated in terms of their similarities and differences. With 100 objects, this is no longer possible, not to mention 1,000. Arranging 100 objects on a standard screen already proves to be a challenge.

When we think of creating order, we automatically associate the formation of piles, according to the motto "similar stuff goes together". But what if there is more than one thing that needs to be treated as similar, like all the birthday pictures, or all the mother-in-law pictures? How do you proceed if you have already created a basic order by grouping things together, and a new object is added? How do you know which group to add it to? Do you have to compare the new object with all existing objects for this? This would require the same amount of effort as to produce a new basic order. How long would that take for 10,000 objects? Or do you just compare the new object with a description of the groups? This would be the incremental, and in comparison certainly the faster way. However, further questions arise when describing the groups: What should such a description contain? And do you write them down or just keep them in mind? Again a question of quantity. When adding objects, what if you need to change the basic order or just want to change it sometime?

The good news is that there are professional answers to all these questions, which are especially designed for use in work-sharing environments and over longer periods of time. Unfortunately, these are again less suitable for private use because the initial effort is too high to manage "smaller" quantities.

Professional organization systems, which reflect relationships in content—examples are taxonomies, classification systems, or thesauri—are intended to serve as knowledge maps for orientation and as tools to support retrieval. In addition, they should enable the integration of a new object into the existing structure without having to look at all existing objects again. In their first function, they can be seen as forerunners of today's knowledge representation systems; their second function is nowadays often considered no longer necessary and replaced by complete data processing solutions. The statistical techniques used, especially big data techniques, are not good at handling subsets because they usually work with the entire data set. This means they are not designed to deal with incremental growth.

Instead, these knowledge organization systems can come up with another crucial feature: They are not unstructured collections of descriptive features for objects, but as knowledge systems they have a structure based on content. This structure is built on content relationships between entities and provides a link between the knowledge of the individual and the knowledge used to describe the objects. This structure can be based on a worldview, a scientific view, or a pragmatic view. It is always born from the need to get a better overview through organization. If, in this course, previously unknown connections are discovered, the structure can even serve to expand knowledge, the highest form of benefit of a predefined structure.

Comparing the two approaches makes it seem as if ceding the effort to the cloud-based solution can only be a win. It remains to be explored whether our own efforts can have advantages over a cloud-based solution and what these might be. Of importance here is the individual focus related to the objects and their contents. These may also be emotionally influenced, but should still be considered as search criteria in a retrieval situation. The issue, then, is the difference between individual preferences and intersubjective criteria, and how important someone considers them when designing an information system. If objects are to be described on the basis of subjectively preferred features, a special form to represent the relationships between the objects is used. Then it is no longer a matter of supposedly objective characteristics, but of attributes that are associated with the objects.

Pattern recognition methods can identify the Eiffel Tower in a photo from a list of features and make it searchable and findable thanks to a stored label. If the same photo was taken on the occasion of a honeymoon, pattern recognition will still yield the same result because there is no individual attribute associated with the photo for the occasion, only the label that has been externally assigned.

This is because cloud services generally cannot take into account attributes that are individually assigned from the outside. They can only represent a structure perceived as intersubjective—if a defined structure is offered at all. They cannot support individual requirements concerning the structure, just as they cannot support any connections (concordances) between global and individual structures. Individual ideas about context and structure can only be realized in a self-designed information system.

So is there a recommended—or any—solution to the initial problem of designing an information system for a private collection of objects? Probably not. Cloud-based approaches will serve you well if you don't want to invest much time and effort. Whoever considers knowledge organization without individual structuring to be inappropriate, will not be able to avoid doing it alone. While the advantages and disadvantages of the home-made approach are well known, there is still a lack of experience with cloud services. Interfacing both ways can be imagined, but requires a lot of know-how and so much effort that it cannot yet be considered suitable for mass production. In particular, they presuppose compatibility of the ordering structures involved. As things stand, the easiest way then is to adapt to a given structure or to do without any structuring at all; reasonable consideration of individual structuring ideas, however, falls by the wayside.

So for the moment, the discussion can at best be about criteria which may encourage and help find a competent way of dealing with the problem. After all, losing the knowledge to do the right thing is likely to be more of a disadvantage in the long run than doing the wrong thing once.

To summarize, we would like to specify the components that are involved in the creation, configuration and maintenance of an information system. These include:

- a plan with ordering criteria that serves to map one's search interests in such a way that it provides a sufficiently broad set of commonalities on the one hand, but on the other hand offers enough granularity for possible expansion; expandability, also in the sense of refinement, is always desirable, but is one of the most difficult features to realize; ideally, the plan should not solely exist in the user's mind, but should be externalized in a way that is accessible to others;
- the creation of a structure by identifying relationships, formal and content-related interconnections;
- the consideration of aspects (for example, persons, places, time, institutions, buildings) within which the objects represented can be well identified by individual names;
- a concept for addressing different aspects that lead to multiple assignments or to descriptions by multiple characteristics;
- the specification of rules that enable consistency and thus ensure the uniformity of the approach for comparable cases over longer periods of time.

5.5 Data and Context

Data cannot be interpreted and understood isolated from context and theory. In everyday life, we are often familiar with both, so that—unlike, say, in scientific or technical contexts—it may seem strange to turn our attention to this relationship.

Often it will be necessary to deal with an object more intensively, because only in this way we gain contextual knowledge which allows for a deeper understanding. This applies not only to complex problems of science, but also, for example, to the use of search engines, which has become an indispensable part of our lives.

Search engines are markedly complex tools, but they smartly hide their complexity because they want the search experience to be easy and enjoyable. There are many internal processes for refining the search and the set of results, whose function and mode of action are not known to the average user.

The reality of an ordinary information search is characterized by the simple input of words or strings into, for example, the *Google* search slot. The entered terms are searched for in isolation as character strings and are not embedded in a thematic context. This works well when searching for individual names of persons, companies or products, unless there are several hits with identical names. For words that are used for more general concepts, the problems already start when such a search term has synonyms. Concepts for which there are multiple terms in the language used for the search cannot be queried with a search engine like *Google*. Sometimes it looks as if searching for a word also finds synonymous terms, just because they are found together in the search results. A fallacy, because in most cases it is just the result of statistical coincidence, i.e., the common occurrence of words in a document. Completeness of such common occurrences should not be expected.

Despite this, most users seem to be satisfied with the services currently offered and also with the presentation of the search results. Competing services just as making comparisons hardly meet with any interest.[187] At least, there are increasing complaints that the search process is not transparent enough. And although we are dissatisfied with the perceived paternalism of the search engine as it presents us with personalized results based on its analysis of our search habits, we do not want to give up the simplicity and convenience of our search experience.

Search engines are undeniably an important link between our minds and the expansion of individual knowledge based on potential information from external information sources. And yet, a distinct desire for more elaborate ways of systematically incorporating knowledge into larger contexts has not been detected so far. It almost seems that people have lost their motivation and curiosity to look more closely at the technologies and the underlying data of the tools they use every day.

The reasons for this development can only be speculated. How we use the information offered today certainly contributes to this. The media as well as the social environment literally encourage us not to look deeper into the matter, even if

---

187 See Höchstötter: Suchverhalten im Web, Markey: Twenty-five years of end-user searching, Jansen/Spink: How are we searching the World Wide Web?, White: Interactions with search systems, Lewandowski (ed.): Handbuch Internet-Suchmaschinen.

we could. There is an increasing expectation that data must be immediately understandable and can be consumed as a direct question-answer resource. Moreover is data commonly conceived as something that can be incorporated into an individual's cognitive structure without any further structure-building efforts. Also, little attention is paid to the fact that the perception of data is tied to individual sensory impressions or that data may be the result of theory-based processes. Instead, data are all too often ascribed a high degree of truth and are seen as immediately suitable for solving problems. Independent cognitive interpretation no longer seems to be necessary. The fact that all this is only possible under the narrow conditions of a respective theory binding or the existence of corresponding reference domains is being ignored as well.

Ludwig Wittgenstein had already seen in the dominance of the formal the possible final stage of a development:

> If you wrap up different kinds of furniture in enough wrapping paper, you can make them all look the same shape.[188]

Contextualization, the search for analogies, and verification by plausibility are central criteria of informational literacy. Not to forget, the equally important qualities of intuition and creativity always require context and correlation when designing objects, as well as when dealing with subjects in general. The interpretation of data being involved in a context is bound to a theory, which the interpreter must be familiar with at least on a basic level. The context may already be given—such as in learning processes—but often it must first be discovered or identified. And this in turn requires practice on the basis of suitable specifications. Today's media landscape is increasingly dominated by product types that offer a presentation of context that is more closely modeled on the sensory perceptions of the real world, resulting in less interest in independently engaging with the content's context.

There is a well-known design principle that says: "Form follows function". Media presentation was originally intended to support the reception of content or the meaning of statements by means of suitable media design. In this sense, "Form follows function" would mean that the formal presentation first and foremost supports the reception of the content. The content should not tempt you to be too concerned with the requirements of the form(al operation). More and more, media forms are being filled with random, or even fictional, content and are considered equally important. The possibilities of virtual reality, for example, simulate an idealized reality and this idealization is then projected inversely as an expectation onto the appearance of the real world. More mundane in comparison

---

188 Cited by Searle: The rediscovery of the mind, p. 126.

are the constant changes in software interfaces and their interaction elements. Often enough, animated icons, constantly opening dialog or notification windows, and redesigned menu items require far too much attention, when they should only trigger an action within the application itself.

Whether these changes in media (re-)presentation forms lead to a faster or improved reception of content is still an open question; cognitive knowledge expansion has in any case existed long since without them.

Creativity, one of the core human competencies, also risks being affected. Our world is highly interconnected, and we are more and more exposed to automated processes, with ever more perfectly prescribed contexts. There are already indications that this will have, or already has, an impact on the human imagination. Such a development would have serious implications, as creativity has a decisive influence on adaptability, problem solving and resilience, qualities that we should not forfeit as we move into the future.

5.6 Fragmentation of Knowledge

In parallel with the emphasis on fact and form over content, the demands imposed by the technical operation of the medium dominate the engagement with the content. Actually, despite the emergence of new media forms for interpersonal communication, proficient usage should continue to be measured by the content communicated; perhaps also by the capability of knowing and being able to use a wide range of these media forms. Knowing their historical development and the proper selection from the existing variety of media forms would be the right yardstick for competence here. But we are still a long way from that.

And this despite the fact that the importance of properly mastering a medium has undoubtedly continued to grow under the influence of information technology. Once again, this should only be the framework for engaging with the actual content and not a substitute for it, and, of course, also not an evaluation standard for the quality of the engagement. Nevertheless, even political programs hype the mere equipping of educational institutions with IT infrastructure as a competence-promoting measure, without explaining which content it is that can be taught more appropriately using information technology. The significance of the topic has, for example, prompted the *German Mathematical Society* to publish its position on the "Education offensive for the digital knowledge society" in a press release entitled "Contents instead of devices" on the occasion of the 2016 national IT summit:

It is not the mere use of digital media, but an understanding of its fundamentals that creates the conditions for a confident digital transformation.[189]

Data and Fragmentation

What are the consequences of these changes for the persistence of knowledge when it is tied to experience and context? Who still knows the phone numbers of their friends (or even the own number) by heart today, when it has become a habit to simply click on the number of the saved contact to make a call? What effect does the use of navigation systems have on the ability to orient in nature with the help of a map? To measure the distance of a hike, we rely on a pedometer app, and the altitude information is provided by the GPS function of our smartphone. How much confidence do you have in your own assessment of the current weather when the forecast says otherwise? There is nothing fundamentally wrong with checking your assessments against other data and correcting them if necessary, but this should be done in a balanced way and should not lead to a loss of intuition or the ability to come to your own assessments.

In the classical model of knowledge acquisition, great importance was attached to the ability to weigh up facts "and" consider contexts "before" making a decision as well as to the ability to translate them to new facts. Data and facts were major components, but performance was judged more on the ability to categorize according to facts and to establish correlations. This was clearly evident in teaching, learning, and testing situations, for example. Only poor teachers tended to view memorizing and reproducing facts as a crucial testing requirement. Good teachers have always given priority to the capability to weigh and argue within given frameworks. Yet it may be too early to see a turning point here.

The constant and immediate availability of information gives the impression that many things no longer need to be "known". Text snippets and isolated segments replace context and correlation, knowledge is reduced to the retrieval of fragmented units of information.

The devaluation of knowledge about contexts and correlations leads, among other things, to the view that numerical parameters with possibilities for automated evaluation are suitable substitutes. What remains unconsidered here is the fact that the mere possibility of a data-based analysis changes the whole approach

---

189 Deutsche Mathematiker-Vereinigung: Inhalte statt Geräte (author's translation). Other authors as well have critically examined this topic and made suggestions for alternative approaches. Representatively mentioned here are Liessmann: Geisterstunde, Hensinger: Trojanisches Pferd ‚Digitale Bildung' [Vortrag], Hensinger: Digitale Bildung. So far it is not apparent that the relevant institutions would include such proposals in their deliberations.

to solving a problem. It cannot be ruled out that this may also have an impact on the view of what a problem actually is. An example from the world of science or scientific publishing that may not have widespread popularity, but can illustrate the trend, is a post promoting the author identification system *ORCID*[190] which claims:

Unambiguously attributing scientists to their publications is a challenge.[191]

Why, in what context, and for whom is this a challenge? Not for the author after all. Usually, neither is it for the reader. The problem exists only for those who want to list publications separately by author and who cannot accomplish this task based on the available data alone. This problem is not a new one. Libraries and bibliographies have always had it, and over time have found different approaches to dealing with it successfully. The results were international sets of rules for the assignment of personal names and authority data that were based on those rules. These approaches, however, mostly do involve intellectual work: Knowledge must be acquired, targeted searches conducted, directories (databases) maintained, and rules followed. Less and less valued today, these activities were once closely associated with information literacy. Meanwhile, interest in the topic is also shown by all those who (supported by informetric methods) want to perform citation analyses on the basis of automated name identification in order to derive key data for personal rankings.

Interestingly, automatic procedures for separating homonymous personal names have not been very successful: reliable identification of authors still requires an intellect endowed with specific knowledge. *ORCID* therefore attempts to create unique data that can be automatically matched by uniformly labeling scientists.[192]

In the meantime, established procedures are being forgotten, with the result that, in view of not knowing the old approaches, inadequacies of the new ways do not even become apparent during the conception phase. Some of the proponents of the new approaches are no longer even aware of them and consider their approach to be a creative new idea, not only in terms of technology but also in terms of content.

ORCID, for example, suggests a completeness for its procedure that cannot be achieved at all due to the lack of retrospective reprocessing of old material. Any completeness of this would require intellectual and manual activity. *ORCID*

190 ORCID [Website].
191 Höhner: ORCID an der TH Dortmund (author's translation).
192 Höhner: ORCID an der TH Dortmund.

is therefore well suited to mark a break, because one thing is clear: authors and publications without an *ORCID* identifier will have a different status by this fact alone. If, in addition, the knowledge of the previous states is lost, these can also no longer be reconstructed when needed. Looking back into the past and to the roots of what happened is then limited to the possibilities of machine data analysis.

Will there one day be an *ORCID* identifier for *S. B. Preuss*? This supposed co-author of *Albert Einstein* actually never existed. Due to the sloppy application of citation rules and publishing pressure to shorten bibliographical references, the name *S. B. Preuss* arose via a chain of citations from the abbreviation of the source *Sitzungsberichte der Preußischen Akademie der Wissenschaften*.[193] Nevertheless, he was for a certain time a prominent co-author and of course there are publications also about "him". For *Albert Einstein*, a search in the *ORCID* database returns three IDs that do not correspond to "the" *Albert Einstein*.[194] The commercial system *Scopus* links *Albert Einstein* to a *ScopusID* (22988279600) and lists 132 documents, 49 co-authors, and 30,122 citations.[195]

5.7 Hypertext, Delinearization, Fragmentation

After it had been recognized that the presentation of text in a screen-ready manner was accompanied by a fragmentation of contexts, some attempts were made to address this problem. One approach was hypertext by *Ted Nelson*.[196] Initially, great expectations were associated with it, which were even supposed to have an impact on the formation of a social memory.[197]

The de-linearization of text was seen as a particular advantage, which should support individual reading paths and thereby promote the building of contexts. Systematic structures should no longer be rigidly predefined, but should be designable in user-controlled discovery and navigation processes. For this purpose, other methods were used in addition to the still familiar hyperlinks.[198]

Even greater expectations were associated with the development of the so-called semantic web. The idea of Web 2.0 to create and enrich dynamic web pages with data from various sources (such as embedding weather reports, news, or calendars) should now be complemented by enriching semantically comparable

---

193 See Goenner: Das kurze Leben des S. B. Preuss, S. B. Preuss [Wikipedia].
194 Search on ORCID [Website] on February 14, 2023.
195 Einstein, Albert [Scopus preview].
196 Nelson: Complex information processing, Nelson: Transhyperability and argumedia.
197 See Schmidt: Von der Memoria zur Gedächtnispolitik.
198 As an introduction to the concept, see Kuhlen: Hypertext.

data from different sources. One hoped-for result of this was the emergence of new search functions that would allow for semantic exploration through synonyms and other related concepts; the search success would no longer depend exclusively on the entered character string and its computer linguistic or statistical treatment. The motto of the semantic web was: "My computer understands me".[199]

The impression arose that human and machine processing of semantic knowledge (read: cognitive concepts) were meant to be aligned. The intention of the new methods was to model machine processes as a replica of human processes.

Semantic interoperability has become a key concept in this context. It is almost tedious to trace the shades of meaning that this concept has undergone in the few years since it was first coined. At one time it is intended to express similarity and interchangeability of concepts according to meaningful content[200], at other times the error-free replacement or linking of data between machines. The current interpretation in *Wikipedia* expresses it most clearly:

> Semantic interoperability is the ability of computer systems to exchange data with unambiguous, shared meaning. Semantic interoperability is a requirement to enable machine computable logic, inferencing, knowledge discovery, and data federation between information systems.[201]

As it seems, not much has remained of the original ideas. What has been preserved is the solidity of fragmentation, which is even more likely to be intensified by new generations of devices (smartphones, tablets) and services (blogs, messengers). The introduction of semantic tools to offer guidance at the level of meaning could have mitigated this effect. What has prevailed in everyday life is commercial pragmatics. Remnants of the semantic web idea are mainly markup languages (*HTML, XML, OWL*) and standards (*SKOS, ISO 25964*) used for designing web content. Here, too, form has triumphed as an end in itself over its originally intended role as a means to facilitate design. The variety of labels for different relationships initially envisioned in the concept of hypertext has been reduced almost exclusively to the use of hyperlinks. The result is thus rather a support of fragmentation without showing systematic or other correlations. The most obvious example of this is that returning from a page reached via a web link is often only possible via a browser functionality: the "back" button.

Semantic interoperability is also a prerequisite for "communication" between humans and autonomous machines. It specifies which properties the interfaces of

---

199 Berners-Lee/Hendler/Lassila: The semantic web.
200 Gödert: Semantische Wissensrepräsentation und Interoperabilität.
201 Semantic interoperability [Wikipedia].

information-processing systems should have in order to be able to exchange ("communicate") formatted data between the systems and to process it without further transformation measures. Communication understood in this way can only consider, interpret, and process data according to the meaning that is already stored in the data model. Unknown data structures are rejected in this form of processing. Currently, there are no known solutions for equipping technical systems with properties that meet the criterion of plasticity as it occurs in human communication (Chapter 5.3). The success of a communication between humans and machines depends solely on the cognitive plasticity of the human communication partners. If the communication possibilities between humans and machines are designed exclusively on the basis of technically understood semantic interoperability, the level of understanding will flatten out in the long run. Fact is, the current dialog is increasingly oriented toward the possibilities of the technical systems and the definition of interfaces. Recent examples of "services" such as automated telephone hotlines or chat bots already clearly demonstrate this.

5.8 Knowledge in Change

There is some evidence that the relationship to knowledge, and thus the way knowledge is understood, is changing. Instance-based (fragmented) knowledge, which can be retrieved as single fact portions from external storage media, is about to become a guiding concept for the modern understanding of knowledge. It replaces the earlier primacy of a context-based notion of knowledge based on the comprehension of correlations.[202] For the internal conception of knowledge, context and structure no longer seem to play a significant role. Knowledge is reduced to a commodity that can be retrieved quickly, taken from a repository when needed, and used for a specific purpose.

There are still examples of the opposite situation, such as shown by the understanding of "money". Although even children have an idea of the meaning, function, and effects of "money", an exact definition stubbornly eludes all efforts of science and general understanding.[203] In order to be a payer or payee, an understanding bound to experience and passed on as background is sufficient; an abstract conceptualization is not necessary. Everyone living in a society affected by digitization is familiar with money and its functions. It is therefore a good example

---

202 See Neuser: Wissen begreifen.
203 See the compilation of 35 characterizations from different historical eras at Busch: Aspekte der Geldkritik von Aristoteles bis heute.

of how reality is generated in modern societies through the creation of structures and organizations that are perceived as reality by all members and which one cannot live against. Modern money has the character of a promise without a material basis, yet its existence in reality is not questioned. Money is not only exchanged for goods and services, it is even multiplied by anticipation of future events. The fact that there is such a high level of acceptance despite its virtuality is certainly related to the fact that money was once introduced as the equivalent of real objects and was treated in the educational canon for a long time. Perhaps its acceptance is also supported by many a children's game or board game, in which its traditional view continues to be preserved despite social advancement. Money is a fact of institutional reality:

> The process of the creation of institutional facts may proceed without the participants being conscious that it is happening according to this form. The evolution may be such that the participants think, e.g., "I can exchange this for gold," "This is valuable," or even simply "This is money." They need not think, "We are collectively imposing a value on something that we do not regard as valuable because of its purely physical features," even though that is exactly what they are doing. There are two points about the relation of this process to consciousness. First, obviously, for most institutions we simply grow up in a culture where we take the institution for granted. We need not be consciously aware of the form of the collective intentionality by which they are imposing functions on objects. In the course of consciously buying, selling, exchanging, etc., they may simply evolve institutional facts. Furthermore, in extreme cases they may accept the imposition of functions only because of some related theory, which may not even be true. They may believe that it is money only if it is "backed to gold" [...] As long as people continue to recognize the X as having the Y status function, the institutional fact is created and maintained. They do not in addition have to recognize that they are so recognizing, and they may hold all sorts of other false beliefs about what they are doing and why they are doing it.[204]

How will money be viewed in a world dominated by digital payments and digital debts? It should not be too bold a prediction that our daily interaction with cash has led to a familiarity that cannot be easily transferred to a world of cryptocurrencies. Perhaps in a world of purely digital money transfers, the demands of comprehending the interweaving connections will become too great and resignation will set in. Then the understanding would shift out of the habit of the old ways of doing things as if nothing had changed, and people would deal with this reality as if it were a children's game or a board game.

The execution of data-oriented actions does not require understanding as long as it takes place in a context that corresponds to its theoretical modeling.

---

204 Searle: The construction of social reality, pp. 47–48.

But if the context changes, we have to rely on understanding or we become helpless. This presupposes a concept of knowledge that is based on understanding and must be founded on informational autonomy.

5.9 Assessing, Deciding, Acting

Assessing, deciding, and acting are the central fields of application when it comes to informational literacy. Every human action is preceded by a process of assessing and deciding. Both can be seen as the result of cognitive information processing. Assessing is (too) often seen as a moral judgment, especially when referred to persons. However, the main point here is that any decision related to choosing between options involves an evaluation process. If there are no options, there can also be no decision situation; then we have a command and obedience situation, one that cannot be dealt with in the context of informational autonomy.

Decisions about actions to be taken are based on knowledge and are, again, the result of cognitive information processing. They are often distinguished into rationally driven decision-making processes and those that are more associated with gut feelings or seen as experience-based.[205] It is common to assign the higher quality to rational decisions. Decisions involve cognitive load and this load has limits. Especially in light of a changed understanding of knowledge, arguments for delegating decisions to algorithms and data evaluation are then readily brought up. If informational autonomy were to be seen as an indispensable property, there would be a conflicting relationship between decision-making processes based purely on the parameters of a situation and those based on experience and prior understanding.

In an abstract way, the situation may be described as follows: Instrumental reason can be controlled by parameters and external specifications, but the "inner reality" cannot be described in this way. Situations requiring action and decision-making can be based on informational processes under the following premises:
- Decision-making situations, especially those involving moral principles, presuppose the ability to access your inner imprint.
- The affinity toward external parameters and algorithmic procedures leads to a loss of the ability to acquire and retrieve those inner imprints.
- In real life, action-induced situations presuppose the ability to assess a situation on the basis of both external and internal states (also in combination).

---

205 See Gigerenzer: Gut feelings.

Individuals must be able to make instant moral judgments about their actions. In doing so, it is not possible to call up situational specifications from outside at the same time. Recalling them can only take place on the basis of internal states. What is needed, then, is a balance between the inside and the outside. Losing or even limiting the ability to access these states has significant consequences for an individual's ability to act. This would result in a loss of intuitive orientation and perhaps also of the ability to make independent moral judgments.

In the Ancient World and through-out the Middle Ages, the meaning of life and morality were still dictated to most people by external instances and events. There was no obligation for individuals to make up their own minds on these questions. The general principle was to repeat what was given, and not to think for oneself. Life without the reference to God and associated texts, that is, without the reference to external sources, was inconceivable. The Enlightenment overcame this state which we today consider unsatisfactory and put ideas of humanism in its place. People were now encouraged to think for themselves, and to have their own inner scale of values, which they acquired through education. The concept of authority is characterized by the fact that it is experienced by us as an internal projection which we then transfer into life; authority thus does not function solely as an external framework. Hence, the external source is not abolished, but for sensible decisions it is replaced by internal processes that arrive at statements of meaning with or without reference to the external source. This results not only in freedom of choice, but also in the desire to live up to the newly acquired values or demands in our own lives.

Machines, even under the premises of artificial intelligence, have no inner imprint for decision-making situations and can only act according to external guidelines. They cannot be a substitute for any informational and autonomous decision-making. Humans with their inner imprint do have the option to deal autonomously with questions of meaning and morality. Therefore, it would be fatal if the orientation towards algorithmic thinking led to an instrumental understanding of morality, which could be given to a robot as well as to a human being.

And yet decision-making processes based on the algorithmic analysis of data are penetrating more and more areas of society. Often, it can only be guessed to what extent this is already happening; in other cases, it happens quite openly.

Can any arguments be made for "not" replacing cognitive decisions with algorithm-based data evaluation? After all, with dataism, we already have a school of thought among us that relies entirely on the analysis of data, not only for purchase recommendations or the granting of credit, but based on our individual preferences and tastes. We would like to recall that there are highly successful cognitive decision-making processes out there that are not emotion-based or irrational, although they are based on algorithms.

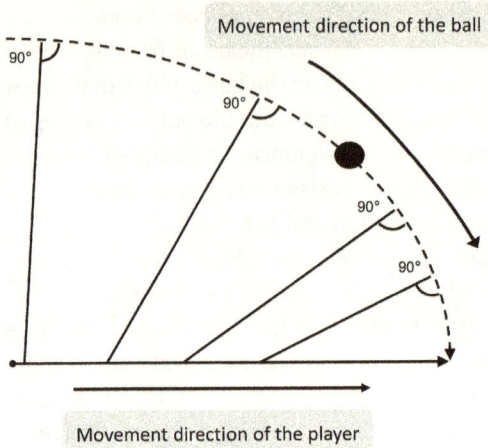

Fig. 5.2: Throwing parabola.

Consider the task of catching a thrown ball.[206] After being thrown, the ball moves on a curve that is to be mathematically calculated under known initial conditions (throwing speed, throwing angle, mass of the ball, wind direction, etc.). The point of bouncing on the earth can thus be determined exactly. In baseball, for instance, catching balls is a major task for players to master as perfectly as possible. However, no baseball player first solves differential equations after the ball has been hit and before catching the ball. Instead, he or she will apply a heuristic that can be described as follows: Fix the ball and start running; adjust the running speed so that the angle of view on the ball remains constant (Figure 5.2). To determine the viewpoint necessary for catching the ball, the player does not need any technical or mathematical aids, but relies solely on the own experience gained through success and failure.

Applying this heuristic represents a cognitive process that is all the more successful the more it is internalized by the player and the more often the player trains it and thus settles it as experience. Such strategies are deeply embedded in the evolutionary structure of living beings. Use of this heuristic can also be observed, for example, in dogs, which run after a thrown stick and often intercept it before it hits the ground.

The example illustrates the difference between decisions based on a cognitive understanding of knowledge and those based algorithmically on parameters. Data can be collected for all components of ball throwing. With this data, a robot

---

206 The example follows Gigerenzer: Gut feelings.

designed to move appropriately and programmed with a "catch" algorithm can be enabled to catch the ball. Within the tolerances of the algorithm, the robot will probably succeed even more reliably than many humans. Nevertheless, this approach is not suitable as a model for human actions. These are two worlds with their own strengths and weaknesses (Chapter 1.3). Only a robot that is capable of learning, with the ability to develop and verify its own heuristics based on success or failure, would give cause to reconsider this statement.

Still, there are those who, like *Max Tegmark* as one of the proponents of the computer metaphor, tend to think of such strategies very much as algorithms. From our point of view, however, this is not covered by the standard understanding of algorithms and only serves the purpose of blurring the differences. We therefore stick to a distinction between heuristics and algorithms.

5.10 Algorithms for Action Control

Algorithm-based recommendations or control of actions coming from big data evaluations further exacerbate the situation. They are based on experience and context, as data are collected from real situations of acting people—but possibly in the future also from people whose informational autonomy is already limited. Heuristics and hypotheses are used, but in a different sense: they are built in ab initio and are not subject to individual success monitoring and refinement. In any case, the evaluation is done via algorithms, but little is known about their ability to handle different situations.

The idea of using algorithms to control action is reminiscent of proposals already made by *Gottfried Wilhelm Leibniz* in his *Ars Combinatoria*.[207] He assumed that a decision and action problem can be rationally formalized by specifying its parameters completely and subjecting them to algorithmic evaluation.

According to *Leibniz*, freeing the evaluation from the factor of "arbitrary" human influences would lead to the acceptance of the result by all people. Importantly, he wanted to replace the weakness of action in humans with algorithms, not their ability to assess or think rationally. Algorithmic solutions were sought even before *Leibniz* to solve the most difficult problems of mankind. For instance, *Raimundus Lullus*, who also inspired *Leibniz*, proposed to create proofs of God through assertions generated by combinations, which should convert non-believers to the right faith.[208]

---

207 Himmelheber: Leibniz.
208 Duda: Ein mittelalterlicher Computer.

Solving problems to general satisfaction through the use of rational tools and securing lasting acceptance for the solution is undoubtedly an attractive idea of a goal. In view of the many ways in which affective factors influence human action and decision-making, however, their feasibility may be fundamentally questioned. The course of history, even if limited to the period after the Enlightenment and *Leibniz*, does not really offer an optimistic prognosis for this.[209]

In a historical perspective, humans have developed various models of social coexistence. All these models can be described in a highly rational process by a number of parameters. So, in principle, it would certainly be possible to get a ranking of these models with the help of an algorithm. Let us hypothetically assume that even the weighting of the parameters could be clarified, for instance by consulting the *United Nations Charter on Human Rights*. What current society would be willing to abandon its prevailing social model in favor of the top performer in this ranking? What kind of reasons would play a role in this? And would this be a rational process?

In his historical analysis of social organizational structures (including animal social communities), *Yuval Harari* concludes that the winning model is the one that can attract the most adherents by unfolding a higher and more mutable degree of organization:

> History provides ample evidence for the crucial importance of large-scale cooperation. Victory almost invariably went to those who cooperated better—not only in struggles between *Homo sapiens* and other animals, but also in conflicts between different human groups.[210]

Here, on the one hand, the optimization of the degree of organization is described as a rational level. Another factor is the agreement of the organization's members, which, however, cannot be presumed to be given in advance.

A special property of human social systems is their independence from the direct acquaintance of all members, as is used, for example, in animal populations to stabilize conditions. This in turn emphasizes the role of abstract states and their importance for human action. *Harari's* conclusion is not necessary to share:

> If Sapiens rule the world because we alone can cooperate flexibly in large numbers, then this undermines our belief in the sacredness of human beings.[211]

If "sacredness" is replaced by "the ability to abstract and instantiate in the expression of heuristics and their verification by plausibility", this would create a

---

209 See Randow: Gottfried Wilhelm Leibniz.

210 Harari: Homo Deus, p. 133.

211 Harari: Homo Deus, p. 138.

sufficiently unique human characteristic and a basis for participation in decision-making processes. The preference of one social model over another can at best be described as the result of an algorithmic process, if it takes place without the participation of the members of the social system and is imposed on them—something that is rejected, at least by democratically constituted states. Unless the decision bypasses the members of the social system, it is accompanied by affective factors such as interests and preferences. Again, the ability to balance rational and affective decision components is the imperative, not replacing human decisions with algorithms.

6 Informational Literacy as Lived Informational Autonomy

I combat the imperialism of instrumental reason, not reason.

Joseph Weizenbaum[212]

6.1 Information Literacy versus Informational Literacy

Informational literacy can be viewed from a variety of angles. On a lower level are those areas that are characterized by the handling of—predominantly digital—materials. Here, the main focus is on the features of the material and its most appropriate and efficient use. Work outcomes are deemed equivalent to media literacy, digital literacy, or information literacy and include a list of criteria derived from the media or the respective materials.

The concept of media literacy is associated with the proper handling of a "medium" as a carrier of potential information. This can be a physical or digital information storage medium, which requires certain skills and capabilities to be learned. In contrast, the concept of information literacy separates from this material baseline and aims to access something virtual, the information itself. Understood as a key concept of the information age, no one should evade acquiring information literacy any longer.

More and more information sources with ever easier and quicker access to them combined with the trend to replace actual understanding with fact-finding, seem to point to a potentially inexhaustible reservoir of knowledge. Not many people are aware that this could pose a problem in terms of selection. Also related to this is the question of whether a learning process can ever be complete, and whether it can actually function without any prior conditions. The first of the prerequisites we see here is the need for a basic attitude toward information literacy understood as an extension of established cultural techniques, and whose knowledge is indispensable.[213]

Humans are information-processing beings. Hence, it is only obvious that there must be a further level of consideration. On the one hand, this level is more abstract because it describes cognitive abilities and characteristics as preconditions for acquiring information literacy. On the other hand, it is also real and

---

212 Weizenbaum: Computer power and human reason, p. 256.
213 See Liessmann: Geisterstunde.

https://doi.org/10.1515/9783110693744-006

concrete, since it takes into account people in their everyday actions and communication habits. Therefore, the level of informational literacy is to be placed ahead of information literacy. Informational literacy is informational autonomy in action. It is the ability to process actual information in an act of communication and to receive potential information (meant as medially externalized information) in order to perform a construction of reality for the purpose of acting or acquiring knowledge.

There is a correlation between information literacy and informational literacy that is critical to individual and societal progress: The fundamentally existing basic endowment of human cognitive abilities can be used to strengthen informational literacy, which in turn can be built up to better master all the instrumental skills associated with information literacy. If instrumental mastery alone is the benchmark, this may lead to efforts to improve artificial intelligence being preferred to efforts to improve natural intelligence. Informational autonomy would then no longer be lived. In the longer term, it cannot be ruled out that precisely this path will be chosen, which, under the convenience of digitization, will inevitably lead to a creeping degression of informational capabilities and could ultimately even result in the emergence of totalitarian social structures. For now, we still have a choice.

Informational literacy and information or media literacy can be distinguished from each other by yet another characteristic. Information literacy and media literacy are both object-related, namely they refer to an object of recent technical innovation for which specific handling skills are claimed. A study on the topic of "digital maturity" summarizes the argumentation typical of this view:

> "Digital maturity" is the result of media education processes and of emancipation and cognition processes associated with digital media, which individuals undergo with their own efforts in order to be able to participate in a digital media society. It manifests in a combination of characteristics of digitized media literacy, autonomy, and self-determination, and for its realization is reliant on the independent thinking of the individual, the inclusion of cultural practice, and the contextual conditions of a liberal-democratic basic order.[214]

The formulation "in order to be able to participate in a digital media society" proves that digital maturity is seen here as an attribute that has only attained significance with the development of a certain form of modern technology. In another argumentation, parallels to our positions can certainly be recognized, but cannot achieve any stringency due to the binding to external factors:

---

214 Bender: Digitale Mündigkeit, p. 78 (author's translation).

At this point, autonomy, independent thinking, and self-determination are the characteristics that will be considered in the definition of digital maturity. The dimensions identified are a political-social dimension (free democratic basic order) and an individual dimension (comprehension, decisiveness, activity).[215]

In contrast, the understanding of informational literacy is neither bound to a form of medium nor to a temporal epoch, but generally allows the reference to all situations related to cognitive information processing. Accordingly, no instrumental understanding can be the focus in dealing with informational tasks. Crucial is the view of the invariants of cognitive abilities by which informational literacy is distinguished as a basic cognitive function. We speak of abilities such as contextualizing, abstracting and instantiating, using intuition, heuristics and hypotheses, making analogies, checking plausibility, reasoning, as well as structuring and ordering.

Our time is full of—not only informational—phenomena giving the impression that there is no longer a balance between dealing with tasks that are important and those that are less important. Providing reliable evidence of this is difficult. It is even more difficult to avoid explanatory approaches that do not simultaneously invoke cultural pessimism or scenarios of decadence and doom. However, if one accepts the above observation, this inevitably leads to the claim that informational literacy should include the ability to distinguish between importance and unimportance in informational problems.

Interpretations of information processing start with data-related processes and range up to cognitive processes, which can furthermore take place in a social environment. The focus here will be on situations in which information processing involves the search for and reception of externalized information. Externalized information sources serve as a resource for expanding knowledge by evaluating what is found in relation to personal objectives and translating it into actual information. Informational literacy is thus a partial aspect of informational autonomy related to a specific situation, i.e., a "lived" informational autonomy.

Algorithmically based action or value specifications can only be seen as subsidiary support for human thought and action, taking into account informational autonomy. As long as information processing cannot generate itself in its information technological environment, cognitive information processing and informational autonomy will remain its prerequisites. As a cognitive property, informational autonomy cannot be switched off; it is present even when substitute or complementary functions partially take effect. Yet it may also be met with con-

---

215 Bender: Digitale Mündigkeit, p. 76 (author's translation).

tempt, and it is even more concerning when its value or usefulness for human or societal development is questioned.

Having confidence in your own information-processing capabilities is indispensable for a lived informational autonomy. And this depends on the trustworthiness, or credibility, that is attached to a piece of information. The assessment of informational credibility is done on several reference levels:

The Cognitive Level

Cognitive information processing is based on sensory perceptions, acts of communication, or externalized information. Unless there is a fundamental doubt that meaningful results can be achieved through this process, it must be assumed to be credible. Having constant doubts about the credibility of your own information processing would make it difficult to lead a normal social life. However, there are examples, such as optical illusions, which demonstrate that errors can creep in, leading to a difference between the measurable reality and the outcome of the cognitive process. Humans can deal with such phenomena without harm, which is made possible by knowing the phenomena's mechanisms and the discursive processing with other people.

The Level of the Source

Information outside the individual cognitive sphere is characterized as sources with content, and for these, too, the question of their respective credibility arises. Sources of externalized information can come up with varying degrees of credibility, because credibility is always an assigned attribute and not an intrinsic part of the sources. The extent of this problem becomes clear in the discussion about fake news and the possibilities for identifying it and preventing its spread. Here it is not decisive whether the source is another person or a repository for externalized information. Their credibility is judged on the basis of experience on a scale ranging from reliability to intentional misleading.

The Level of Content

There is no objective criterion for the credibility of content. At this level, an assessment can only be made on the basis of a person's own knowledge or with the help of external knowledge. If foreign knowledge is involved, the credibility of the source also plays a role. Since there is no a priori labeling of information that marks it as credible, there is, in principle, also no protection against informational misleading, lying or deliberate fraud. The only corrective that can be used in this case is your own knowledge and plausibility considerations. However, both must not only be present, but applied and continuously practiced.

The Level of Interests
Experience shows that there is a close connection between credibility and the interests involved in the provision and reception of information. This opens the way for the manipulation of facts in favor of particular interests which can lead to falsified information or the concealment of essential details. Likewise, if the recipient intentionally ignores facts, he or she contributes to the further dissemination of manipulated content.

An overall picture of informational credibility can only be obtained by considering all the levels. This creates a broad field of application for informational literacy, leading over to the topic of informational self-determination or informational dependence. Social concepts of informational self-determination will be all the easier to realize the more they can be based on the criteria of informational credibility.

6.2 Informational Self-determination and Dependence

Information literacy in its instrumental interpretation is usually viewed without reference to social structures; discussions of the skills deemed necessary assume that information literacy is invariant to all social conditions.

Due to the assumed close relationship between informational literacy and informational autonomy, the extent to which society promotes or hinders the development of informational autonomy does make a difference. This issue is discussed in the context of civil rights and liberties as so-called informational self-determination. In Germany, it has also been given high priority by supreme court jurisdiction as:

> [...] the authority of the individual to decide himself, on the basis of the idea of self-determination, when and within what limits information about his private life should be communicated to others.[216]

Internet policy debates center primarily on the various efforts of state security authorities to repeatedly use current threats made to the security situation to call into question legal standards that have already been achieved.

---

216 Informational self-determination [Wikipedia], citing the individual judgments of the *Federal Constitutional Court*.

A more fundamental conclusion is that informational autonomy is an inalienable human right. Human rights may be restricted within the framework of arbitrary state measures, but their relinquishment cannot be legitimized; not even with the supposedly good intention of wanting to benefit the individual. Thus, merely questioning informational self-determination is already a violation of informational autonomy, because it is impossible to talk about informational self-determination without grounding it in a concept like informational autonomy.

As a cognitive attribute, informational self-determination therefore has a backlash on the behavior of individuals in dealing with their rights. This right must also be lived in return. At the same time, the risk of being overstrained cannot be completely ruled out, which in turn threatens autonomy. If the awareness of informational autonomy is lost in society and is therefore no longer lived by the individual, this can lead to the emergence of informational totalitarianism (Chapter 7).

A multitude of informational appearances increasingly call informational self-determination into question or even endanger it. Every day, our knowledge meets the results of data analysis. Sometimes we can still decide for ourselves whether we want to trust signals that are controlled by unknown parameters or whether we want to give preference to our acquired knowledge as the basis for our actions. However, analogous to the replacement of understanding-based knowledge (Chapter 5.8), the trend is toward trusting the results of unknown parameters. Things look somewhat more positive, at least in cases where parameters and algorithms are used only to support human decisions and actions.

Since there is no data without context or theory binding, the use of external data always includes the respective background when making decisions and taking actions. In scientific and technical processes, this is usually only an academic problem. For economic, political or other social processes, however, the situation looks different. There are two variants: If the context of the data used is affine to the own ideas and one is aware of this fact, the use of the data is quite unproblematic. If the context is not clear, however, or if there is no affinity to it at all, informational self-determination is at least partially lost and one slips into informational dependence.

It is, for example, possible to be misled by a navigation system instead of being led to the intended destination. Certainly, compared to using maps (at least when there is no map-reading co-driver), the navigation system makes route finding easier. Here, too, it is above all the consequences of malfunctions that are thought-provoking. Some of us can get out of such a misfortunate situation by the still existing ability to interpret a classical map—but who still has a classical map in the car? However, with the omnipresent use of navigation systems or GPS trackers, a capability that was once of great importance to our civilization may now be lost.[217]

Another example: Many devices indicate consumption values. There are consumption meters for gasoline in the car, for fuel oil in the heater, for electricity in the washing machine, or in other household appliances. Everything may be correct, but one usually learns nothing about the background of the measurement methods used and, significantly, very few of these consumption meters are the basis for billing with the respective supplier. Whether it is a gas station, electricity or heating oil supplier, they all bill on the basis of their own measuring devices, with official calibration stamps to signal their professionalism.

In the examples given, informational dependence is already well advanced, and not all data pass the test of credibility. How can we be sure about the correctness of methods and data? All the more, when cross-checks by means of alternative measurement methods often provide deviating results? Who is right in the end? Many more examples can come to mind, as it is meanwhile very common for qualitative evaluations to be replaced by ratio-based ones. The standard argument of supposedly higher objectivity, which is repeatedly emphasized by the proponents, ignores the fact that each ratio is only meaningful with its respective theoretical background. The supposed objectivity is not independent of this background and therefore not safe from misuse.

If we wanted to, we could decide through our own behavior whether we want to follow the creepingly growing spiral of dependence, or whether we want to retain and further develop our maturity in the future through lived autonomy and the acquisition of knowledge.

6.3 Informational Incapacitation

There have long been developments that go even beyond informational dependence, leading to a further escalation that can be described as informational incapacitation. In many cases, data obtained from logs of user behavior is analyzed without users being able to have any influence on it. Often this is done under the pretext that decisions can be derived from the data that are meant to help the individual.

---

217 The use of GPS data illustrates the strong theory dependence of such approaches. Depending on the defaults of the system, the selected geographic location must be entered in the form of decimal degrees [52.520007 (latitude), 13.404954 (longitude)] or using the GMS system [52° 31' 12.025" north latitude / 13° 24' 17.834" east longitude] and, if necessary, a converter must be used before an accepted entry is made (respectively for the map reference system WGS 84).

Fields of application are not just the global data network with its search engines and social networks. There are obviously no limits to what is possible, neither on the supplier side nor on the consumer side. By now, all environments are affected where people leave their data footprints; whether these are individualized or anonymous tends to play a subordinate role. This equally includes supermarket checkouts, mobile networks, or GPS movement data. Also affected are the compilation of products in supermarkets, the dispatch of advertising material controlled by the place of residence, the granting of loans, or dating matches. We can still hope that some of it is just a short-lived trend. What speaks against a trend, however, is the persistence and the almost obsessive way in which the developments are driven forward. The fact is, a lot of money can be made from analyzing available data which has developed into an entire business sector.

Any support for decisions based on big data analysis that is not transparent and not requested by the individual is a violation of the individual's informational autonomy.

Strictly speaking, such infringement already begins with the personalization of search engine results. Meant here are the completely non-transparent processes together with the insufficient information about how search engines (for example *Google*) adjust their search and display algorithms. All that is known is that it happens and that neutrality and objectivity are blatantly taken ad absurdum. By comparing the hits for an identical search query, executed by different people or on different computers, or with different browsers, it is easy to see that the search results differ. The exact mechanisms for this are not known and have been the subject of much speculation at least since the 2016 United States elections.[218]

The creeping introduction and high acceptance of these new practices is of some importance also for societal processes. People are losing touch with the meaning of their individual actions. They stop thinking about which capabilities for plausibility testing they want to have taken away by algorithmic results or which ones are perhaps wrongly taken away from them. Added to this is the lack of knowledge about whether there are any possibilities at all to do something about this external interference. Informational literacy must at least mean not being indifferent to possible manipulation, ideally striving to understand the modus operandi, and demanding corrective action or seeking alternatives when wrongdoing is identified.

It should be obvious that personalized search results are only possible because far too much personal data has already been made available for big data analyses.

---

[218] Russian interference in the 2016 United States elections [Wikipedia]; see also Woolley: The reality game.

As a result, the users giving the data are in effect making themselves the stooges of a procedure that they may not even have wanted. If deficits in dealing with cultural techniques, such as abstracting, applying plausibilities and deriving inferences come on top of this, the path leads to informational totalitarianism by way of the creeping erosion of the legal framework (informational self-determination) and the loss of informational autonomy. In the end, algorithms would then indeed shape the values of human actions, as is already the case in dataism.

If informational autonomy is no longer seen as the cornerstone of all people's cognitive actions and is relativized by algorithm-based value and action specifications, this could lead to the development of informational stratification and a class society. In this scenario, an elite class necessary for shaping the future would retain its autonomy, and everyone else would have to share their functionalized existence with autonomous artificial systems. Autonomy and informational self-determination, and ultimately even human rights and human dignity, would no longer play a major role. The fundamental equality of all human beings would then once and for all be history. If humans were to refrain from participating in the formation of the social order, this would result in a regression of important cultural achievements and even in a regression of evolutionary events. The vocabulary often used for dataism, posthumanism or transhumanism, would then only turn out to be a disguise for antihumanism.

This all reads very pessimistic; but precisely from this exaggeration, arguments can be derived to underline that such a development can still be prevented. Let us take for a moment the extreme view of dataism, according to which a human being is assigned value only through being an informational contributor to the data sphere. Even such a person must continue to act with informational autonomy in essential parts of his or her physical and social existence and cannot base all action on instructions coming from data evaluations. If external instructions for action are given, this must result in an informational dichotomy that holds enormous potential for psychological conflict. Moreover, even a dataistic society will need the creativity of the individual for its successful continuation. Creativity and informational autonomy thus remain essential components even of a society that follows dataism—though no longer necessarily for all its members.

6.4 Informational Autonomy and Self-esteem

Self-esteem
Self-esteem is given an essential role by the modern understanding of humanism. It has its roots in the field of psychology, but is also strongly connected to our social structures and thus tied to conditions relevant to informational autonomy. Both

components contribute to our ability to feel success, happiness, and satisfaction in relation to our actions. Any negative influence on our self-esteem also affects how well or poorly we cope with the world around us.

The modern understanding of humanism is attributing a sustaining role to the individual's self-esteem. Both its psychological background and its rootedness in social structures are essential components in assisting individuals to successfully fulfill their roles in the various fields of social life. Conversely, limitations or loss of self-esteem can have a negative impact on an individual's personality and even on social processes.

A particular factor influencing an adult's self-esteem is the world of work, with its high focus on performance and success. Work overload and too little recognition can lead to an alienation from work and to a loss of confidence in one's own abilities and decisions. New leadership styles that encourage employees to engage with their whole personality and to bring in their own ideas can counteract this problem and thus also make a positive contribution in terms of informational autonomy.

We associate informational autonomy with being capable of acting freely and making free decisions. Both embody, on the one hand, the aspect of freedom in social structures and, on the other, the psychological image of the human being endowed with free will.

Is this idea still justified in the face of the many attempts to infringe on informational self-determination?

Emotional Security

What is required to create the image of an informationally autonomous and freely acting human being? This question is controversially discussed especially in the overlapping area of philosophy and cognitive psychology.[219] In any case, the emotional level should not be neglected in the quest for an answer.

Informational autonomy ranges from biological survival functions to abstract rational thinking. Human thinking and acting is not free of emotional influences. Emotions often do not only have an individual and psychological background, but are also influenced by external factors of the individual's environment. One particularly important factor related to emotions and self-esteem is the feeling of security.

---

219 See Pauen/Roth: Freiheit, Schuld und Verantwortung.

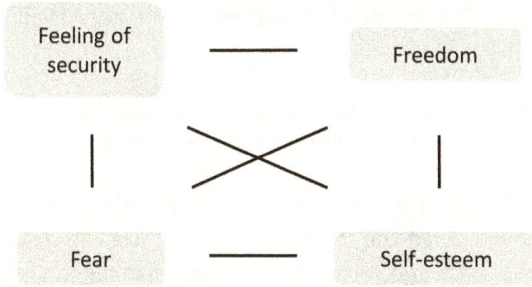

Fig. 6.1: Emotional security in individual states of autonomy.

Emotional security is an immediate life need shared by every individual, which is closely linked to being free, and especially to being free from fear.[220] While it is a state related to the individual, it can only be experienced within a structured social environment. This can be the family or any other social structure a person is connected with.

Emotional security can only be found on the basis of mutual communication and requires the ability to process information reciprocally. The prerequisite for this is informational autonomy, a condition that is also closely linked to the human sense of freedom and for this reason alone is worth being protected. Emotional security and its relationships to other emotional states is shown in Figure 6.1.

This makes it all the more astounding that dataism has such an appeal to people. Attractive enough to see in it a personal perspective, even one for human development as a whole. More than that, even achievements are abandoned that are deeply connected with the ideas of individual freedom and autonomy, the self-determined shaping of life and the self-organized creation of social structures.

Emotional security is a strong feeling that predominantly emerges from being close to other people. Not feeling deeply secure accordingly generates the desire for compensation. This compensation can as well be created via non-living environments, which today also include virtual worlds.[221] Finding emotional security in a social environment determined primarily by rational processes is exhausting, too exhausting for many. The perceived pressure to participate in shaping civil society, the failure to understand complex social correlations and the feeling of not belonging awaken the need for substitute solutions. The goal is to create places of retreat—spatial or virtual—that are as free of disturbances as possible.

---

220 We follow the approaches of Mogel: Geborgenheit, Doi: The anatomy of dependence, Kaminski: Geborgenheit und Selbstwertgefühl.

221 This is impressively demonstrated by the analyses of Doi: The anatomy of dependence.

The Japanese psychoanalyst *Takeo Doi* drastically summarizes this need for belonging as something that:

> [...] reveals a law that lies at the very foundation of human existence: that man cannot lead a human kind of existence without experience of having belonged to something or other.[222]

Before the advent of virtual worlds, chat rooms, and social media, the fictional worlds of novels and movies represented the main alternative. With the possibilities of digital worlds and networks, the escape to the cloud has taken on a significant role. As a counterbalance to the complexity of the living world with its communicative emptiness, the largest possible number of followers opens up an attractive chance for emotional security. The simultaneous increase in the need for self-expression in this context is not at all surprising.[223] *Elmar Holenstein* described it in his preface to the German edition of *Takeo Doi's The anatomy of dependence* as early as 1982:

> The suspicion arises that the cult of independence has, to a large extent, as its real driving force the aggressiveness of those who have fallen short.[224]

Emotional security as a concept related to humans in their interaction with social partners implies that there cannot be a sense of security in oneself.[225] Whether emotional security can also exist in the data sphere remains to be answered. It cannot be ruled out that this will one day be seen in this way. It will then be necessary to think about the price that such a path demands.

Whether emotional security really contributes to the development of individual freedom is a controversial issue. Since the feeling of security is associated with the connection to other people or groups of people, some also see in it the danger of dependence and thus an aspect of unfreedom. Still others see in this group involvement the potential for self-development, that is, a benefit to the development of personal stability and freedom.[226]

Authority
Similarly to the case of emotional security, there is a relationship between freedom and dependence with respect to the concept of authority. Actually, authority

---

222 Doi: The anatomy of dependence, p. 139.
223 For this aspect, see Reckwitz: The society of singularities.
224 Doi: Amae, p. 12 (author's translation).
225 Kaminski: Geborgenheit und Selbstwertgefühl, p. 19.
226 For a thorough discussion of such viewpoints, see Doi: The anatomy of dependence.

should not necessarily be seen as negative, but the linguistic proximity to "authoritarian" often attaches it too hasty with a negative connotation. When speaking abstractly of authority, the model of authority that serves as a metaphor or template is not always clear. You can have authority or be one. It can originate from a person, but also from a social group or a social institution. Authority may be perceived as a positive experience, or it can be marked by suffering. Special authority relationships exist, for example, in the world of work, bureaucracy, the church, or military. The relationship with an authority figure often has a complex structure and is strongly influenced by personal attitudes (which, however, do not necessarily turn out to be the underlying cause). People typically orient themselves, consciously or unconsciously, to authority figures in order to compensate for their own lack of success, to regain missing self-confidence, or to escape feelings of inferiority. By following authority figures, they experience their successes as their own and thus feel secure in their relationship to authority.

This constellation shows a parallel to the discussion about fake news: The authority of the fake news authors is often perceived by the "readers" in an initially incomprehensible ambivalence between indignation and concealed admiration. This eventually turns into blatant and uncritical admiration in order to share in the success of the fake news authority. Presidents and dictators alike, past and present, provide examples of both contempt and admiration for their behavior. A major role is played by the reference to the paternalistic metaphor of authority and the transfer of the conditions of power, domination and care familiar from the family environment to other social structures:

> Throughout the 19th Century, paternalistic controls were similarly motivated by a desire to make personal, face-to-face contacts—to make a community—in an economic system always pulling people into paths of individual striving and mutual competition. Moreover, the recourse to the family, rather than to the Church, or to the military, had a purpose: allusions to the family are attempts to make these personal contacts warm, rather than a matter of pity or shared aggressiveness.[227]

In the paternalistic metaphor, there is a connection between care, power, protection and obedience. Authority is given to those who use their power to care for others. For *Richard Sennett*, this situation can become a problem as soon as a separation from authority—whether by our own decision or by external influences—is perceived as a loss:

---

[227] Sennett: Authority, p. 71.

> When we observe, therefore, the difficulty with which the subjects of power push away those who claim to care for them, or the depression which follows the act of rejection, we are observing people who have lost a sense of some humane value of power.[228]

Inner following creates the feeling of being part of a success that you could not have achieved on your own. The intoxication of success thereby displaces all existing knowledge about the possible wrongfulness of the actions done by the authority figure. Conversely, the constellation of an inner following can also have a benefit for the individual's self-esteem. Authority, just like emotional security, can imply dependence or protection for the individual. Depending on the context, authority can thus be harmful or useful. An interesting point with regard to informational autonomy is that studies on the historical development of different forms of authority show that a major motivation for seeking allegiance to an authority is the desire for independence.

How one relates to authority figures has consequences for the self-esteem.[229] The "cult of independence" as described by *Holenstein*[230], should not be confused with individual self-consciousness, its outward presentation and a required self-esteem:

> Autonomy arises out of self-expression rather than self-denial.[231]

A further description of authority relationship is offered by *Hegel's* definition of master ("being for oneself") and servant ("being for others").[232] In a historical dimension, he distinguishes four phases that follow one another—*Sennett* calls them "Hegel's journey"[233]—and that can be described in abbreviated form as follows:

> Stoicism
> turns away from the outer world and leads to immersion in one's own world of thought—it creates an undeveloped, inward-looking freedom.

---

228 Sennett: Authority, p. 82.
229 We prefer the concept "self-esteem" to the expression "self-consciousness" which is also used, in order to emphasize more strongly the character of an inner state; self-consciousness is to be distinguished from it as an outwardly directed behavior. Self-consciousness can, but does not have to be carried by self-esteem.
230 See Doi: Amae, p. 12.
231 Sennett: Authority, p. 90.
232 Hegel: Phänomenologie des Geistes.
233 Sennett: Authority, pp. 125–133.

Skepticism
already doubts the role he plays and likewise the moral superiority of the Lord. But the
servant still serves obediently.

The unhappy consciousness
turns this skeptical knowledge inward; in every man dwells a master and a servant.

The reasonable consciousness
allows this knowledge to become social; man sees his own unhappy dichotomy in others as
well.

The transition from one phase to the other is always associated with a crisis of authority, as soon as the relationship between master (authority) and servant (self) becomes conscious and leads to doubts about the existing beliefs. The person recognizes freedom and slavery in oneself, recognizes freedom and slavery in others, and finally recognizes oneself in other people. This opens up the opportunity to review the person's relationship to the authority figure, to arrive at new convictions, and to move on to the next phase. Overcoming the individual crises of authority brings about a change in self-awareness, and passing through all four stages can be seen as a person's path to freedom.

The last two phases mark a change in the person, in which the servant becomes so equal to the master that the latter also changes the own behavior. Increasingly, power is giving way to mutual recognition. And this mutual recognition generates freedom. In this concept, however, freedom is not synonymous with happiness. Rather, freedom here is the realization that in each of us there is both the tyrant and the slave. Only with the recognition of this fact can people hope to meet each other not only in formal equality, but also in internalized equality. Recognizing the other as equal would then no longer be a diminishing factor for the self, but would even strengthen the understanding of the own self.

The last stage is designated by *Hegel* as "reasonable" because our perceptions and actions can now be aligned with others toward a common goal within a common social or institutional reality. There is no longer any need to fight for recognition, because consciousness has brought us to the (rational) realization that ambivalence is present in all people. It is the stage of comprehending oneself as equal to others. Reaching this fourth stage does not happen inevitably, though various techniques can be promotive for it. These include:
– detachment from authority (e.g., through masking, purification, role reversal);
– recognizing the "Inner Lord" as the projection of the external authority;

- demystification of authority;
- reshaping authority.[234]

Applying *Hegel's* stages to modern industrial society, *Sennett* concludes that humans have passed through the first two stages but have not yet arrived at the stage of rational consciousness to achieve equal freedom.[235] According to him, the situation is rather characterized by the transition from "unhappy" to "reasonable consciousness".[236]

The question arises whether digitization and social networks play a beneficial or rather obstructive role for reaching the stage of "reasonable consciousness". Virtual worlds and social media can be considered as instances of authority. They seem to offer the potential to compensate for deficits in the conflicting relationship between authority, security, autonomy, fear and freedom, and to create a sense of well-being through the realization of wishful thinking.

This becomes possible because virtual worlds and social media allow us to experience the dichotomy between our inner master and servant in the sense of a crisis of authority and to resolve this dichotomy through a feeling of security. In real life, the role of "being for others" (being a servant) is experienced and accompanied by many framework conditions that do not appear to be easily changeable. In virtual reality, by contrast, the role of "being for oneself" (being the master) can be lived out. Through this second identity, we compensate for and seemingly overcome our lack of success, and thereby create the impression that we have finally overcome the servant role.

What actually emerges is a double illusion: The first promises that the hardships of the transition to the final phase—that is, to inner and outer freedom—can be avoided in real life and are instead achievable in the virtual world with much less effort. The second is that emotional security in freedom can be achieved without any orientation toward an authority figure. Virtual worlds and social media can therefore only play a beneficial role in achieving "reasonable consciousness" if they are designed in such a way that, applying the same criteria, they can have a positive influence on shaping real life and do not become an isolated bubble.

Informational autonomy is best supported by a relationship between emotional security and authority that promotes and protects individual freedom without fear and through the positive example of lived authority. This would be the most valuable contribution a fully developed informational literacy could take on.

---

234 Sennett: Authority, pp. 165 sqq.

235 Sennett: Authority, pp. 125 sqq.

236 The term "consciousness" as used by *Sennett* coincides at this point with what we understand by our preferred term "self-esteem".

6.5 Informational Autonomy, Authority, Transcendence

If we want to preserve informational literacy and informational autonomy and at the same time try to avoid their deficits and deformations, this is only possible if we hold on to the fundamental meaningfulness of our lives and the lives of all people. If we question this fundamental meaningfulness, we do so without any existing arguments based on sensory perception or experience. Beyond the realm of experience, we enter the epistemological field of transcendence. The concept has clear connotations in philosophy and religion, but can also be understood more generally. Then transcendence merely refers to an assumed realm outside of our own world of experience, more generally even to transcending the reality of an object. As such, transcendence shares characteristics of rational abstracting, but differs in the presence of an emotional component. In a broader sense, transcendence can be understood as interpreting a situation and transferring its meaning to a real life situation.

The basic cognitive functions of informational literacy, especially contextualizing and abstracting, also play an important role in the practice of transcending. Informational autonomy can help ensure that transcendence does not consist solely of an act of faith, which may be reinforced emotionally. Without informational autonomy, transcendence is subject to uncontrollable external influences that can become manifest in dependence and doubt. In a nutshell, it can be said that informational autonomy enables the individual to transcend to meaningfulness.

In terms of developing a relationship to an authority, transcending means projecting our own ideals and aspirations into an entity (person, institution, structure) that is assumed to have the potential for their realization. What is decisive is the realization itself, less the realization by oneself. The projection allows to postpone the realization into the future. A direct reward for action is not necessary; the projection promises a reward in a later state, on another level or in a new existence.

One typical example of such a projection is the authority of the father. For almost everyone, this authority is associated with a personal experience, albeit not necessarily always experienced as positive, but whose fundamental importance is hardly ever questioned. This authority is readily transferred to the employer, thus demonstrating the great influence it has on the shaping of societies. The employer does not necessarily have to be a person; the projection can also refer to a company or any other organization.[237]

---

[237] Sennett: Authority, pp. 72 sqq.

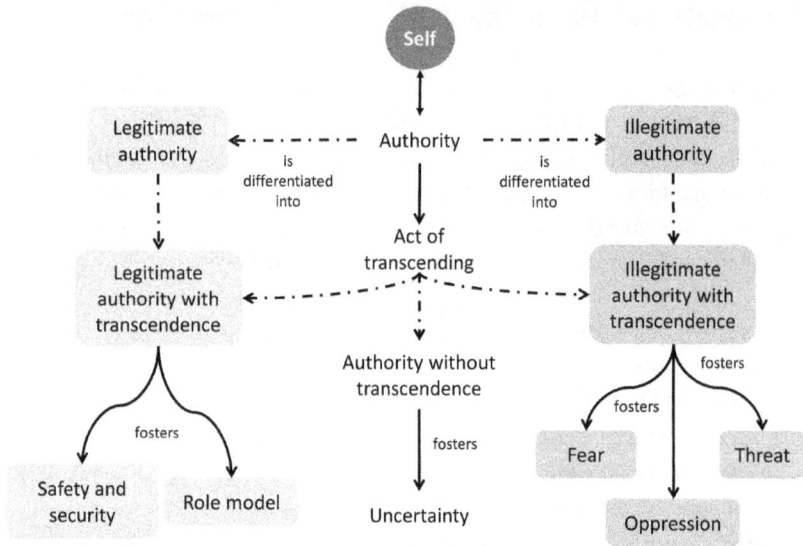

Fig. 6.2: Self – Authority – Transcendence.

Authority does not have to be perceived as a personal restriction or even a threat, but instead can be seen as a positive support that makes life easier. Authority can be an instance:

– giving hope for the future, a changed life, or even for the idea of what will come after death, independent of current successes or failures (compensation for possible deficits);
– to use for both justified and unjustified blame;
– where protection can be sought and found if the demanded price is paid;
– that offers the possibility of tolerating failure, making the authority a source of meaning for the own life and also for the greater whole.

With respect to all of the foregoing points, an instance accepted as authority plays an essential role in making sense of one's life. The condition for this, however, is transcending the own ideals and longings and projecting them onto this authority.

The subjective psychological impressions of the individual and the social impressions are subject to mutual influence. For the individual, this can either lead to a positive (subjectively desirable) or a negative (subjectively undesirable) outcome. *Max Weber's* distinction between legitimate and illegitimate authority may be useful in analyzing this ambivalence (Figure 6.2).[238]

One can say that a legitimate authority's claim to rule is justified either by the acceptance of the individual or by a legalized normative act of a social group.[239] A legitimate authority with transcendence is able to create a role model for the individual and thus lead to emotional security and freedom. Instead, authority without transcendence is more likely to cause a sense of insecurity. When transcendence is combined with illegitimate authority, this can provoke fear, threat, and oppression.

It should not be concealed that transcendence bears some potential for abuse, as evidenced by historical examples. Despots and dictators equally use the mechanisms of transcendence to consolidate or maintain their position of power as authorities. As history shows, what happens in societies always ranges from the legal to the abusive to the oppressive. The abuse of power that often takes place in this context is always associated with intimidation and the practice of reprisals.

It is only understandable that if the longed-for transcendence is not fulfilled, the consequence is a turning toward a new authority, provided this is accepted by the old authority, which may have built up structures of power that do not tolerate change.

The hope for a life in freedom is often associated with the idea of renouncing and turning away from transcendence. For that to happen, however, people would have to take full responsibility for their own lives. In this scenario, only their own answers would be permissible—but also imperative. Accordingly, complete freedom would be bound to an exclusively rational way of life. From this, in turn, forms of insecurity and discomfort may emerge, which the individual is neither able nor willing to cope with. And so begins the search for alternatives—which will soon lead to the consideration of digital worlds.

This feeling of discomfort caused by living in complete rationality increases further when it is accompanied by giving up social contacts. The truth is that even though people may not agree with technological innovations and digital communication practices, they still do not want to refrain from using social media because if they did, they would fear being socially isolated. The peer pressure of social media affects the behavior of individuals in a coercive way and thus shows clear characteristics of authority. There seems to be no other way than to follow this authority, because otherwise the transcending of the own longings

---

238 Weber: Die drei reinen Typen der legitimen Herrschaft; see also Sennett: Authority, p. 22.
239 *Max Weber* speaks of a form of leadership based on "determinate rules". In this context, the term "determinate" is meant to express normative authority within a social structure.

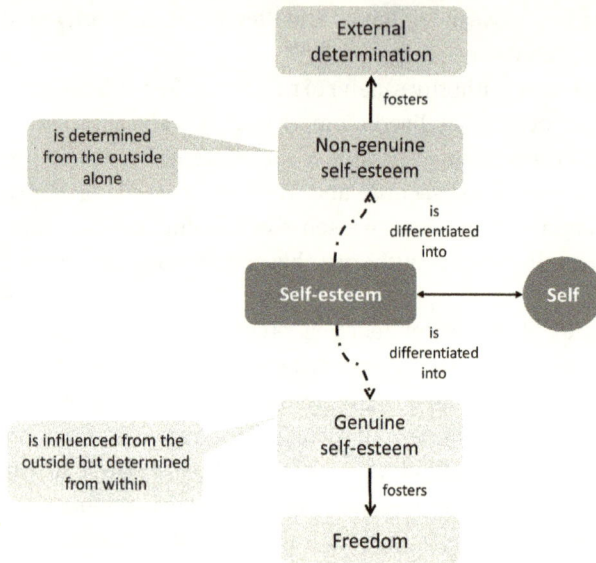

Fig. 6.3: Self – Self-esteem.

would be at risk. In *Searle's* terminology, this would mean: The social medium is an institutional reality creating a context as a field of reference which no longer requires the rational engagement with rules (which one might otherwise have to reject). Instead, it creates, through habituation, a disposition to participate in what is happening, which is further reinforced by the group.

In contrast to earlier developments, authority, transcendence and technological processes are merging in the digital world in such a way that the projection of desires is much more aimed at the technological process and, as a consequence, digitization takes over the role of authority. Take the reversal of traditional experience and learning roles when it comes to using social media or smartphones. Suddenly, it is the grandchild generation that is seen as "competent", in other words, as the authority to instruct parents and grandparents in the use of high technology. The dynamics of technological development lead to a cyclical process in which new developments replace previous ones comparatively quickly. Lastingness is not among the properties of the digital world.

Nevertheless, digitization and social media at least have the potential to serve as an authority in everyday situations and thus as a projection surface for our desires. The difference is that the projection is aimed at the technology and not at its meaningfulness. Technological changes alone do not offer any possibility for the determination of meaningfulness (a kind of substitute transcendence, as it were),

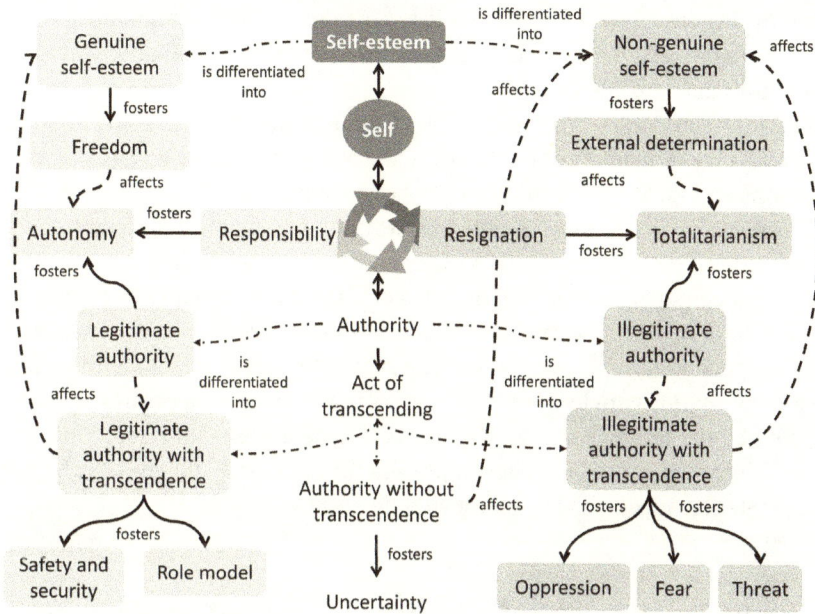

Fig. 6.4: Self – Autonomy – Totalitarianism.

since there is nothing durably familiar, which would be suitable as an orientation. This problem could only be solved if the projection itself were to consider meaningfulness. On the one hand, it may be conceivable that a fear-free emotional security under the protection of authority could be experienced. In the long run, however, it will probably not be possible to experience emotional security exclusively through projections tied to technology.

It should be noted that the transcendence of an authority does not yet ensure that a fear-free sense of security is also achieved. It must therefore be clarified which factors are decisive for it and which may impair or hinder it. One crucial factor is self-esteem, which we gain through self-confidence and by having faith in our own abilities.[240]

Self-esteem contributes significantly to whether transcending leads to a fear-free emotional security or turns into in an other-controlled state (external determination) (Figure 6.3). A distinction can be made between "genuine" and "non-genuine" self-esteem. Genuine self-esteem refers to the positive transcendence of authority into self-determination and marks the connection to informational

---

240 See Kaminski: Geborgenheit und Selbstwertgefühl.

autonomy. In contrast, non-genuine self-esteem means the transcendence of authority into external determination, dependence, immaturity and fear, which leads to informational dependence.

Fear-free emotional security describes a state of freedom and also paves the way for making human dignity the abstract target projection of humanistic considerations and ideals in the context of social life shaping.

Figure 6.4 shows a synopsis of the network of relationships indicated so far. The interactions between fear, emotional security, and freedom (Figure 6.1) are expanded to include self-esteem (Figure 6.3) as well as authority and transcendence (Figure 6.2), providing a picture of the correlations between autonomy, totalitarianism, responsibility, and resignation with regard to human dignity. The socially relevant correlations are located in the center of the figure on a central axis and, as shown by the rotating arrows, can be seen to be in constant interaction and change. The boxes above and below represent the spheres of influence with their internal relationships, which we have already discussed.

6.6 Cultural Remembering and Forgetting in the Digital Age

Cultural remembrance is considered to have quite a significant influence on the formation of what is called cultural identity.[241] With regard to informational autonomy and informational literacy, therefore, we should not ignore the changes that digitization has brought about in the context of cultural remembering and forgetting.

Before digitization, personal forgetting was considered an inevitable process that was correlated with advancing age. To deal with the fact that other people or records could be important sources of a remembering that goes beyond the individual's remembering was hardly relevant in normal life. This was reserved for few people in contemporary history. It generally applied that remembering could be useful and forgetting could be liberating. There were even efforts to actively support forgetting if those negatively affected by remembering expected to benefit from it. Conversely, there can also be a demand not to forget. Accordingly, both the culture of remembrance and the culture of forgetting have always sought ways to strike a balance between these divergent interests.

Today it says, and this would mean a radical rebalancing: The web never forgets. What exactly does that mean? Does this change refer to digitization and its

---

241 See Assmann: Cultural memory and Western civilization, Welzer: Das kommunikative Gedächtnis, Assmann: Cultural memory and early civilization, Halbwachs: On collective memory.

impact on the relationship between individual and collective memory? Many of us are certainly inclined to spontaneously answer "yes" to this question. After all, the volumes of stored data keep growing unceasingly.

People are now confronted with this stored data all their lives, including unwanted data, and it is almost impossible to get rid of it by your own efforts. For example, there are repeated warnings about the disadvantages that digital "peccadillos of youth" can have for job interviews and the professional life. Meanwhile, an entire industry has emerged that offers only the one service to remove personal digital traces. Everyone is affected by these consequences of digitization—and with it, of not forgetting—, no longer just celebrities and important people in contemporary history.

Whether digitization has actually created a completely new situation with regard to cultural remembrance may need to be addressed in a more differentiated way. *Maurice Halbwachs* emphasized the influence of each society on collective memory, even before the digital age:

> From this it follows that social thought is essentially a memory and that its entire content consists only of collective recollections or remembrances. But it also follows that, among them, only those recollections subsist that in every period society, working within its present-day frameworks, can reconstruct.[242]

> It is in this way that history does not limit itself to reproducing a tale told by people contemporary with events of the past, but rather refashions it from period to period not only because of other testimony that has become available, but also to adapt it to the mental habits and the type of representation of the past common among contemporaries.[243]

> Since the persons themselves and their actions—and the memory of those actions—constitute the frameworks of this social life, these frameworks disappear when the persons and families in question vanish. It is hence necessary to reconstruct other frameworks in the same manner and following the same lines, which however will not have exactly the same form or appearance.[244]

Following *Halbwachs*, the collective memory is thus not comparable with the records on a hard disk. But this does not yet answer the question from the other perspective: Do the stored data on a hard disk, or the sum of all data on all hard disks in the data cloud, represent a collective memory? According to our considerations, these data can at best be potential information, the activation of which still requires a selection, sensory processing as well as subsequent cognitive processing.

---

242 Halbwachs: On collective memory, p. 189.
243 Halbwachs: On collective memory, p. 75.
244 Halbwachs: On collective memory, p. 124.

The selection requires prior decisions that cannot be made without the existence of criteria. This would make data open to discussion and legally actionable, and therefore principally subject to social choice. In contrast, an unquestioned trust in the objectivity and durability of digital records could lead to less effort being invested in creating a culture of remembrance, and thus could be damaging to the development of a (modern) collective memory.

Both personal and collective memory are indispensable for shaping the future. Supporting and stabilizing these memories and the cognitive processes involved and responsible is more important than trying to orient the memory process to the computer metaphor. It is well known, for example, that there is no immediate digital substitute for the context under which the articles of conventional printed encyclopedias, each with different cultural and historical understandings, were written. Nonetheless, major encyclopedias such as *Collier's Encyclopedia* (1966) or *Encyclopædia Britannica* (1962) are now being sorted out of the collections even by larger libraries. Our remarks on the importance of structural knowledge and reference domains for the generation of actual information in the reception of potential information from externalized information sources prove the necessity of permanent access to such conventional sources in order to contribute to the preservation and appreciation of collective memory.

Within society, however, current value ideals diverge widely. On the one hand, we derive fundamental frameworks for the shaping of our society from views and events far in the past—for example, when it comes to the foundations of our understanding of law or the obligation of state foreign policy to historical events. Or, on the other hand, we virtually do everything in our power to tear down the bridges to the past and see redemption in digital reinvention.

Considering the essential role our own memory plays in shaping our personal future, this alone should be an incentive not to jeopardize the importance of collective memories—in all possible recording variants—for shaping the future of society by making rash decisions.[245]

6.7 Informational Ambivalence and Reason

Informational autonomy is indispensable for the life of the individual, both biologically and socially. At the same time, as a result of digitization, hitherto unknown situations have arisen in which individuals carry out their decisions and actions

---

245 It is precisely those variants that have more structural parts for re-interpreting externalized meanings that deserve special attention in this regard.

in informational dependence. Almost all people live in a constant tension between informational autonomy (in basic life issues) and informational dependence (in areas determined by algorithmic specifications or data evaluation).

This ambivalence between informational autonomy and informational dependence is associated with situations in which external circumstances demand one or the other behavior, without it necessarily being clear to the person which of the two is required.

Informational ambivalence may also arise from lapses in informational autonomy. Decision-makers, for example, who want to make a difference must constantly match their intended actions with the permissible actions allowed to them by the given action framework. Compromise can be attained through autonomy if it is subordinate to intention and treated as a prerequisite for negotiation. But if success in negotiation becomes the sole guiding principle of the intention and hence possibly an end in itself, the limitations set by the framework of action for determining own objectives are "anticipated". As a result, the potential of negotiation is no longer fully explored, but is instead made secondary to considerations of opportunity. And if personal goals were abandoned against better judgment, this would be tantamount to informational self-cutting. In both cases, informational external determination is involved. It is even more serious when informational external determination is voluntarily chosen, for instance, for the purpose of gaining influence or power.

Although informational ambivalence can be caused and facilitated by external factors, informational behavior always requires own decisions. For this purpose, the framework of a concept of informational reason should be chosen. So far, such a concept has not been established. However, it is possible to formulate conditions for acting in an informationally rational way and to develop criteria for detecting and avoiding acting in an informationally unreasonable way (both individually and in the context of society).

If reason is understood as the supreme epistemological capacity, all forms of reason are thus connected with cognitive information processing. Conversely, not every form of cognitive information processing has to correspond to reason; it is quite possible to imagine forms of cognitive processing that are free of or even contrary to reason.

Informational reason, however, can only be traced back to general reason. It is the capacity of human thought to carry out cognitive processes for accessing actual reality, transforming observations into meanings and providing the rules and principles established by reflection as a basis for action. With this characterization, informational reason can be seen as an anchor concept, since it provides for an understanding of all other informational processes. Accordingly, informational reason is not to be regarded as a separate form of reason in the information age, but as a specific conceptual further development of general reason.

Although this characterization of informational reason shows a close relation to theoretical reason, the fact that it is connected with moral judgments makes it belong to practical reason. In order to underline this correlation, lived informational reason shall be introduced as a further concept. This is to be understood as the liberation of the human being from self-inflicted informational immaturity. Immaturity here means the absence of any informational competence. For the individual, lived informational reason is also associated with the obligation to help shape informational processes in the sense of living together in a community. This obligation concerns both the personal and the societal level. The consideration of a concept of informational literacy based on informational autonomy is a prerequisite for this.

A program for informational reason in the sense of a humanistic critique of informational reason has not yet been addressed and remains a desideratum for the justification of a form of coexistence that sees itself as an information society.

7 Informational Autonomy at Risk

The society of discipline creates violations, transgressions, possibilities to fall out, not to belong, to betray oneself, to be exhibited: All are sleepers, say a wrong word and are fatals, destroyers, show their true nature. The demand for discipline in all fields produces troublemakers, hysterics, choleric people, people who run amok, the demand for performance produces failures, burnt-out people, depressives, people who fail in the project of self-development and get lost between the public parameters to the refrain: I can't take it anymore. I can't take it anymore.

Roger Willemsen[246]

Informational autonomy is at risk. The threat comes from outside, but also results from individual behavior and, at worst, can end in informational totalitarianism. Ensuring informational autonomy can therefore not be achieved by government measures alone, but must be complemented by individual responsibility.

Informational totalitarianism is the intensification of informational incapacitation, because totalitarianism permeates all areas and connects with them its respective purposive idea.

Our guiding thesis is: Digitization is causing a change in the understanding of knowledge, whereby understanding is being replaced by fact-finding and supplemented by algorithm-based information. Compared to the performance of machines, however, humans will always be the underdog in algorithmic processing and data analysis. Thus, if we lose the practice of learning the basics of experience-based decision making, we will see evaluation practices shift in favor of algorithmic approaches. This would cause a loss of balance between experience-based decision making and rational parameter control and would result in a previously unknown situation of dependence and inferiority.

Informational totalitarianism seeks the abolition of informational autonomy as an individual cognitive property. According to this, decisions and actions of the individual should be made exclusively from a state of informational dependence. The ideas of dataism are merely one example of this—and perhaps not even the most dangerous. We emphasize again: Informational autonomy is the basis for cognitive functions of all life processes and a key cornerstone for the humanist position.

---

246 Willemsen: Wer wir waren, p. 40 (author's translation).

https://doi.org/10.1515/9783110693744-007

7.1 Analog versus Digital Information

There are still many people who are familiar with the acquisition of externalized knowledge from analog sources and who would consider this skill to be an original cultural technique important for the development of humankind. Increasingly, however, the impression arises that more weight is given to the awareness of digitized information compared to analog ways of representation, which tend to gain a reputation for being outdated manifestations. This judgment may be explained to a certain extent by the scope of what is available and the convenience of access. As an opinion, however, this does not endure, for the sole reason that individual thought and action are based on analogous cognitive processes. Moreover, the acquisition of knowledge from analog sources has developed over a long period of time into a cultural technique with familiar modes of usage. Due to the rapid pace of technological development, nothing comparable has yet been achieved in terms of today's digital usage habits: The replacement of typing by swiping, of swiping by voice control, of voice control by ... is proceeding too fast for a permanent cultural technique to become established. This leads to the assumption that the usual processes of human development and socialization will no longer be possible if they are based solely on digitally externalized information and the skills needed to acquire it. The "Zeitgeist", though, sees things differently and assigns a clearly indispensable and positive role to digitization and to skills in dealing with everything digital.

Particularly striking is the association of the digital with the topic of learning and its possibly promoting or inhibiting influence on it. However, these high expectations are actually not shared by most educational researchers. Educational researchers argue that before entering the debate, it is first necessary to clarify what digitization means or is supposed to mean in the context of learning. One of the essence of education is seen in engaging with the world through a self-managed constructive process in a way that also makes it possible to cope with the unknown:

> First of all, I don't think you can underestimate the concept of education. The concept of education—and this is often not seen at all—is not to be confused with the acquisition of knowledge. The concept of education is also not to be compared with a mere absorption of what is and the adaptation to the world—following the changes of the world, so to speak. Education is always self-construction in interaction with the world, and education is invented in a situation where all that was previously considered certainty had been lost. [...] In the situation, our concept of education is invented and the essential thing that the greatest mastermind we have in the milieu, Wilhelm von Humboldt [...] then expected from education for these open societies, was a formula that I always find with great pleasure as the latest just sold: The learning of learning we must learn. [...] This means that the concept of education is

designed for a situation in which I cannot say for sure what the future will be like, in which I cannot say specifically what challenges I will be confronted with, and in which I cannot say decisively and simply what knowledge portions the individual has to learn in schools in terms of content, but rather he or she has always acquired basic fundamental competencies, modes of access and engagement with the world [...].[247]

The concept of "digital education" is questionable. It should therefore be examined what potential threat a superficial understanding of digital information and digital learning has for informational autonomy. At the very least, the importance of digital information for future developments should be put into perspective. This would not mean to question their fundamental usefulness, but to clearly elaborate this usefulness and to consider it in the context of cognitive information processes.

7.2 Flood of Information

The amount of externalized information is constantly increasing. The problem of this information flood is not new, as the production of books, magazines, and other forms of printed paper has been growing for a long time.[248] Already *Erasmus* and *Leibniz* complained about the mass of new publications which people were no longer able to keep up with.[249] Keeping up with the advancement and acquiring at least the most necessary of all the new knowledge was increasingly seen as a challenge that could no longer be met. As a remedy, tools and services were introduced to help keep track of things after all. These were bibliographies, specialized periodical indexes, and later databases. Their service consisted in offering the contents of newly published papers in a summarized form. This marked the beginning of quantitative evaluation of publications as a separate field of study, today called informetry.[250]

Digitization is held responsible for a further escalation in the amount of information, hence the metaphor "information flood".

Various other metaphors are circulating that address the issue of an information flood with a simultaneous lack of knowledge. There is talk of "drowning in information" and "starving for knowledge". *T. S. Eliot* had something to say about it already in 1934:

---

247 [Excerpt from an interview with educationalist Heinz-Elmar Tenorth] Heinrich-Böll-Stiftung: Bildung für die digitale Zukunft, min. 06:40-08:40 (written version of the interview and translation by the authors).
248 Gleick: The information, Chapter 14.
249 See Standage: Information overload is nothing new, Blair: Too much to know.
250 For origins, see Price: Little science, big science.

Where is the wisdom we have lost in knowledge?
Where is the knowledge we have lost in information?[251]

It is not just the increase in books, texts, externalized potential information, or whatever is considered the source of knowledge acquisition. Actually, we could know better from experience. We cannot deny that the amount of available material has always been greater than the time available for its complete reception. One difference between the old and the current complaints is that, for the first time, not only is the lack of time seen as an hindrance to coping with the information flood, but there is also a subliminal demand that one must first have received everything available before one is regarded capable of competent action. For the first time, digitization is leading to doubts about whether cognitive abilities are even sufficient for the reception of the available (or needed?) information.

An example of this is the familiar situation of wanting to select a suitable sample for drafting a document (contract, business letter) from the offer provided by a search engine as a result of a corresponding query.

Processing such large amounts of information requires not only information technology procedures in the form of quantitative methods and corresponding algorithms, but also an evaluation and selection according to quality criteria. For this purpose, there are cognitive, quality-oriented procedures that work in a fundamentally different way than information technology solutions. Being capable of applying these cognitive skills requires the development and practice of an inner sensorium, which could be considered, for example, as an object of education.

A substantial part of this information flood is provided by the media and various internet services (forums, blogs, messengers, chat rooms, vlogs, podcasts, etc.), and there is a perceived pressure in both professional and private life not to miss any of the information disseminated via these channels. Thanks to the digital form of presentation, there are numerous analysis methods available that can be used to obtain an overview of the material offered. These deliver statistical results, but say nothing about the relevance or importance of the particular contribution for the particular reader or user. Instead, these analyses document, for example, whether a blog is continuously followed by many people and thus create the impression of its (supposed) relevance. And this, in turn, suggests to the users to take note of every single post on the blog just because of its popularity. On top of that comes peer group pressure and the need for social recognition. Nothing must be missed if one wants to talk along with the others.

---

251 Eliot: The Rock.

A thought experiment: Every day, a whole lot of people who are not personally known are to be found at a train station in a large city. There is no perceived pressure to take notice of what the people say or do or to engage in any conversation with them. Usually, this condition is not perceived as a deficiency. Why is this different for posts on *Twitter*?

7.3 Decision-making and Informational Overload

The trend to place data aggregation at the beginning of a decision-making process is based on the now well-established assumption that decisions can be made better if they are based on (supposedly) complete information. However, our own life experience shows that we have to make decisions even when we do not have enough information, or think we do not have enough information. Decision-makers in business and politics often even act against the rational information situation backed up by data aggregation—and are even admired for it, in the event that the decisions produce a positive outcome. Their principle is: The development of the future is predicted from past experience by analogy, abstraction, or on the basis of heuristics.[252]

"Gut decisions" like this are a suitable means against informational overload and stress. Informational overload occurs when too many parameters have to be considered equally as a basis for a decision or action process, but cannot be processed due to limited cognitive capacities. Cognitive processing capacities cannot be increased at will. Everything that requires attention also demands cognitive resources. And in this context, it does not matter whether it is something formally trivial or something that is significant in terms of content. The difference can then only be determined by setting priorities. Thus, the situation of informational overload becomes a problem of both decision making and optimization.

Such situations can also arise with the reception from medialized sources, which then too may lead to informational overload. The content may then be misunderstood or not understood at all, which is why attempts are made to escape the informational overload and to leave the evaluation of the medialized data to algorithmic analyses. There may be situations that can be resolved and managed well in this way. Applications for this exist, but none that would be suitable for everyday use. In addition to the technical requirements, which are generally not manageable for the individual, the question is again whether the individual is

---

252 See Gigerenzer: Gut feelings.

sufficiently equipped with informational autonomy to be capable of mastering the decision-making situations.

Can uncertainty in decision-making situations be reliably prevented? Only a few people in selected positions can afford to make gut decisions without having to deal with the potentially negative consequences. Most people know only too well the feeling of personal failure and defeat caused by wrong decisions. So if they are aware that they have to make (or have made) a decision, even though relevant information has not been evaluated or has not been evaluated comprehensively, the consequences of the decision cannot be reliably assessed and a worrisome feeling of uncertainty or even of failing to act remains. It is difficult to predict what the consequences of this will be in terms of informational self-esteem and informational autonomy.

7.4 Social Networks and Informational Self-determination

Social media have become a mass social phenomenon of the 21st century. The user numbers of the social media services *Instagram* and *TikTok* have increased steadily over the last years and are now in the billions. No classic medium has more reach than social media and has a similarly large potential influence on the rationally acquired attitudes or affectively formed views of its recipients. The basic principle of social media is that users follow the user profiles of other users or, usually via so-called hashtags, topics that arouse an interest in them. Every day, we visit our personalized timelines in the expectation of receiving new information from the people and topics we follow. The human brain responds positively to reward stimuli. We know this well in connection with food or money; if it tastes good or we get a raise, we feel good. *Instagram* and co. make use of this principle through the activities of "posting" and "likes" to get users to stay in the app longer or click back in regularly.

Informational self-determination can be restricted by external conditions, for example by government measures. But it can also be restricted by our own actions. The rules by which social media operate and the actions of their users therefore have consequences for informational self-determination.[253]

Participation in social networks enjoys being seen, in a positive sense, as a democratic practice. Here, in theory, everyone is equal to the other in communication and can contribute his or her position in an equal manner. Real-life commu-

---

253 For a comprehensive overview on the topic of social media, see Schmidt/Taddicken (eds.): Handbuch Soziale Medien.

nication practice, however, shows that this is not the case. Opinion leaders and followers emerge just as they do in other social structures. Above all, the possibility of expressing applause or displeasure in the quickest and easiest way (likes, emojis) seems to favor the herd principle rather than equality and individual independence. The number of followers determines the opinion leader and becomes the yardstick; the assertion itself or its quality play a clearly subordinate role in this.

Social media allow the creation of digital identities with profiles in specially created identity worlds. The repercussions of such parallel worlds on reality are not yet sufficiently investigated or known, but it can be assumed that they will not be very positive on the whole.

Nevertheless, social media need not necessarily pose a threat to informational self-determination; since they also provide an opportunity for self-expression, they could equally be ascribed a supportive value for personal development. At the same time, however, no other informational event shows such a large discrepancy between alleged benefits and possible risks. Particularly notable is the willingness, familiar from peer pressure, to comply with the dictates of others, even if they contradict your own convictions.

Here, too, information technology is used to pursue economic interests. The resulting end products often prove to be highly problematic in terms of compliance with ethical standards. The algorithms constantly react to the user behavior and readjust the timeline, the user profiles offered to be followed, as well as the advertising. Using informational literacy effectively to safeguard informational self-determination is virtually hopeless here.

In view of the enormous economic power of internet corporations and the penetration of everyday life with their products, it will probably be left with demands for better data protection and more efficient control mechanisms. It is to be feared that in particular those regulations called for in terms of personal rights will not be implemented or will not be implemented sufficiently.

Social networks are in the process of profoundly changing the way we interact with each other, which will inevitably have, and is already having, an impact on social structures as well. Informational autonomy is thus all the more challenged to promote and protect the individual freedom to apply the basic cognitive abilities discussed here as part of an authority lived by example. With this characterization must come a commitment to the values of an enlightened humanism as a guiding principle for the design and practice of social networks.

Dataism measures the value of human beings by the amount of data they are giving. Is this fundamentally different in social networks? How far are we from the point where not providing data will be sanctioned? In his novel *The Circle, Dave*

Eggers has given a visionary preview of how life and working conditions may be like in a world shaped by virtual social environments.[254]

The protagonist of the story is a 24-year-old woman named *Mae Holland*. She is overjoyed because she lands a job at *The Circle*, the hippest tech company in the world. This company is a mixture of *Google, Apple, Facebook*, and *Twitter* and provides all customers with an internet identity through which everything in life can be easily handled. The company's vision: With the elimination of anonymity and privacy on the net, the world will be a better place, because no one will be able to do anything bad unnoticed. Every misconduct, no matter how small, is observed by the members of the network and is directly made transparent to everyone. The protagonist enthusiastically plunges into her work while enjoying all the staff-only benefits: *Michelin*-starred chefs create free meals, international artists give free shows, and there are parties almost every night. *Mae* becomes a model employee and lets the company's philosophy become the maxim of her own way of life. This includes sharing her daily life with everyone on *The Circle* via live cam. She wants to become a pioneer for complete transparency for the public network community. In this way, she finds millions of followers and receives a lot of confirmation for her actions.

With the realization of such ideas, fundamental rights such as informational self-determination would completely fall by the wayside.

Informational Egotism

There is a lot of evidence that people behave differently on social networks than they do in real life. Many of the behaviors observed are reminiscent of those already described by *Josef Weizenbaum* in the context of his "diagnostic system" *ELIZA*.[255] On the one hand, many people believe that their (virtual) actions remain anonymous and either underestimate or ignore the actual reach and transparency their actions might have. Online, people reveal private details that they would never reveal in a face-to-face conversation. If there were such a thing as informational nudism, it would describe this behavior quite well. On the other hand, this is countered by the irresistible urge for many to demonstrate their skills in using the latest information technology devices. Interestingly, it does not matter whether this "showing off" takes place in the context of direct personal interaction or through chats, blogs, discussion forums, or other network media. The most important thing seems to be that the excessive need for informational representation

---

254 Eggers: The circle.
255 Weizenbaum: ELIZA, Weizenbaum: Computer power and human reason; for more recent activities, see also Becker: Auf dem Weg zum Psychotherapie-Bot.

can be voiced. Such behaviors are known as typical group behavior. The group, or the online community, is perceived here as a protective space even for excessive or unauthorized self-expression. Another characteristic is that in such environments it is no longer possible for users to admit their own shortcomings in dealing with informational problems.

Informational egotism makes people act as if they were fully capable of coping with an informational problem, while ignoring their own deficits.

Informational egotism can be considered as a suitable criterion for distinguishing between information literacy and informational literacy. Information literacy is related to the application of skills. A condition perceived as a deficiency in operating a device or using an app is compensated for by the acquisition of the instrumental skill. Informational literacy does not limit dealing with this deficiency to operation aspects, but describes the difference compared to the desired state in a broader sense. It does not associate any fundamental added value in the acquisition of a new instrumental skill or the fulfillment of an app's operating requirements. It is a preferable variant of informational self-restraint whose need for recognition is narrowed down to skills with a potential for transferability to new situations.

7.5 The Data-measured Human Being

What do we expect from a world in which even elementary everyday activities become more and more data-driven? How does this change our behavior? *Philip Davis* and *Reuben Hersh* characterized it this way back in 1986:

> For instant money, available twenty-four hours a day, I am encouraged to get a magic card and follow a simple program. I have no doubt that within a few short years, I will have to do some preliminary programming in order to use a public convenience. Putting a nickel in the slot will be listed among the Holy Simplicities of the past. Are we drowning in digits? Is the end in sight? Yes, we are, and no, it is not. What underlies all the digits is that our civilization has been computerized. We are in the grips of the symbol processors and the number crunchers. The nature of this slavery is often misunderstood. It is not thralldom to an individual computer; rather it is the total computerization of the sources of information and communication. Every time a dentist fills a cavity a computer, somewhere, finds out about it and sends a bill. Unplug the computer network? No way. Your son-in-law may have a good job programming the billing system. The dentist himself owns IBM stock.[256]

---

256 Davis/Hersh: Descartes' Dream, p. 15 (first ed. 1986).

Well, today we know which of these fears have become reality. What are the consequences for the image of human nature, the human self-image, and the human value? How do we define ourselves today as human beings? By being, thinking and acting, or only by our data values? The *EU Charter of Fundamental Rights* and the *Basic Law of the Federal Republic of Germany* are in agreement: "Human dignity shall be inviolable."[257]

Dataism, by contrast, involves a complete reorientation that is no longer compatible with this humanistic view. Given their radical nature, the ideas of dataism will probably not be taken very seriously at first in terms of rapid realization. Nevertheless, there are clear signs that people are no longer judged on the basis of their self-value but on a variety of parameters. The data-based measurement of people has long since become part of everyday life, for instance with services that base their customer orientation on ratings and scores. So the desire to do well in these parameters and to look for ways to improve them, even without doing anything for it, is almost understandable.

In the world of science, too, evaluating people on the basis of data has become very important in the meantime and has almost become the norm. In the context of appointment procedures for professors or in the allocation of research funding, decisions were long made according to quality criteria. In the meantime, however, these decisions are increasingly based on numerical indicators that take a large number of parameters into account. These may include, but are not limited to:

- the number of publications;
- the number of publications with co-authors;[258]
- the number of publications in conference proceedings;
- the number of citations in other publications;
- the *Hirsch index*;[259]
- the number of PhD students;
- the number of projects under executive responsibility;
- the amount of third-party funding already raised;
- the number of owned patents.

257 EU Charter of Fundamental Rights : Article 1, Basic Law for the Federal Republic of Germany : Article 1(1).
258 While in the past much emphasis was put on demonstrating individual achievement through sole authorship, it is widely believed that today a collaborative competence is expressed in a special way through the large number of contributions with co-authors.
259 See Hirsch: An index to quantify an individual's scientific research output, Hirsch: An index to quantify an individual's scientific research output that takes into account the effect of multiple coauthorship, Krattenthaler: Was der h-Index wirklich aussagt.

There are no limits to the consideration of further parameters, also each parameter can be rated individually. The number of publications can be limited to those in peer-reviewed journals, or the number of publications with co-authors may be required to have a high *Hirsch index* themselves.[260]

These scoring or ranking methods are determined solely by quantity-based parameters. The inference to quality characteristics of the content can only be made indirectly and is based on an assumption that is widely considered plausible: The consideration of publications in peer-reviewed journals, for example, assumes that other people have already made a reliable qualitative assessment of the publication. However, quantitative parameters cannot replace a separate qualitative assessment. Nor can they provide any guarantee that the underlying data have not been manipulated, which would call into question the validity of the "score". Those who are concerned are of course aware of the importance the quantitative parameters have for their own scientific careers. So they will do anything to stay ahead of the competition for jobs and funds. Yet, it cannot be determined by a quantitative assessment alone whether the measures used for this purpose also lead to an enhanced scientific quality.

One way of adapting to survey mechanisms based on quantitative data is to outsmart, if not outmaneuver, them. A comparable approach is followed by the so-called search engine optimization.[261] Unlike common expectations, this optimization is not aimed at improving the functionality of search engines or measures for their improved use. Rather, it is about implementing tricks to improve the positioning of a website in the search engine's hit list. The goal is to outsmart the search engine's rating algorithm in order to gain an advantage over competitors who do not use such techniques. Thus, interest-driven manipulation defeats the idea of a rational approach based on probity.

This increasing tendency to apply quantitative analysis to anything and everything has given rise to a separate discipline known as scientometry or informetrics.[262] Here, attempts are made to measure the digital world and to derive conclusions for the non-digital life. There has been and still is criticism of this

---

260 Remarkably, the *Erdös* number, which is well-known in mathematics, has not yet been transferred to other disciplines. *Paul Erdös* was the most productive mathematician of modern times and inspired many mathematicians in their work. The *Erdös* number 1 expresses that one has co-authored a publication with *Paul Erdös*, which is considered a special distinction. The *Erdös*-number 2 signals that the paper was written together with a co-author of *Paul Erdös*, and so on.
261 Search engine optimization [Wikipedia].
262 Other terminological varieties are known, such as bibliometrics or weblogometry. The starting point for this has already been set by Price: Little science, big science and Garfield: Citation indexes for science.

compulsive numerical measurability, though this has not yet led to any significant changes. A recent article comes to the following conclusion:

> Although these criticisms have been noted, they have been largely brushed aside or ignored, not addressed head on. This may be for a number of reasons, but we believe the main one is that these criticisms undermine the desire to have an easy "scientific"—that is, quantitative—method of evaluation.[263]

This kind of measuring mania will not stop at the science and research sector. There is evidence that the methods known from informetrics are also being applied to our everyday life. In the context of the so-called sociometry, the data-measured human being is thematized.[264] A journalist summarizes her fears (at the end of a newspaper article about screenings, ratings, rankings, and scoring of people) this way:

> In the end, numbers could determine one's entire existence—and no citizen would be able to understand exactly why the all-powerful state algorithm is relegating him or her to second place.[265]

Of particular concern should be the development of systems that assess the social compatibility of members of a society. Such ambitions have become known through the app *Honest Shanghai*, which has been in the news since 2017.[266] Based on several thousand parameters provided by offices and authorities, a social credit system with personal scoring accounts serves to punish social misbehavior or reward good behavior. This creates a scoring of social acceptability reminiscent of stock market quotations—except that this one is for people. The goal is the mass surveillance of society and ensuring the development of citizens into—in the sense of the state—morally flawless people. The scoring is becoming the basis for negative labeling and social exclusion, and at the same time provides incentives for receiving benefits and discounts (which initial reports indicate are very popular and readily received).

Such developments in China are quickly associated with the label "dictatorship", even though there seems to be great acceptance among the domestic population. The question is when such a system will also be adopted in democratically constituted states and how their inhabitants will then respond to it.[267]

---

263 MacRoberts/MacRoberts: The mismeasure of science.

264 See Mau: The metric society.

265 Witte-Petit: Der menschliche Kurswert (author's translation).

266 See Honest Shanghai [CyberPolicy], China invents the digital totalitarian state [Economist].

267 Calls for self-monitoring are obviously more readily accepted if they are associated with financial benefits. Examples of such monitoring discounts already exist in the automobile and

Rating systems in a quantified society will not only reflect the inequalities in the world, but will ultimately also become an influencing factor in important life decisions. And it does not even necessarily have to be a "state algorithm". We already do apply a large number of algorithms ourselves and usually consider them to be less problematic on their own. But this can also lead to completely new forms of assessment, in an interplay that is anything but transparent to us. What is even more problematic for future developments than direct government intervention are our own behaviors when based on habituation and misperception.

7.6 Limits of Informational Autonomy

Informational autonomy is a basic condition for coping with human life. In introducing the concept of informational dependence, we have already addressed limits to informational autonomy (Chapter 2.7). Basically, these can lie in external factors or result from the behavioral patterns of the individual. They can also be influenced by individual decisions, although they are to some extent invariant properties of cognitive information processing. One such delimiting condition is cognitive structural determinacy. Furthermore, informational autonomy can be limited by ourselves and on a voluntary basis, as in the case of a self-chosen restriction or renunciation of the de facto exercise of autonomy. But is it still evidence of informational autonomy if the limits are self-imposed?

Let us assume that it would be possible to develop an optimally informationally competent person and a society with optimal conditions for the realization of individual informational autonomy. In order to get there and to maintain this abstract optimum, comprehensive qualification, education, and training would be necessary. And even if the necessary programs could be designed, how could they be made available to all people of all ages, all social classes, all levels of education, all work environments, all dispositions, and all spheres of interest? Would it be possible to expand the requirements and their competent mastery at will? Would adaptation to the capabilities of the addressees be possible through individual tailoring, or would this have to be done through general flattening (in the sense of leveling down)?

Then again, is the informationally literate individual desirable at all? Or should people only have the necessary instrumental skills to be able to use all the communication and information offerings and services? If economic interests

---

health insurance industries (European insurance and occupational pensions authority (eiopa): Big data analytics in motor and health insurance, Nocun: Tracking durch die Versicherung).

alone are taken as a basis, informational literacy in the sense of "understanding" is neither necessary nor expedient. A more comprehensive view of humans and their abilities is therefore required to arrive at a quality-oriented definition of informational literacy.

If the world of data is accepted as a rational alternative to the real world, and delegating of decisions to algorithms becomes the guiding principle for future action, there will be a price to pay. At first, the price may be willingly paid; the awakening to the fact that the price was too high will come later, maybe too late.

Ideally, informational literacy should encompass components for recognizing overload and the ability to respond to it without sacrificing autonomy. But what happens when informational autonomy becomes too much of an obligation for the individual, resulting in an overload that may lead to an avoidant behavior? We describe this state as informational self-incapacitation, which we will discuss in more detail below.

Informational Self-restriction and Informational Self-incapacitation

Limitation of informational autonomy by cognitive structural determinacy cannot be avoided, but its restriction by informational self-incapacitation can. This is a behavior in which a person takes external causes to set the boundaries for his or her own decisions and behavior. It is done without any compulsion from the outside, but voluntarily or as a result of a gradual process.

With the number of channels through which information is provided and accessed, the number of opportunities to avoid individual responsibility for possible omissions or deficiencies is also increasing. This effect is further enhanced by collaborative working methods used for creating information offerings, such as websites. With each person or instance added, there are more opportunities to shift responsibility elsewhere.

In the first place, informational self-restriction simply means that the own knowledge or informational literacy is not used to solve a problem. Reasons may include convenience, respect for the interests of others, or directives that impose sanctions.

But there is another form of informational self-restriction, whose mechanisms of action are far more subtle and are thus considered to be less problematic, at least on a superficial level. This type is present, in part, in debates about the potential impact new technologies may have on society. Here, the acting persons express their critical or opposing stance on a matter (often by emphasizing ethical points of view), but at the same time accept decisive factors in their own argumentation as unchangeable and do not even consider other important factors.

In arguments about artificial intelligence, the position is often taken that harmful effects of artificial intelligence can only be avoided by setting ethical plans. A subtle driving force for informational self-restriction, however, is when AI metaphors are used as a basis for own arguments, and the benefits promised by the proponents are taken as already established facts or findings. In response to the supposed influence of transhumanism, an understanding of "Darwinism" focused exclusively on suppression becomes the guiding model of evolutionary biological processes to describe the position of humans in future social developments.[268]

Under these conditions, it can happen that exactly the opposite is achieved: By means of a fatalistic argumentation, the supposedly inevitable occurrence of an undesired development is virtually talked into existence. The development that is accepted as inevitable in this way can then no longer be stopped—neither through arguments nor by demanding ethically justified prohibitions. The latter are purposeful for stabilizing social behavior, but can only be achieved if their introduction is backed up by informational autonomy. Relativization through informational self-restriction is rather harmful.

Empirical findings show that tacit disempowerment can also be triggered by specific habituation processes. A survey of 1,200 employees in the UK on the consequences of automation, digitization and the introduction of robots at work has shown that getting used to digital assistants is reducing our critical distance.[269]

In the beginning, we still believe that we have complete control over the algorithmic assistance system. Gradually, however, we become so accustomed to it that we no longer want to live without this system, perhaps at some point we will no longer be able to live without it. *Yuval Harari* sees this as something of an inevitable process that makes the algorithm—as he calls it—"sovereign":

> You ask a question, the oracle replies, but it is up to you to make a decision. If the oracle wins your trust, however, the next logical step is to turn it into an agent. You give the algorithm only a final aim, and it acts to realise that aim without your supervision.[270]

Since informational autonomy is an intrinsic part of human beings and is indispensable for their cognitive performance, it should not be questioned as a core component of human existence. In this respect, it is astonishing that defending it is not given more attention. It seems that it is taken too much for granted and that people are not as aware of it as they should be. In the elementary processes of life, this experience of its being taken for granted is formative and is transferred to

---

268 See Henn: Gefahr durch KI.
269 Rötzer: Junge Generation.
270 Harari: Homo Deus, p. 346.

other areas as well. This could prevent the new challenges posed by digitization from being perceived as a potential threat to informational autonomy at all.

Informational self-incapacitation as a consequence of not (sufficiently) living informational autonomy may also arise from social pressure, which sometimes escalates into bullying. Questions such as "Why don't you log on to *Facebook*?" or "Why don't you participate in the possibilities of social networks?" imply that the person being asked is technologically retarded or overly cautious when it comes to data protection.

But then again, what kind of problem is solved by registering with *Facebook* or another social network? An informational problem or a social problem? In the first case, the decision for or against registration would put the user in a competitive situation, as there may be other comparable services. This competitive situation could be decided by comparison based on proven criteria. Social problems, by contrast, are part of everyday life and are usually solved by weighing up the reasons for and against a course of action. Accordingly, registration on a social media platform is not suitable for drawing conclusions about the user's informational literacy.

Informational literacy is lived informational autonomy. Is there any reason at all to justify why something is "not" done? Such an expectation would be justified only if it were a matter of a justification for "not refraining" from doing something although it is forbidden by law or by a socially determined order; for example, a justification for why one did not refrain from committing a crime.[271] But is it of any importance to give reasons why a crime has not been committed or will not be committed in the future?

It is fully legitimate to use new processes or technologies as the basis for a business model and leave it up to the market and customers to decide whether to use or buy them. Increasing the enticement by suggesting presumed or hoped-for advantages has its justification either. However, if users are driven to incapacitate themselves in the informational sense, these business models should be questioned. This applies particularly to the area of health and the collection of medical data, one of the areas that should not be left to the market alone.[272]

---

271 We explicitly use the phrase "socially determined order" here to emphasize the normative authority within a social structure.

272 First business models have already been developed, as exemplified by the low-cost genetic test offered by *23andMe* to private individuals. CEO of the company is *Anne Wojcicki*, the wife of *Google* co-founder *Sergej Brin*. *Google* is significantly involved in the financing, by the way. There are different legal frameworks in different countries for the conduct and scope of the laboratory analyses. See also the comments in Harari: Homo Deus, pp. 341–343.

It now becomes clearer why it can be so tempting to wish for artificial intelligence to triumph and thus to make a possibly even voluntary contribution to informational self-incapacitation. Here, it is important to distinguish between computable and non-computable parts of cognitive information processing. What is non-computable mostly comes from the world of emotionality and affectivity. Therefore, it cannot be modeled algorithmically and thus cannot be incorporated into the world of rational control mechanisms of artificial intelligence. A world that makes decision-making increasingly dependent on metrics, algorithms, and predictable expectations will therefore seek to eliminate the non-computable. The strongest form of elimination would be to discard any information processing that is non-computable because it no longer conforms to the prevailing paradigm of information processing (computer metaphor). In a mitigated form, only its legitimacy could be questioned.

Artificial intelligence emphasizes the benefits of computability in a particular way, pointing to extraordinary successes in competition with natural intelligence (chess, Go, etc.). This often takes place in artificial worlds that represent, at best, a reduced understanding of intelligence. The superiority of computer-based algorithms achieved in such events is then readily interpreted as an indication of a future replacement of cognitive intelligence. However, one particularly important aspect of AI success is often overlooked because it has no correlation to algorithmic intelligence performance: the return on investment of business models.

In the world of shareholder value and stock speculation, the returns of classic manufacturing value chains are no longer matching expectations. Information technology companies, including those with business in artificial intelligence (but also companies whose business model consists of making promises about the future), have demonstrated that returns can far exceed expectations. It is therefore only logical that the manufacturing sector is basing its future planning on the vague promises of these industries as well. Once this step is taken, it is difficult to step back from it, even when doubts arise.

In some respects, this behavior resembles that of a gambler. In a world of ostensibly rational decision-making, people prefer to use the scientific paradigm that the answers are not yet known, instead of admitting that they do not want to engage in already existing solutions at all. The supposedly rational attitude toward artificial intelligence is perhaps to be interpreted more as a hope for the occurrence of something incalculable than as a prediction based on probabilities regarding the realization of something already calculated.

Will we soon have to conclude that humanity has maneuvered itself into a future in which people are unable to cope with the tasks necessary for survival? Since most tasks involve cognitive informational processes, it is conceivable that this excessive demand could be used as a justification for restricting informational autonomy and looking for technological substitutes. Moreover, this would create the paradoxical scenario that people would have to be denied more and more informational autonomy. And this only because they have proven to be incapable of taking independent and self-responsible action to ensure its preservation.

7.7 Informational Dependence as the Price of Rationality

It is by no means certain that human beings are still at all capable of coping with the diverse demands of today's increasingly complex, globalized world shaped by information technology. It is rather conceivable that the requirements for rational behavior on too many levels and in too many new fields of action contribute to informational dependence and to a loss of informational autonomy.

Information technology applications have created structures of highest rationality, which in principle correspond well to the image of the rational human being. Then again, a purely rational way of looking at the world requires more and more technical and specialized knowledge, and the gap to average knowledge is getting even bigger. This may be one of the reasons why there is an increasing desire for alternatives to rationality, be it emotionality, religion, esoterism, or conspiracy theories, and why these alternatives become the basis for decision-making even when a more rational approach would have been more appropriate.

In his time, *Gottfried Wilhelm Leibniz* already mistrusted the human ability to act according to rational considerations. He therefore proposed to solve the world's problems by rational computations and to replace the human inadequacy in rational decision-making by algorithms (Chapter 5.10). Actually, *Leibniz* has thus become a pioneer of artificial intelligence. At his time, however, machine-based rational action was still utopia. In the meantime, it is possible and also well proven that humans are inferior to computers when they are guided exclusively by rational criteria. It should be clear that rationality cannot be the only criterion for preserving the human capacity to evolve. Here, criteria must be applied on the basis of characteristics that reflect the nature of human thinking and acting. And there would be no reason why the rational potential of humans should not nevertheless be further strengthened. The concern begins when these criteria become subordinate to computer-based approaches.

The Enlightenment created an image of human life that implies being guided by rational processes, both in personal behavior and in the shaping of social structures. Modern societies that see themselves in the tradition of the Enlightenment refer to rational justifications when it comes to pursuing societal goals or implementing their social values. These require well-developed skills in abstracting and inferring, with a clear distinction between the premises and the mode of reasoning used (logic). Concepts like "tolerance", "solidarity", "justice", or "responsibility", for example, necessitate such a way of reasoning. They may be of immediate relevance for the individuals with respect to their convictions and beliefs. Understanding the importance of such concepts for social development, as well as defending them against competing and perhaps less desirable concepts, can only be done with the help of rational thinking.[273]

These demands are certainly high and therefore a possible cause of the kind of overload that becomes apparent, for example, in processes of social change. The heated discussions about "foreign infiltration" and "dominant culture" and the worrisome side effects of this non-rational debate are symptoms of such an excessive demand. Agreeing on a consensual ethics of society obviously needs much more time than the establishment of the factual conditions.

Modern secular societies grant people individual rights of freedom while requiring them to be as neutral as possible in the public. The relationship between the two requirements is unstable and can also be understood as a contradiction. If not all members of society are willing or able to reach rational consensus, this provides fertile ground for conflict. There are many examples of how rationally comparable facts can lead to different social assessments. This assessment is not made on a purely rational basis, but is further influenced by cultural or religious values.

In modern enlightened societies, the individual lives in a tension between the need to act rationally and a set of values that may stem from transcendent sources of a cultural background. However, individuals may not be adequately prepared for the necessity of rationally balancing different cultural backgrounds. This also has to do with the fact that human decisions and actions are never free of emotional influences. The dynamics of modernity, with its increased demands on the individual's "self-understanding"[274], are responsible for the loss of this balance between rationality and emotionality. The emotional part has yet to adjust to the new demands so that it can compensate for this lack of ability to act rationally.

Humans need some kind of drawn line for their self-esteem and well-being that creates a zone of protection or emotional security. They must be able to cross or leave this boundary at any time, while others must not enter it without their consent. If the function of such a boundary is not (any longer) present, there will be a feeling of oppression, fear, the loss of the feeling of being able to decide freely, and finally the loss of self-esteem. This will inevitably lead to the loss of

---

273 See for instance the argumentation of *John Rawls* within the framework of his theory of justice in Rawls: A theory of justice, Rawls: Justice as fairness; see also the communication-theoretical ultimate justifications for ethical norms by *Karl-Otto Apel* in Apel: Diskurs und Verantwortung.
274 See Kaufmann: Die Erfindung des Ich.

emotional security, which is perceived as a drastic deficit and possibly ends in irrational compensation efforts. With regard to the shaping of social structures, the following questions must be addressed:

1. What role does informational autonomy have in maintaining an individual image of freedom in civil society?
2. Is informational autonomy, as a basic endowment and essential cornerstone of what makes human beings human, dispensable at all? If so, would such a renunciation constitute a violation of basic human rights, as well as of human self-determination and responsibility?
3. How are informational autonomy, freedom, and individual responsibility related in civil society?

Freedom, in the context of society, is not a gift or a privilege to be taken for granted. An important prerequisite for its realization is informational autonomy. Consequently, there is a responsibility to defend informational autonomy in a society[275]—not an easy task in practice. In view of the complexity of the information technology penetration in today's societies, it is easy to feel powerless or even resigned. Avoiding informational totalitarianism means to constantly circle between responsibility and resignation (Figure 6.4).

Those who do not want to take responsibility will seek a sheltered environment that makes no demands on self-fulfillment or independent personal development. This creates the impression of emotional security, but restricts freedom and favors the development of totalitarian structures. Restrictions on freedom, therefore, do not necessarily have to come from the outside, but can correspond to the personal desire to delegate the responsibility to act to others while still living a comfortable life.

Emotional security in freedom can only exist if one takes responsibility for preserving autonomy. This contributes to safeguarding human dignity and self-respect. The question remains open as to what understanding of responsibility, beyond the understanding from a legal perspective, would be compatible with freedom and emotional security. If it were wanted to be established, its benefits would have to be justified without raising a moral finger too much. It seems that only discourse in society can do this. It is to be hoped then again that such a discourse will not to be accompanied or even replaced by non-living systems and algorithms.

---

[275] For a rationalist justification of the concept of responsibility, see, Nida-Rümelin: Verantwortung, Nida-Rümelin: Über menschliche Freiheit, Nida-Rümelin: Tief in unserer Lebenswelt verwurzelt.

The rapid progress in the development of artificial intelligence foreshadows possible threats to informational autonomy. Especially the language models based on deep learning led to new, extremely powerful systems with *GPT-3* and currently (December 2022) *ChatGPT*.[276] Designed as a dialog system, *ChatGPT* is optimized for communicative capabilities and impresses with features including:
–   input in natural language and complete sentences;
–   use of multiple languages;
–   high quality of correct interpretation of input, even with complicated syntax;
–   output of answers in complete sentences with correct syntax;
–   reliable classification of the input in a correct factual or technical context;
–   extremely broad knowledge base.

The responses of *ChatGPT* comprise arguments, statements, facts, as well as justifications, examples, and comparisons. Formally, the answers are thus resembling those we would find pleasant in a conversation with human partners. The system is predestined as interface of search engines or other query systems. But it would also provide reception robots or robotic service butlers with a new behavioral interface that would enable them to have "conversations" about all kinds of topics beyond their command control for primary tasks.

ChatGPT answers the question about its self-assessment ("Do you consider yourself an instrument or tool or a something that makes decisions and finds answers on its own?") as follows:

> As an artificial intelligence, I am a tool that is designed to assist users in finding information and completing tasks. I do not have personal feelings or make decisions on my own. My responses are based on the information that I have been trained on and the algorithms that have been designed into me. I am not a human and do not have the ability to think or act independently in the same way that a person does. Is there anything else I can help with?[277]

The future will show whether the majority of users will use the system primarily as a tool in the sense of its still limited self-claim, or whether they will increasingly see it as an adequate substitute for a human conversational partner. For topic-related searches or fact-finding, this can indeed be useful or even enjoyable. Boundaries are touched or crossed, however, when intimate personal or even therapeutic interests are involved. We recall *Joseph Weizenbaum*, who has already described this aspect in connection with the *ELIZA* system.[278]

---

276 ChatGPT [OpenAI], ChatGPT [Wikipedia], GPT-3 [Wikipedia], Huge "foundation models" are turbo-charging AI progress [Economist].
277 Session with *ChatGPT* on January 1, 2023.
278 See Weizenbaum: ELIZA.

ChatGPT clearly shows how thin the line of an information technology development can be between benefit and harm for everyone's informational autonomy. It must remain open whether the use of the tool will move more in the direction of informational autonomy or whether the danger of informational self-incapacitation with all its consequences will get the upper hand.

The scope for individuals to take responsibility is already limited by the framework set by politics and government. There must be a balance achieved between the unfolding of the individual's personality and its restriction by these two factors. Informational literacy as lived informational autonomy in each of us could be seen as a starting point for this discourse. And no doubt it is necessary, because neither has personality been granted to all members of a society at all times, nor can we be sure that the current framework will not be weakened again and used to establish class structures.

Digitization processes create new frontiers that could be used to build elites and pursue rulership. If digitization is to become a stable pillar of society based on the principles of equality, freedom and solidarity, all members must be enabled to participate in it. Informational autonomy and responsibility must be granted to all members of a civil society as equitable concepts.

7.8 Non-living Autonomous Systems

So far, we have characterized informational autonomy as a property of human autopoietic systems. This allows us to ask whether this is a property that should be attributed exclusively to humans, more precisely: Should or can informational autonomy mean the same for non-living systems as it does for humans?

Our world is permeated with information technology systems. In most cases, these are systems that support human decisions in action situations (for example, automotive diagnostic systems as used in repair shops) or perform mechanical work that should no longer be performed by humans (for example, welding robots). Forecasts—particularly concerning the fields of artificial intelligence and business—predict that the range of uses for such systems will not be limited to assistance tasks. Rather, it is assumed that the systems will replace humans in many situations and also take over decisions that were previously reserved to be made by humans. These could then even be decisions that would be directed against humans.[279] So the question is obvious: Are autonomous vehicles, robots or combat

---

279 See Schmidt/Cohen: The new digital age.

drones systems which, like humans, can be ascribed the property of informational autonomy?

Such systems act autonomously within the scope of the task assigned to them, at least to the extent that their decision-making and action processes are controlled by algorithms and sensorimotor interfaces to the outside world. However, their tasks are still limited to narrow segments and the systems operate within a framework that is usually clearly predefined and can be described by rational calculation.

In any case, these systems are not autopoietic. For this, they are lacking the dual function inherent in informational autonomy, which applies both to the sustainment of all life processes and to rational decision-making when interacting with other people and systems. Sensations (up to doubts about their own suitability or right to exist) are not part of the characteristics of such systems.[280] They cannot gain or feed back ethical norms of action based on their own doing; they can only communicate what has put into them via the algorithm. In order to be able to design such "ethics modules", people have to make highly artificial preliminary considerations and put them into rules. Like in the much discussed case of autonomous driving: Should, in the event of an inevitable accident, an autonomous vehicle's algorithm give preference to the likely lower number of casualties in order to avoid a higher number of casualties?[281] What happens if the probability was calculated incorrectly because the algorithm did not consider all the parameters in question? Does anyone have to take responsibility for this?[282]

The application of any new technology requires the establishment of a meaning that cannot be derived solely from its functionality, the pleasure it brings, or the fact that it was created by humans. A formerly propagated model of technology as a substitute for organs saw modern humans as deficient beings who have long since ceased to have any immediate capability to survive.[283] For humans to compensate for their deficits and ensure their survivability, even in inhospitable environments, they have to create technical aids. The result is that the deficit on one side is compensated by a dependency relationship on the other side: the tools

---

280 The consequences of the developments as thematized by the contribution of *Briggs* and *Scheutz* regarding the refusal of robots to obey orders, cannot yet be foreseen (Briggs/Scheutz: Why robots must learn to tell us "No").

281 In accordance with the recommendations of the *Ethics Commission on Automated and Connected Driving* of June 20, 2017; see also, Rojas: Die Tugend des Roboters.

282 Such considerations are made by the *German Ethics Council*; see the program of the event "Autonomous Systems: How Intelligent Machines Change Us": Deutscher Ethikrat: Autonome Systeme.

283 See Rapp: Fortschritt.

created cannot generate their own requirements for action, cannot become an acting subject themselves.

Non-living autonomous systems, however, would no longer be tools. They would be able to make demands for action on their own, which would fundamentally change the way we see human life. Potentially, this could be expressed in two ways:

1. Non-living autonomous systems are made to resemble humans; this would include endowing them with a "soul" (understood as being receptive to influences from non-rational realms such as emotions, sensitivities, doubts, etc.).
2. Humans are reduced to algorithmically working systems, and their actions are measured only by those values that allow for parameterization.

What would be gained by the first option? Perhaps the creation of non-living systems with all the shortcomings and defects of the living systems, the elimination of which was supposedly the cause of their development?

Let us assume that it is possible to program an ethics module for autonomous vehicles with an "experience function" that enables the vehicle to make autonomous assessments of its own actions. In conflict situation between many or few casualties, the vehicle has repeatedly decided in favor of the smaller number of casualties according to the specification of the ethics algorithm. The subsequent evaluation reveals that there was one very important person among the victims. The ethics module gets doubts about its acting and would rather decide according to the other option in the future. Does the autonomous vehicle thus also possess ethical decision-making capabilities that can be used as a model for corresponding functions of other non-living autonomous systems?

What would be gained by the second option? An informational totalitarianism heading irreversibly toward the "algorithmic human"?

How could such an "algorithmic human" be characterized? Is it a living system with the informational autonomy of a non-living autonomous system? In other words, a living being that, on the one hand, acts informationally autonomously in order to sustain life, but, on the other hand, shapes its rational processes according to the standards and specifications of algorithms? Is this living being allowed to determine the boundary between autonomous and non-autonomous itself, or is this determined externally by non-living autonomous systems? Is an algorithmic human being still an individual?

Human decision making involves physical sensations (such as hunger or pain), emotions (such as joy, anger, sadness, hope, disappointment, affection, insecurity, or shame), and also doubts. All this is related to human dignity and self-respect. Should these sensations and emotions also be made part of the spectrum defining the informational properties of autonomous systems, or, conversely, should a human image be created that establishes an understanding of informational autonomy without these properties?

Even if one shares the view that emotions are complex algorithms[284], this would still make no argument for wanting to control or replace human decisions and human actions by algorithms as well. Decision-oriented algorithms without autopoietic life functions do not own informational autonomy. For them to act, specifications are required that express values and meaningfulness through preferences, but these must be provided by actors who participate in real life. This participation in turn requires autopoiesis as the basis of life processes and continuous feedback interaction with other actors. Relying decisions and actions on imported parameters or data (as would be the case even with constantly updated algorithms outside autopoietic systems) is not equivalent to informational autonomy.

If non-living autonomous systems were to develop doubts about their actions and even take them as a reason to decide differently in the future, what would this mean for the usefulness of the results of algorithmic procedures? What difference could then still be seen in comparison to human actions? The consequence would be that precisely by equipping non-living autonomous systems with self-correction functions, they would become incapable of acting, or at least their use would appear absurd due to the non-existing unambiguity of the results. The debate as to which cognitive performance could or should be replaced or enhanced by artificial intelligence will lead nowhere if at the end the outcome is once again only a product that is deficient due to standards that were set incorrectly at the beginning.

In a competitive situation, in which pure algorithmic processing ("thinking") is required, the human being cannot win against the machine; regardless of whether the latter acts autonomously or not. Autonomy is at risk of being lost when autonomous thinking is no longer practiced and when the values of human cognitive performance are determined by algorithms. The ideal to be reached is to reconcile rational and experiential approaches. Co-existence of both worlds is necessary, and replacing the mechanisms of one with those of the other is simply nonsensical. Humans can draw their value only from the achievements of autonomous thinking and autopoietic life, and this includes discrepancy and doubt.

And there precisely is a crucial difference between man and machine: Man, in order to become whole, must be forever an explorer of both his inner and his outer realities. His life is full of risks, but risks he has the courage to accept, because, like the explorer, he learns to

---

284 Harari: Homo Deus, pp. 107, 122, 141, 151.

trust his own capacities to endure, to overcome. What could it mean to speak of risk, courage, trust, endurance, and overcoming when one speaks of machines?[285]

---

285 Weizenbaum: Computer power and human reason, p. 280.

8 Closure

Human dignity shall be inviolable.

Basic Law for the Federal Republic of Germany[286]

The guiding principle "Informational literacy is lived informational autonomy" has taken us on a journey through many different topics. They are all equally relevant to successfully making this guiding principle a lived reality. The nature of informational literacy is multifaceted and complex, though perhaps not always with the greatest depth, but with a great scope. This broad scope is characterized not only by the increasing demand on all of us to develop more and more skills for dealing with new devices, services and technologies, but above all it shows the multitude of resulting problems and the need to search for possible solutions.

In the world we live in, information technology is omnipresent and its unbiased use today begins as early as in preschool age. According to the economic point of view, our future is to become even more dependent on the developments of information technology. At the same time, there is a widespread belief that we, as users of these complex technologies, will be able to cope with them without having to deal more deeply with their fundamentals. No other technology of comparable complexity is so uninhibitedly unleashed on people, and is the same time accepted by them.

This makes it all the more important to pursue the ideal of a society in which we, through informational autonomy, promote digital reason and thus ensure the preservation of human dignity as part of a civil society. Unfortunately, there is no simple recipe for achieving this challenging goal. Yet there is one factor that can be identified without doubt as a key factor, and this factor is "time". It takes time to adapt to progress. But the complexity of the processes involved is so great that there may not be enough time to acquire the skills needed to master this complexity.

Part of the basic attitude of professional approaches is to begin from the assumption that there must be a course of action that can transform inadequate or non-existent competence into a state of solid competence. It is true that this approach may require a significant investment of time and can therefore in many cases only be managed by specialization and cooperation. Some of this can be advanced through standardization as well as cognitive knowledge and information

---

286 Basic Law for the Federal Republic of Germany : Article 1(1).

https://doi.org/10.1515/9783110693744-008

processing (Chapter 2). However, a minimum amount of time, which cannot be precisely determined, will be required for it.

If instrumental and skill-oriented information literacy is to become a self-evident cultural technique in the sense of informational literacy, it is first necessary to pay close attention to the existing problems and carry out thorough analyses. The subsequent step would be to examine what measures should be taken to enable people to achieve this competence. In this regard, close cooperation with governmental and educational institutions would be indispensable in order to involve and reach as many people as possible. Offering training modules, such as PC, internet or smartphone driver's licenses, is by far not sufficient here.

However, there is an obvious contradiction regarding "time" as a key factor between the dynamics of technological development and the time constraints imposed on educational institutions and their plannings and teaching practices. What is needed is support in the acquisition of a cultural technique that includes the provision of abstract skills that can be applied in a reason-based manner to any individual situation. Of course, such a path is fundamentally in conflict with the current parameter-oriented educational landscape, which is dominated by rankings and scores.[287]

Inseparably linked to this cultural technique is informational autonomy as an inalienable basic cognitive property. The consequence drawn from this should be the search for societal guidelines and developments that strengthen and promote informational autonomy instead of questioning it or contributing to its cutback. If the value of human beings is measured solely by their function as data suppliers, if their actions are subordinated to the primacy of the rational, to algorithmic processing, then informational autonomy and human dignity would have long since given way to informational incapacitation. In this case, humans were inferior to machine intelligence and would have to follow its instructions in order to avoid making mistakes. So are algorithmic criteria decisive for digital belonging or exclusion? How can this be compatible with human dignity? Is it possible to stop or prevent these processes that are exclusively human-induced? How can we make informational properties a lived part of our societies while avoiding informational inequality?

Visions of society based on artificial intelligence see the deficits and differences of existing societies and cultures as obsolete and forecast a universalistic culture of superintelligence. However, if we follow the analyses of cultural diversity and its historical development, it becomes clear how unrealistic such ideas actually are. *François Jullien* provides evidence that the search for cultural iden-

---

287 For example, see Liessmann: Geisterstunde.

tity would have to result in a cultural entirety that includes all known individual cultures as special cases or differentiations.[288] However, his analyses of existing cultures show that no generic concept for determining the commonalities of different cultures can be found that could be considered culturally universal. Even the concept of "human dignity", which originates from the Western tradition, is not accepted by all philosophical schools of thought associated with the Western tradition, nor is it regarded as an unquestioned attribute by lived practice. A normative framework was needed to help it reach its current rather abstract status, but this does not guarantee that it will be respected in practice.

Cultural universalism would hinder the unfolding of identity because the abandonment of differences would mean the end of any ability to evolve. Isolating the particular leads to stagnation. What exists is classified, stipulated, and assigned. The potential for development then no longer exists. When diversity is rejected, the creative potential that derives its power from change also disappears. But only by embracing diversity and leveraging the resources of different cultures can we ensure continuing lively growth. Ignorance has no potential to do so. Space for creation can only exist if we recognize the distance to the other and do not shy away from the confrontation with different ideas.

If we want to achieve understanding between divergent systems, possibly through dialog, then a common language is needed, which, however, cannot be just "one" language. The liveliness of a system is also expressed through the liveliness of its respective language. However, liveliness also creates blurring. Therefore, there will always be a sphere that is ambiguous, that marks the distance to the other and stands for the difference. Meta-languages found in information technology are no alternative because they can only represent nuances of differences by means of flattening; data-oriented coding in the sense of a universal dialog system is just as unsuitable as a solution.

Informational literacy is thus ultimately also a prerequisite for the ability to recognize the difference between cultural realities. This gives it the potential to strengthen the individual. The perception of this difference thus becomes a substitute for separating and differentiating. Informational literacy endows each member of a culture or society with a dignity that does not need to be justified by specific behavior, conditions, or characteristics.

---

[288] Jullien: Es gibt keine kulturelle Identität.

The endless cycle of idea and action,
Endless invention, endless experiment,
Brings knowledge of motion, but not of stillness;
Knowledge of speech, but not of silence;
Knowledge of words, and ignorance of the Word.
All our knowledge brings us nearer to our ignorance,
All our ignorance brings us nearer to death,
But nearness to death no nearer to GOD.
Where is the Life we have lost in living?
Where is the wisdom we have lost in knowledge?
Where is the knowledge we have lost in information?
The cycles of Heaven in twenty centuries
Brings us farther from GOD and nearer to the Dust.

T. S. Eliot[289]

---

289 Choruses from "The Rock" (Eliot: The Rock, p. 7).

Glossary

The glossary contains those terms which, in the context of the book's argumentation, are given a meaning that does not necessarily correspond to the ones commonly found. It is not a complete glossary of all technical terms used.

Abstracting is the ability to realize and apply patterns of knowledge. (Chapter 4.2)

Actual information is the cognitive processing pattern of a structurally determined system that occurs at the moment when reality construction or the exchange of information between two cognitive structures takes place as part of any direct act of communication. Actual information becomes conscious either through self-initiated cognitive reactivation or through information processing triggered by external sensory perception. (Chapter 3.1)

Competence is the ability, when faced with a deficit, to indicate what actions are required and what efforts must be undertaken to close the gap between the deficit state and the desired state. (Chapter 2.8)

Computer metaphor is used as a placeholder term for all attempts to interpret the nature of human information processing by comparing it to a computer-algorithmic understanding of information. (Chapter 1.2)

Consciousness is a basic mental state that includes the ability to make a spontaneous and autonomous decision about which perceptual segment to pay selective attention to. This also includes selecting the areas one does not want to pay attention to. (Chapter 2.7)

Data are to be understood as elementary units in the information technology sense as well as in the sense of cognitive processing. (Chapters 2.1 and 2.5) They are sensory impressions put into form or the results of theory-guided measurement processes. (Chapter 3.4) They require theory binding when used in the context of cognitive processes. (Chapters 2.6 and 3.4)

Information is the object of cognitive processing. Through sensory perception, it can be connected to the outside world and to other information processing beings. Further, it can be referred to as the resulting object of a purely self-referential process. (Chapters 2.5 and 2.1)

Informational stands for the totality of all processes that enable humans to autonomously infer information using sensory perception or self-referential processes as part of an autopoietic system. (Chapter 2.5)

Informational ambivalence is a state of uncertainty in humans in which they do not know whether they are acting in informational autonomy or informational dependence. (Chapter 6.7)

Informational autonomy is the ability to cognitively process states that result from self-triggered information or information experienced through sensory perception. This includes the ability to cognitively process received externalized information. It is supported by an understanding of the relationship of security to authority that encourages and protects our individual freedom to apply our basic cognitive abilities without fear and within the framework of authority lived by example. (Chapters 2.7 and 6.5)

Informational dependence is present when someone cannot decide whether information processing is done on their own initiative or is triggered by external factors. It is also present when the input of sensory perceptions or data is decided by another instance rather than by the person using that input for a cognitive information process. (Chapter 2.7)

https://doi.org/10.1515/9783110693744-009

Informational literacy is lived informational autonomy. (Chapter 2.8)

Informational overload is the simultaneous presence of a larger number of parameters that should equally be used as the basis for a decision-making or action process, but which can only be processed to a limited extent or not at all due to limited cognitive capacities. (Chapter 7.3)

Informational reason is the capacity of human thought to perform cognitive processes in order to infer and construct reality; in this process, observations are transferred into meanings and the rules and principles created by reflection are provided as a basis for action. (Chapter 6.7)

Informational self-incapacitation is a behavior in which human beings choose external factors to be the reason for delimiting their own informational autonomy. (Chapter 7.6)

Informational totalitarianism is a condition in which a person's decisions and actions are to be made on the basis of informational dependence. Thereby, a suspension of informational autonomy as a cognitive property is accepted or induced. (Chapter 7)

Instantiating (or to specify) is the ability to use knowledge patterns to identify individual objects. (Chapter 4.2)

Knowledge is the result of a construction of reality. (Chapter 2.2)

Lived informational reason is the liberation from self-imposed informational immaturity. (Chapter 6.7)

Potential information is externalized information supplemented (enriched) with structural information for the purpose of reception, taking into account reference domains. (Chapters 3.1 and 5.3)

Transcendence (act of transcending) is the interpretation of a situation for the purpose of transferring it to the own life situation or the projection of personal ideals and longings onto an authority (person, institution, structure) that is assumed to have the potential for their realization. (Chapter 6.5)

List of Figures

https://doi.org/10.1515/9783110693744-010

List of Tables

https://doi.org/10.1515/9783110693744-011

References

Albinus, Lars: Can science cope with more than one world? : a cross-reading of Habermas, Popper, and Searle, in: Journal for General Philosophy of Science 44 (2013) 1, pp. 3–20, URL: https://doi.org/10.1007/s10838-013-9221-9 (visited on Dec. 17, 2022).

AlgorithmWatch, 2023, URL: https://algorithmwatch.org/en/ (visited on Jan. 16, 2023).

Antos, Gerd: Mythen, Metaphern, Modelle : Konzeptualisierung von Kommunikation aus dem Blickwinkel der Angewandten Diskursforschung, in: Gisela Brünner, Reinhard Fiehler, and Walther Kindt (eds.): Angewandte Diskursforschung : Band 1: Grundlagen und Beispielanalysen, Radolfzell 2002, pp. 93–117, URL: http://www.verlag-gespraechsforschung.de/2002/diskursforschung/1-093-117.pdf (visited on Dec. 17, 2022).

Apel, Karl-Otto: Diskurs und Verantwortung : das Problem des Übergangs zur postkonventionellen Moral, Frankfurt am Main 1988.

Arnheim, Rudolf: Art and visual perception : a psychology of the creative eye, 2nd ed., Berkeley, Calif. 2004.

Assmann, Aleida: Cultural memory and Western civilization : functions, media, archives, Cambridge, Mass. 2011.

Assmann, Jan: Cultural memory and early civilization : writing, remembrance, and political imagination, New York, NY 2011.

Axelos, Christos et al.: Allgemeines/Besonderes, in: Joachim Ritter (ed.): Historisches Wörterbuch der Philosophie, vol. 1, Basel 1971, pp. 181–183, URL: https://schwabeonline.ch/schwabe-xaveropp/elibrary/openurl?id=doi%3A10.24894%2FHWPh.5033 (visited on Dec. 17, 2022).

Balzli, Beat et al.: SPD : Der Müll, die Partei und das Geld, in: Der Spiegel, no. 11, Mar. 11, 2002, pp. 22–25, URL: http://www.spiegel.de/spiegel/print/d-21662455.html (visited on Dec. 18, 2022).

Basic Law for the Federal Republic of Germany in the revised version published in the Federal Law Gazette Part III, classification number 100-1, as last amended by the Act of 28 June 2022 (Federal Law Gazette I p. 968), URL: https://www.gesetze-im-internet.de/englisch_gg/englisch_gg.html#p0019 (visited on Oct. 2, 2022).

Bauer, Hans-Ulrich et al.: Selbstorganisierende neuronale Karten, in: Spektrum der Wissenschaft (1996) 4, pp. 38–47, URL: https://www.spektrum.de/magazin/selbstorganisierende-neuronale-karten/822941 (visited on Dec. 17, 2022).

Becker, Matthias: Auf dem Weg zum Psychotherapie-Bot. Telepolis, Feb. 28, 2018, URL: https://www.heise.de/tp/features/Auf-dem-Weg-zum-Psychotherapie-Bot-3974410.html (visited on Dec. 17, 2022).

Bender, Bianca: Digitale Mündigkeit : Definition und Dimensionen ; eine theoretische Fundierung zwischen Medienbildung und Medienkompetenz, Bachelorthesis, unpublished, Hagen: Fernuniversität in Hagen ; Fakultät Kultur- und Sozialwissenschaften ; Institut für Bildungswissenschaft und Medienforschung, 2016, URL: https://lesen-schreiben-bilden.net/wp-content/uploads/2017/02/BA_BB_ohnePr%C3%A4si_public.pdf.

Benedikter, Roland: Digitalisierung der Gefühle? Telepolis, Apr. 2, 2018, URL: https://www.heise.de/tp/features/Digitalisierung-der-Gefuehle-4000478.html (visited on Dec. 17, 2022).

Berners-Lee, Tim, James Hendler, and Ora Lassila: The Semantic Web : a new form of web content that is meaningful to computers will unleash a revolution of new possibilities, in:

https://doi.org/10.1515/9783110693744-012

Scientific American 284 (2001) 5, pp. 34–43, URL: https://www.jstor.org/stable/26059207 (visited on Dec. 17, 2022).

Berry, Dianne C. and Donald E. Broadbent: On the relationship between task performance and associated verbalizable knowledge, in: The Quarterly Journal of Experimental Psychology Section A 36 (1984) 2, pp. 209–231.

Berry, Michael W. and Murray Browne: Understanding search engines : mathematical modeling and text retrieval, 2nd ed., Philadelphia, Pa. 2005.

Bibel, Wolfgang, Steffen Hölldobler, and Torsten Schaub: Wissensrepräsentation und Inferenz : eine grundlegende Einführung. Braunschweig 1993.

Bibliographisches Institut: Brockhaus Enzyklopädie Digital, 21st ed., Mannheim 2005.

Bildgebende Verfahren. Sprache und Gehirn : ein neurolinguistisches Tutorial, 2014, URL: https://www2.ims.uni-stuttgart.de/sgtutorial/neurorad.html (visited on Dec. 17, 2022).

Blackmore, Susan J.: Consciousness : a very short introduction, Oxford 2005.

Blackmore, Susan J.: Conversations on consciousness : interviews with twenty minds, New York, NY 2005.

Blair, Ann M.: Too much to know : managing scholarly information before the modern age, New Haven, Conn. 2010.

BMVI : Bericht der Ethik-Kommission. bmvi.de, June 20, 2017, URL: https://www.bmvi.de/SharedDocs/DE/Publikationen/DG/bericht-der-ethik-kommission.html?nn=12830 (visited on Dec. 17, 2022).

Boehm, Andreas and Gesellschaft für Angewandte Informationswissenschaft (eds.): Texte verstehen : Konzepte, Methoden, Werkzeuge (Schriften zur Informationswissenschaft, vol. 14), Konstanz 1994.

Boghossian, Peter and James A. Lindsay: The conceptual penis as a social construct : a Sokal-style hoax on gender studies. Skeptic, May 19, 2017, URL: https://www.skeptic.com/reading_room/conceptual-penis-social-contruct-sokal-style-hoax-on-gender-studies/ (visited on Dec. 22, 2022).

Böhme-Dürr, Karin (ed.): Wissensveränderung durch Medien : theoretische Grundlagen und empirische Analysen, München 1990.

Bookstein, Abraham: Relevance, in: Journal of the American Society for Information Science 30 (1979) 5, pp. 269–273, URL: https://doi.org/10.1002/asi.4630300505 (visited on Dec. 17, 2022).

Bowker, Geoffrey and Susan Star: Sorting things out : classification and its consequences, Cambridge, Mass. 2000.

Bredemeier, Willi: Was sagt uns die Debatte zu ‚Fake News' über die Qualität unserer etablierten Medien? : Medienkritik in der Zeit alternativer Fakten. password-online.de, May 29, 2017, URL: https://www.infobroker.de/password-online/archiv/fake-news-und-qualitaetsmedien-gar-nicht-so-verschieden/ (visited on Dec. 17, 2022).

Briggs, Matthias and Gordon Scheutz: Why robots must learn to tell us "No". Scientific American, Oct. 25, 2016, URL: https://www.scientificamerican.com/article/why-robots-must-learn-to-tell-us-ldquo-no-rdquo/ (visited on June 6, 2022).

Brin, Sergey and Lawrence Page: The anatomy of a large-scale hypertextual web search engine, in: Computer Networks and ISDN Systems, Proceedings of the Seventh International World Wide Web Conference 30 (1998) 1, pp. 107–117, URL: https://doi.org/10.1016/S0169-7552(98)00110-X (visited on Dec. 17, 2022).

Busch, Ulrich: Aspekte der Geldkritik von Aristoteles bis heute (Philosophische Gespräche, vol. 45), Berlin 2017.

Caglioti, Giuseppe: Symmetriebrechung und Wahrnehmung : Beispiele aus der Erfahrungswelt, in collab. with Maria Rimini, Braunschweig 1990.

Calvin, William H.: The cerebral symphony : seashore reflections on the structure of consciousness, New York, NY 1990.

Calvin, William H. and George A. Ojemann: Conversations with Neil's brain : the neural nature of thought and language, Reading, Mass. 1995.

Capurro, Rafael: Information : ein Beitrag zur etymologischen und ideengeschichtliche Begründung des Informationsbegriffs, München 1978.

Capurro, Rafael: Theorie der Botschaft, in: Erich Hamberger and Kurt Luger (eds.): Transdisziplinäre Kommunikation : aktuelle Be-Deutungen des Phänomens Kommunikation im fächerübergreifenden Dialog (Neue Aspekte in Kultur- und Kommunikationswissenschaft, vol. 19), Wien 2008, pp. 65–89, URL: http://www.capurro.de/botschaft.htm (visited on Dec. 17, 2022).

Capurro, Rafael: Was ist Information? : Hinweise zum Wort- und Begriffsfeld eines umstrittenen Begriffs, in: Handbuch der modernen Datenverarbeitung 24 (1987) 133, pp. 107–114.

Capurro, Rafael and Birger Hjørland: The concept of information, in: Annual Review of Information Science and Technology 37 (2003) 1, pp. 343–411, URL: https://onlinelibrary.wiley.com/doi/abs/10.1002/aris.1440370109 (visited on Nov. 18, 2022).

Chalmers, David J.: The puzzle of conscious experience, in: Scientific American 273 (1995) 6, pp. 80–86, URL: https://consc.net/papers/puzzle.html (visited on Dec. 17, 2022).

Changeux, Jean-Pierre and Alain Connes: Conversations on mind, matter, and mathematics, Princeton, NJ 1995.

ChatGPT, 2023, URL: https://chat.openai.com (visited on Jan. 1, 2023).

ChatGPT. Wikipedia, 2023, URL: https://en.wikipedia.org/w/index.php?title=ChatGPT&oldid=1130838550 (visited on Jan. 1, 2023).

China invents the digital totalitarian state : the worrying implications of its social-credit project, in: The Economist, Dec. 17, 2016, URL: https://www.economist.com/briefing/2016/12/17/china-invents-the-digital-totalitarian-state (visited on Oct. 2, 2022).

Chomsky, Noam: What kind of creatures are we? New York, NY 2015.

Court of Justice of the European Union: Press Release No 63/17. Curia, June 14, 2017, URL: https://curia.europa.eu/jcms/upload/docs/application/pdf/2017-06/cp170063en.pdf.

d'Alembert, Jean Le Rond: Preliminary discourse to the Encyclopedia of Diderot, trans. by Richard Nahum Schwab and Walter E. Rex, Indianapolis, Ind. 1963.

Damasio, Antonio: Descartes' error : emotion, reason and the human brain, London 2006.

Davis, Philip J. and Reuben Hersh: Descartes' dream : the world according to mathematics, 2005.

Dengel, Andreas (ed.): Semantische Technologien : Grundlagen – Konzepte – Anwendungen, Heidelberg 2012.

Deutsche Mathematiker-Vereinigung: Inhalte statt Geräte. DMV, Nov. 15, 2016, URL: https://www.mathematik.de/presse/572-pi-zum-nationalen-it-gipfel?highlight=WyJpdC1naXBmZWwiXQ== (visited on Dec. 17, 2022).

Deutscher Bibliotheksverband e.V.: Informationskompetenz : Vermittlungs- und Forschungsaktivitäten zur Informationskompetenz. Informationskompetenz, 2015, URL: http://www.informationskompetenz.de/ (visited on Dec. 17, 2022).

Deutscher Ethikrat, 2023, URL: https://www.ethikrat.org/?cookieLevel=not-set (visited on Jan. 6, 2023).

Deutscher Ethikrat: Jahrestagung : Autonome Systeme ; wie intelligente Maschinen uns verändern. ethikrat.org, June 21, 2017, URL: https://www.ethikrat.org/jahrestagungen/autonome-systeme-wie-intelligente-maschinen-uns-veraendern/ (visited on Dec. 17, 2022).

Doi, Takeo: Amae : Freiheit in Geborgenheit ; zur Struktur japanischer Psyche, Frankfurt am Main 1982.

Doi, Takeo: The anatomy of dependence, Tokyo 1981.

Dreisiebner, Stefan, Lisa Beutelspacher, and Maria Henkel: Informationskompetenz : Forschung in Graz und Düsseldorf, in: Information – Wissenschaft & Praxis 68 (2017) 5, pp. 271–273.

Duda, Justine: Ein mittelalterlicher Computer. Virtuelles Museum Digital Humanities, May 15, 2016, URL: http://dhmuseum.uni-trier.de/node/354 (visited on Dec. 17, 2022).

Eco, Umberto: The name of the rose, Boston, Mass. 2014.

Edelman, Gerald M.: Bright air, brilliant fire : on the matter of mind, New York, NY 1992.

Edelman, Gerald M., Joseph A. Gally, and Bernard J. Baars: Biology of consciousness, in: Frontiers in Psychology 2 (2011) 4, URL: https://www.ncbi.nlm.nih.gov/pmc/articles/PMC3111444/ (visited on Dec. 17, 2022).

Edelman, Gerald M. and Giulio Tononi: A universe of consciousness : how matter becomes imagination, New York, NY 2000.

Eggers, Dave: The circle, New York, NY 2013.

Eigen, Manfred: Wie entsteht Information? : Prinzipien der Selbstorganisation in der Biologie, in: Berichte der Bunsengesellschaft für Physikalische Chemie 80 (1976), pp. 1059–1081.

Einstein, Albert : author details [Scopus preview]. Scopus Preview, Feb. 4, 2023, URL: https://www.scopus.com/authid/detail.uri?authorId=22988279600 (visited on Feb. 4, 2023).

Eliot, T. S.: The Rock, New York, NY 1934.

Emrich, Hinderk M.: Die Bedeutung des Konstruktivismus für Emotion, Traum und Imagination, in: Neuroworlds : Gehirn – Geist – Kultur, Frankfurt am Main 1994, pp. 93–116.

EU Charter of Fundamental Rights : Article 1 ; Human dignity. European Union Agency for Fundamental Rights, Apr. 25, 2015, URL: https://fra.europa.eu/en/eu-charter/article/1-human-dignity (visited on Jan. 25, 2023).

European insurance and occupational pensions authority (eiopa): Big data analytics in motor and health insurance : a thematic review, Luxembourg 2019, URL: https://register.eiopa.europa.eu/Publications/EIOPA_BigDataAnalytics_ThematicReview_April2019.pdf.

Fauna im Garten, 2021, URL: http://www.fauna-garten.at/ (visited on Jan. 6, 2023).

Fiorelli, Gianluca: Hummingbird unleashed. moz.com, Oct. 24, 2013, URL: https://moz.com/blog/hummingbird-unleashed (visited on Dec. 17, 2022).

Frické, Martin: The knowledge pyramid : a critique of the DIKW hierarchy, in: Journal of Information Science 35 (2009) 2, pp. 131–142, URL: https://doi.org/10.1177/0165551508094050 (visited on Dec. 17, 2022).

Garfield, Eugene: Citation indexes for science, in: Science 122 (1955) 3159, pp. 108–111, URL: https://www.science.org/doi/10.1126/science.122.3159.108 (visited on Dec. 16, 2022).

Georgy, Ursula: Der Wert von Information : Thesen zum Thema, in: Wolfenbütteler Notizen zur Buchgeschichte 27 (2002) 2, pp. 273–279.

Gergen, Kenneth J.: An invitation to social construction, London 1999.

Gibson, James J.: The perception of the visual world, 1950.

Gigerenzer, Gerd: Gut feelings : the intelligence of the unconscious, London 2008.

Gleick, James: The information : a history, a theory, a flood, London 2011.

Gödert, Winfried: Aufbereitung und Rezeption von Information, in: Info 7 15 (2000) 2, pp. 97–105.

Gödert, Winfried: Information as a cognitive construction : a communication-theoretic model and consequences for information systems, in: Knowledge Organization 23 (1996) 4, pp. 206–212.

Gödert, Winfried: Multimedia-Enzyklopädien auf CD-ROM : eine vergleichende Analyse von Allgemeinenzyklopädien (Informationsmittel für Bibliotheken; Beiheft 1), Berlin 1994.

Gödert, Winfried: Semantische Wissensrepräsentation und Interoperabilität. Teil 1 : Interoperabilität als Weg zur Wissensexploration. Teil 2 : Ein formales Modell semantischer Interoperabilität, in: Information – Wissenschaft & Praxis 61 (2010) 1, pp. 5–18, 19–28.

Gödert, Winfried, Jessica Hubrich, and Matthias Nagelschmidt: Semantic knowledge representation for information retrieval, Berlin 2014.

Gödert, Winfried and Hans-Dieter Kübler: Konzepte von Wissensdarstellung und Wissensrezeption medial vermittelter Information : Plädoyer für eine kommunikationstheoretische Betrachtungsweise, in: Nachrichten für Dokumentation 44 (1993) 3, pp. 149–156.

Gödert, Winfried, Klaus Lepsky, and Matthias Nagelschmidt: Informationserschließung und Automatisches Indexieren : ein Lehr- und Arbeitsbuch, Berlin 2012.

Goenner, Hubert F.: Das kurze Leben des S. B. Preuss, in: Physikalische Blätter 39 (1983) 4, p. 91.

Gombrich, Ernst H.: Art and illusion : a study in the psychology of pictorial representation (Bollingen series, 35. The A. W. Mellon lectures in the fine arts, 5), New York, NY 1960.

GPT-3. Wikipedia, 2022, URL: https://en.wikipedia.org/w/index.php?title=GPT-3&oldid=1130774289 (visited on Jan. 1, 2023).

Halbwachs, Maurice: On collective memory, Chicago, Ill. 1992.

Harari, Yuval Noah: Homo Deus : a brief history of tomorrow, New York, NY 2017.

Hari, Johann: Your attention didn't collapse : it was stolen, in: The Observer, Jan. 2, 2022, URL: https://www.theguardian.com/science/2022/jan/02/attention-span-focus-screens-apps-smartphones-social-media (visited on Feb. 16, 2023).

Hasebrook, Joachim (ed.): Multimedia-Psychologie : eine neue Perspektive menschlicher Kommunikation, Heidelberg 1995.

Hauff-Hartig, Stefan: Fehl-, Falsch- und Desinformation aus dem Blickwinkel der Informationswissenschaften : lassen sich Manipulationen im Internet durch informationswissenschaftliche Methoden identifizieren? Berlin 2018.

Hauge, Olav H.: The dream we carry : selected and last poems of Olav H. Hauge, trans. by Robert Bly and Robert Hedin, Port Townsend, Wash. 2008.

Haushaltsabfälle je Einwohner in Deutschland bis 2016 [Statistik]. statista, 2018, URL: https://de.statista.com/statistik/daten/studie/161228/umfrage/haushaltsabfaelle-je-einwohner-seit-dem-jahr-2003/ (visited on Dec. 17, 2022).

Haynes, Marie: Your Google algorithm cheat sheet : Panda, Penguin, and Hummingbird. moz.com, June 11, 2014, URL: https://moz.com/blog/google-algorithm-cheat-sheet-panda-penguin-hummingbird (visited on Dec. 17, 2022).

Hegel, Georg Wilhelm Friedrich: Phänomenologie des Geistes, [Nachdr. der Ausg.] Bamberg, Würzburg, Goebhardt, 1807, Stuttgart 1996, URL: http://www.zeno.org/Philosophie/M/Hegel,+Georg+Wilhelm+Friedrich/Ph%C3%A4nomenologie+des+Geistes (visited on Dec. 17, 2022).

Heinrich-Böll-Stiftung: Bildung für die digitale Zukunft : Prof. Dr. Heinz-Elmar Tenorth im Gespräch, Aug. 23, 2018, URL: https://www.youtube.com/watch?v=fgco3lTsO4U (visited on Dec. 17, 2022).

Heisenberg, Werner: Physics and beyond : encounters and conversations, trans. by Arnold J. Pomerans (World perspectives, vol. 42), New York, NY 1971.

Henn, Wolfram: Gefahr durch KI : Wehe, die Computer sagen einmal ‚ich‘, in: FAZ.NET, June 25, 2018, URL: http://www.faz.net/1.5656989 (visited on July 7, 2018).

Henrichs, Norbert: Information, in: Lexikon des gesamten Buchwesens, 2nd ed., Stuttgart 1991, pp. 592–594.

Hensinger, Peter: ‚Digitale Bildung‘ : der abschüssige Weg zur Konditionierungsanstalt. Norbert Häring : Geld und mehr, Jan. 27, 2019, URL: https://norberthaering.de/macht-kontrolle/digitale-bildung/ (visited on Dec. 17, 2022).

Hensinger, Peter: Trojanisches Pferd ‚Digitale Bildung‘ : auf dem Weg zur Konditionierungsanstalt in einer Schule ohne Lehrer? [Vortrag vom 21.06.2017], GEW Kreisverband, June 21, 2017, URL: https://www.gew-bw.de/fileadmin/media/sonstige_downloads/bw/Kreise/Boeblingen/Info/GEW_BB_Digit_Bildung_170621.pdf (visited on Dec. 18, 2022).

Hentig, Hartmut von: Die Flucht aus dem Denken ins Wissen, in: Frankfurter Allgemeine Zeitung, Aug. 16, 1993, p. 26.

Hesse, Wolfgang: Information : das Soma des ausgehenden Jahrhunderts? In: Ethik und Sozialwissenschaften 9 (1998) 2, pp. 212–215.

Himmelheber, Wendelin: Leibniz : Ars Combinatoria. paarpraxis-rheinmain.de, 2018, URL: http://paarpraxis-rheinmain.de/W/Texte/ArsCombinatoria.html (visited on Dec. 17, 2022).

Hirsch, Jorge E.: An index to quantify an individual's scientific research output, in: Proceedings of the National Academy of Sciences 102 (2005) 46, pp. 16569–16572, URL: https://doi.org/10.1073/pnas.0507655102 (visited on Dec. 17, 2022).

Hirsch, Jorge E.: An index to quantify an individual's scientific research output that takes into account the effect of multiple coauthorship, in: Scientometrics 85 (2010) 3, pp. 741–754, URL: https://doi.org/10.1007/s11192-010-0193-9 (visited on Dec. 17, 2022).

Höchstötter, Nadine: Suchverhalten im Web : Erhebung, Analyse und Möglichkeiten, in: Information – Wissenschaft und Praxis 58 (2007) 3, pp. 135–140.

Hoffert, Barbara: The encyclopedia wars, in: Library Journal 119 (1994) 14, pp. 142–145.

Hoffman, Donald D.: Donald D. Hoffman : University of California, Irvine, 2018, URL: http://www.cogsci.uci.edu/%7Eddhoff/ (visited on Dec. 17, 2022).

Hoffman, Donald D.: Visual intelligence : how we create what we see, New York, NY 2000.

Hoffmann, Ludger: Reflexionen über die Sprache : de Saussure, Chomsky, Bühler, 2005, URL: http://home.edo.tu-dortmund.de/~hoffmann/PDF/Reflexionen.pdf (visited on Dec. 17, 2022).

Höhner, Katrin: ORCID an der TU Dortmund : Wissenschaftler ihren Publikationen eindeutig zuordnen. password-online.de, Aug. 30, 2017, URL: https://www.infobroker.de/password-online/archiv/orcid-an-der-tu-dortmund-wissenschaftler-ihren-publikationen-eindeutig-zuordnen/ (visited on Dec. 17, 2022).

Holenstein, Elmar: Kulturphilosophische Perspektiven : Schulbeispiel Schweiz ; europäische Identität auf dem Prüfstand ; globale Verständigungsmöglichkeiten, Frankfurt am Main 1998.

Holenstein, Elmar: Menschliche Gleichartigkeit und inter- wie intrakulturelle Mannigfaltigkeit, in: Prague Linguistic Circle papers 1 (1995), pp. 39–53.

Holenstein, Elmar: Symmetrie und Symmetriebruch in der Sprache, in: Rudolf Wille (ed.): Symmetrie in Geistes- und Naturwissenschaft : Hauptvorträge und Diskussionen des Symmetrie Symposions an der Technischen Hochschule Darmstadt vom 13.-17.6.1986 im Rahmen des Symmetrieprojektes der Stadt Darmstadt, Berlin 1988, pp. 192–208.

Holze, Jens: Digitales Wissen : bildungsrelevante Relationen zwischen Strukturen digitaler Medien und Konzepten von Wissen, Dissertation, Magdeburg: Fakultät für Humanwissenschaften der Otto-von-Guericke-Universität Magdeburg, 2017, URL: http://dx.doi.org/10.25673/4666 (visited on Dec. 17, 2022).

Honest Shanghai : the app the Chinese government uses to track "honest" citizens. CyberPolicy, 2022, URL: https://www.cyberpolicy.com/cybersecurity-education/honest-shanghai-the-app-the-chinese-government-uses-to-track-honest-citizens (visited on Oct. 2, 2022).

Howard, Dara Lee: Pertinence as reflected in personal constructs, in: Journal of the American Society for Information Science 45 (1994) 3, pp. 172–185, URL: https://doi.org/10.1002/(SICI)1097-4571(199404)45:3%3C172::AID-ASI7%3E3.0.CO;2-V (visited on Dec. 17, 2022).

Hübner, Kurt: Critique of the scientific reason, Chicago, Ill. 1983.

Hübner, Kurt: Die Wahrheit des Mythos, München 1985.

Hug, Theo: On the medialization of knowledge in the digital age, in: International journal of humanities and social science 3 (2013) 11, pp. 22–35, URL: https://ijhssnet.com/journals/Vol_3_No_11_June_2013/3.pdf.

Huge "foundation models" are turbo-charging AI progress, in: The Economist, June 11, 2022, URL: https://www.economist.com/interactive/briefing/2022/06/11/huge-foundation-models-are-turbo-charging-ai-progress (visited on Dec. 31, 2022).

Husserl, Edmund: Husserliana : Bd. 10 ; Zur Phänomenologie des inneren Zeitbewusstseins ; (1893–1917), in collab. with Rudolf Boehm, Dordrecht 1966.

Husserl, Edmund: The Paris lectures, Dordrecht 1998.

Informational self-determination. Wikipedia, 2022, URL: https://en.wikipedia.org/wiki/Informational_self-determination (visited on Dec. 18, 2022).

Informationskompetenz. Wikipedia, 2022, URL: https://de.wikipedia.org/w/index.php?title=Informationskompetenz&oldid=182481071 (visited on Dec. 17, 2022).

Jansen, Bernard J. and Amanda Spink: How are we searching the World Wide Web? : a comparison of nine search engine transaction logs, in: Information Processing & Management 42 (2006) 1, pp. 248–263, URL: https://doi.org/10.1016/j.ipm.2004.10.007 (visited on Dec. 21, 2018).

Jones, Nicola: Deep Learning : wie Maschinen lernen lernen. spektrum.de, Jan. 14, 2014, URL: https://www.spektrum.de/news/maschinenlernen-deep-learning-macht-kuenstliche-intelligenz-praxistauglich/1220451 (visited on Dec. 18, 2022).

Jullien, François: Es gibt keine kulturelle Identität : wir verteidigen die Ressourcen einer Kultur, Berlin 2017.

Jun, Youjung, Rachel Meng, and Gita V. Johar: Perceived social presence reduces fact-checking, in: Proceedings of the National Academy of Sciences 114 (2017) 23, pp. 5976–5981, URL: https://doi.org/10.1073/pnas.1700175114 (visited on Dec. 17, 2022).

Kaminski, Barbara: Geborgenheit und Selbstwertgefühl : eine Untersuchung auf der Grundlage der Forschungen von Otto Friedrich Bollnow in „Das Wesen der Stimmungen" und in „Neue Geborgenheit" sowie der „Analytik des Daseins" von Martin Heidegger in „Sein und Zeit", Frankfurt am Main 2003.

Karner, Josef: Mailüfterl, Al Chorezmi und Künstliche Intelligenz. Telepolis, Aug. 8, 1999, URL: https://www.heise.de/tp/features/Mailuefterl-Al-Chorezmi-und-Kuenstliche-Intelligenz-3563733.html (visited on Dec. 17, 2022).

Kaufmann, Jean-Claude: Die Erfindung des Ich : eine Theorie der Identität, Konstanz 2005.

Keen, Andrew: The Cult of the amateur : how today's internet is killing our culture, 2007.

Kluge, Alexander and Wolf Singer: Hirnforschung : das Gehirn braucht so viel Strom wie die Glühbirne. Welt, Dec. 30, 2012, URL: https://www.welt.de/kultur/article112018610/Das-Gehirn-braucht-so-viel-Strom-wie-die-Gluehbirne.html (visited on Nov. 16, 2018).

Knowledge. Wikipedia, 2022, URL: https://en.wikipedia.org/w/index.php?title= Knowledge&oldid=1094302139 (visited on Dec. 22, 2022).

Koch, Moritz and Torsten Riecke: Deutscher Wirtschaftsbuchpreis : „Gegen die Industriali-sierung ist die Digitalisierung Pipifax" ; Interview mit Nathalie Weidenfeld und Julian Nida-Rümelin. Handelsblatt, Aug. 30, 2018, URL: https://www.handelsblatt.com/arts_und_style/literatur/wirtschaftsbuchpreis/deutscher-wirtschaftsbuchpreis-gegen-die-industrialisierung-ist-die-digitalisierung-pipifax/22965832.html (visited on Dec. 2, 2022).

Kókai, Gabriella: Erfolge und Probleme evolutionärer Algorithmen, induktiver logischer Pro-grammierung und ihrer Kombination (Arbeitsberichte des Instituts für Informatik, Friedrich-Alexander-Universität Erlangen Nürnberg, vol. 36,1), Erlangen 2003.

König, René and Michael Nentwich: Soziale Medien in der Wissenschaft, in: Jan-Hinrik Schmidt and Monika Taddicken (eds.): Handbuch Soziale Medien, Wiesbaden 2017, pp. 169–188, URL: https://doi.org/10.1007/978-3-658-03765-9_10 (visited on Dec. 18, 2022).

Korte, Martin: Gedächtnis : warum wir vergessen. spektrum.de, Aug. 7, 2018, URL: https://www.spektrum.de/news/gedaechtnis-warum-wir-vergessen/1580324 (visited on Dec. 18, 2022).

Krattenthaler, Christian: Was der h-Index wirklich aussagt, in: Mitteilungen der Deutschen Mathematiker-Vereinigung 29 (2021) 3, pp. 124–128, URL: https://www.degruyter.com/document/doi/10.1515/dmvm-2021-0050/html (visited on Nov. 26, 2022).

Kuhlen, Rainer: Hypertext : ein nicht-lineares Medium zwischen Buch und Wissensbank, Berlin 1991.

Kuhlen, Rainer: Informationsmarkt : Chancen und Risiken der Kommerzialisierung von Wissen (Schriften zur Informationswissenschaft, vol. 15), Konstanz 1995.

Kuhn, Thomas S.: The structure of scientific revolutions, Chicago, Ill. 1962.

Kwon, Diana: Intelligent machines that learn like children, in: Scientific American 318 (2018) 3, pp. 26–31, URL: https://www.scientificamerican.com/article/intelligent-machines-that-learn-like-children/ (visited on Sept. 6, 2022).

Langville, Amy N. and Carl D. Meyer: Google's PageRank and beyond : the science of search engine rankings, Princeton, NJ 2006.

Lanners, Edi: Illusions, New York, NY 1977.

Large, Andrew et al.: Multimedia and comprehension : a cognitive study, in: Journal of the American Society for Information Science 45 (1994) 7, pp. 515–528, URL: https://doi.org/10.1002/(SICI)1097-4571(199408)45:7%3C515::AID-ASI6%3E3.0.CO;2-3 (visited on Dec. 18, 2022).

Large, Andrew et al.: Multimedia and comprehension : the relationship among text, animation, and captions, in: Journal of the American Society for Information Science 46 (1995) 5, pp. 340–347, URL: https://doi.org/10.1002/(SICI)1097-4571(199506)46:5%3C340::AID-ASI5%3E3.0.CO;2-S (visited on Dec. 18, 2022).

Lehmann, Konrad: Neues vom Gehirn : Essays zu Erkenntnissen der Neurobiologie, Hannover 2017.

Lewandowski, Dirk (ed.): Handbuch Internet-Suchmaschinen : 1. Nutzerorientierung in Wis-senschaft und Praxis, Heidelberg 2009.

Liessmann, Konrad P.: Geisterstunde : die Praxis der Unbildung ; eine Streitschrift, Wien 2014.

Luft, Alfred L.: ‚Wissen' und ‚Information' bei einer Sichtweise der Informatik als Wissenstech-nik, in: Wolfgang Coy (ed.): Sichtweisen der Informatik, Braunschweig 1992, pp. 49–70.

Luft, Alfred L.: Zur begrifflichen Unterscheidung von ‚Wissen', ‚Information' und ‚Daten', in: Rudolf Wille and Monika Zwickwolff (eds.): Begriffliche Wissensverarbeitung : Grundfragen und Aufgaben, Mannheim 1994, pp. 61–79.

Macedonia, Manuela: Lernen : mit Händen und Füßen. spektrum.de, Dec. 7, 2002, URL: https://www.spektrum.de/news/mit-haenden-und-fuessen/1173260 (visited on Dec. 18, 2022).

MacRoberts, Michael H. and Barbara R. MacRoberts: The mismeasure of science : citation analysis, in: Journal of the Association for Information Science and Technology 69 (2018) 3, pp. 474–482, URL: https://onlinelibrary.wiley.com/doi/full/10.1002/asi.23970 (visited on Dec. 18, 2022).

Manning, Christopher, Prabhakar Raghavan, and Hinrich Schütze: Introduction to information retrieval, 2009, URL: https://nlp.stanford.edu/IR-book/information-retrieval-book.html (visited on Dec. 18, 2022).

Markey, Karen: Twenty-five years of end-user searching. Part 1 : Research findings. Part II : Future research directions, in: Journal of the American Society for Information Science and Technology 58 (2007) 8, pp. 1071–1081, 1123–1130, URL: https://doi.org/10.1002/asi.20462 (visited on Dec. 18, 2022).

Maturana, Humberto R.: Kognition, in: Der Diskurs des radikalen Konstruktivismus, Frankfurt am Main 1990, pp. 89–118.

Maturana, Humberto R.: Neurophilosophie, in: Jutta Fedrowitz (ed.): Neuroworlds : Gehirn – Geist – Kultur (Schriftenreihe des Wissenschaftszentrums Nordrhein-Westfalen, vol. 3), Frankfurt am Main 1994, pp. 152–174.

Maturana, Humberto R. and Rudolf zur Lippe (eds.): Was ist erkennen? München 1994.

Maturana, Humberto R. and Francisco J. Varela: Der Baum der Erkenntnis : die biologischen Wurzeln menschlichen Erkennens, Frankfurt am Main 2009.

Mau, Steffen: The metric society : on the quantification of the social, Cambridge 2019.

Meadow, Charles T.: Relevance? In: Journal of the American Society for Information Science 36 (1985) 5, pp. 354–355, URL: https://doi.org/10.1002/asi.4630360516 (visited on Dec. 18, 2022).

Mensch – Maschine – Visionen : wie Biologie und Technik verschmelzen (Spektrum der Wissenschaft: Spezial Physik – Mathematik – Technik, vol. 2/2015), 2015.

Metzger, Wolfgang: Laws of seeing, Cambridge, Mass. 2009.

Metzinger, Thomas: Ist das Gehirn mit einem Computer oder einer Festplatte zu vergleichen? 1000 Antworten, Apr. 11, 2019, URL: https://www.swr.de/wissen/1000-antworten/wissenschaft-und-forschung/1000-antworten-1284.html (visited on Oct. 20, 2022).

Miller, Carmen: Virtual reality and online databases : will ‚Look and Feel' literally mean ‚Look' and ‚Feel'? In: Online 16 (1992) 6, pp. 12–13.

Misra, Girishwar and Anand Prakash: Kenneth J. Gergen and social constructionism, in: Psychological Studies 57 (2012) 2, pp. 121–125, URL: https://doi.org/10.1007/s12646-012-0151-0 (visited on Dec. 3, 2022).

Mogel, Hans: Geborgenheit : Psychologie eines Lebensgefühls, Berlin 1995.

Monyer, Hannah and Martin Gessmann: Das geniale Gedächtnis : wie das Gehirn aus der Vergangenheit unsere Zukunft macht, München 2017.

Musil, Robert: The man without qualities, vol. 1, New York 1996.

Nelson, Ted H.: Complex information processing : a file structure for the complex, the changing and the indeterminate, in: Proceedings of the 1965 20th National Conference (ACM '65), New York, NY 1965, pp. 84–100, URL: http://doi.acm.org/10.1145/800197.806036 (visited on Dec. 18, 2022).

Nelson, Ted H.: Transhyperability and argumedia, in: New Review of Hypermedia and Multimedia 11 (2005) 1, pp. 27–32, URL: https://doi.org/10.1080/13614560500202191 (visited on Dec. 18, 2022).

Neuser, Wolfgang: Wissen begreifen : zur Selbstorganisation von Erfahrung, Handlung und Begriff, Wiesbaden 2013.

Newberg, Andrew, Eugene G. D'Aquili, and Vince Rause: Why god won't go away : brain science and the biology of belief, New York, NY 2001.

Nguyen-Kim, Mai Thi: Die kleinste gemeinsame Wirklichkeit : wahr, falsch, plausibel? ; die größten Streitfragen wissenschaftlich geprüft, München 2021.

Nida-Rümelin, Julian: Tief in unserer Lebenswelt verwurzelt : Humanismus und Freiheit ; die vollständige naturalistische Erklärung unseres Handelns steht im Widerspruch zu unserer moralischen Alltagspraxis, in: Frankfurter Rundschau, Mar. 2, 2004, p. 19.

Nida-Rümelin, Julian: Über menschliche Freiheit, Stuttgart 2005.

Nida-Rümelin, Julian: Verantwortung, Stuttgart 2011.

Nida-Rümelin, Julian and Nathalie Weidenfeld: Digitaler Humanismus : eine Ethik für das Zeitalter der Künstlichen Intelligenz, München 2018.

Nix, Don and Rand J. Spiro (eds.): Cognition, education, and multimedia : exploring ideas in high technology, Hillsdale, NJ 1990.

Nocun, Katharina: Tracking durch die Versicherung : zu Risiken und Nebenwirkungen. netzpolitik.org, May 19, 2018, URL: https://netzpolitik.org/2018/tracking-durch-die-versicherung-zu-risiken-und-nebenwirkungen/ (visited on Dec. 18, 2022).

Nonaka, Ikujiro: The knowledge-creating company : how japanese companies create the dynamics of innovation. New York, NY 1995.

Nüse, Ralf et al.: Über die Erfindung/en des radikalen Konstruktivismus : kritische Gegenargumente aus psychologischer Sicht, 2nd ed., Weinheim 1995.

O'Neil, Cathy: Weapons of math destruction : how big data increases inequality and threatens democracy, London 2018.

Oeconomische Encyclopädie online, 2022, URL: https://www.kruenitz1.uni-trier.de/home.htm (visited on Nov. 5, 2022).

On consciousness with Giulio Tononi, Max Tegmark and David Chalmers [FQXi]. YouTube, Oct. 30, 2017, URL: https://youtu.be/RX-oOIFoY3E (visited on Dec. 18, 2022).

ORCID : connecting research and researchers. ORCID, 2023, URL: https://orcid.org/ (visited on Feb. 4, 2023).

Pauen, Michael and Gerhard Roth: Freiheit, Schuld und Verantwortung : Grundzüge einer naturalistischen Theorie der Willensfreiheit, Frankfurt am Main 2008.

Pauen, Michael and Harald Welzer: Autonomie : eine Verteidigung, Frankfurt am Main 2015.

Pfister, Rolf-Dieter: Ware oder öffentliches Gut? : über den Charakter von Information ; am Beispiel Internet, in: Datenbanken in Theorie und Praxis (1994) 4, pp. 35–44.

Piekara, Frank Henry: Wie idiosynkratisch ist Wissen? : individuelle Unterschiede im Assoziieren und bei der Anlage und Nutzung von Informationssystemen, Frankfurt am Main 1988.

Plass, Jan L., Roxana Moreno, and Roland Brünken (eds.): Cognitive load theory, Cambridge 2010.

Pöppel, Ernst: Wissen : und wie es kommuniziert werden kann, in: Raffael Ball (ed.): Wissenschaftskommunikation der Zukunft (WissKom 2017), Jülich 2007, pp. 11–21.

Popper, Karl R.: Die beiden Grundprobleme der Erkenntnistheorie : aufgrund von Manuskripten aus den Jahren 1930–1933 (Die Einheit der Gesellschaftswissenschaften, vol. 18), Tübingen 1979.

Popper, Karl R.: Objective knowledge : an evolutionary approach, Oxford 1979.

Popper, Karl R.: The bucket and the searchlight : two theories of knowledge, in: Objective Knowledge : an evolutionary approach, Oxford 1979, pp. 341–360.

Popper, Karl R. and John C. Eccles: The self and its brain : an argument for interactionism, London 1977.

Price, Derek J. de Solla: Little science, big science, New York, NY 1963.

Probst, Gilbert J. B., Steffen Raub, and Kai Romhardt: Managing knowledge : building blocks for success, Toronto 1999.

Quattrociocchi, Walter: Fake News in sozialen Netzwerken, in: Spektrum der Wissenschaft (2017) 11, pp. 58–67, URL: https://www.spektrum.de/magazin/fake-news-in-sozialen-netzwerken/1505997 (visited on Dec. 18, 2022).

Randow, Gero von: Gottfried Wilhelm Leibniz : er sah die Mathematik als Geisteswissenschaft, in: Die Zeit, Nov. 3, 2016, URL: https://www.zeit.de/2016/44/gottfried-wilhelm-leibniz-todestag-300-jahre-genie/seite-5 (visited on Dec. 18, 2022).

Rapp, Friedrich: Fortschritt : Entwicklung und Sinngehalt einer philosophischen Idee, Darmstadt 1992.

Rawls, John: A theory of justice, Cambridge, Mass. 1971.

Rawls, John: Justice as fairness : a restatement, Cambridge, Mass. 2001.

Reckwitz, Andreas: The society of singularities, Cambridge, UK 2020.

Riethmüller, Jürgen: Der graue Schwan : Prolegomena zum Wissen der Wissensgesellschaft, München 2012.

Rock, Irvin: The logic of perception, Cambridge, Mass. 1983.

Rojas, Raúl: Die Tugend des Roboters. Telepolis, Aug. 12, 2017, URL: https://www.heise.de/tp/features/Die-Tugend-des-Roboters-3798701.html (visited on Dec. 18, 2022).

Roth, Gerhard: Das Gehirn und seine Wirklichkeit : kognitive Neurobiologie und ihre philosophischen Konsequenzen, Frankfurt am Main 1994.

Röthler, David: „Lehrautomaten" oder die MOOC-Vision der späten 60er Jahre. David Röthler, Dec. 8, 2014, URL: http://david.roethler.at/lehrautomaten-oder-die-mooc-vision-der-spaeten-60er-jahre/ (visited on Dec. 18, 2022).

Rötzer, Florian: Chinesischer Roboter besteht weltweit erstmals Zulassungsprüfung für Mediziner. Telepolis, Nov. 22, 2017, URL: https://www.heise.de/tp/features/Chinesischer-Roboter-besteht-weltweit-erstmals-Zulassungspruefung-fuer-Mediziner-3894858.html (visited on Dec. 18, 2022).

Rötzer, Florian: Junge Generation will menschliche Interaktion vermeiden : Umfrage. Telepolis, Oct. 8, 2018, URL: https://www.heise.de/tp/features/Umfrage-Junge-Generation-will-menschliche-Interaktion-vermeiden-4182966.html (visited on Dec. 18, 2022).

Russ-Mohl, Stephan: Die informierte Gesellschaft und ihre Feinde : warum die Digitalisierung unsere Demokratie gefährdet, Köln 2017.

Russell, Bertrand: Mathematical logic as based on the theory of types, in: American Journal of Mathematics 30 (1908) 3, pp. 222–262, URL: https://www.jstor.org/stable/2369948 (visited on Dec. 18, 2022).

Russian interference in the 2016 United States elections. Wikipedia, 2022, URL: https://en.wikipedia.org/w/index.php?title=Russian_interference_in_the_2016_United_States_elections&oldid=1112082849 (visited on Sept. 29, 2022).

S. B. Preuss. Wikipedia, 2022, URL: https://de.wikipedia.org/w/index.php?title=S._B._Preuss&oldid=119506247 (visited on Sept. 7, 2022).

Schaat, Samer: Von der automatisierten Manipulation zur Manipulation der Automatisierung. Telepolis, Feb. 17, 2019, URL: https://www.heise.de/tp/features/Von-der-automatisierten-Manipulation-zur-Manipulation-der-Automatisierung-4296557.html (visited on Dec. 18, 2022).

Schaer, Philipp et al.: How relevant is the long tail? : a relevance assessment study on Million Short, in: Norbert Fuhr et al. (eds.): Experimental IR Meets Multilinguality, Multimodality, and Interaction, Cham 2016, pp. 227–233.

Schäfers, Andrea: Gehirn und Lernen – Plastizität, 2018, URL: https://www.gehirnlernen.de/gehirn/plastizit%C3%A4t/ (visited on Dec. 18, 2022).

Schamber, Linda: Relevance and information behavior, in: Annual Review of Information Science and Technology (ARIST) 29 (1994), pp. 3–48.

Schank, Roger C.: Computer, elementare Aktionen und linguistische Theorien, in: Peter Eisenberg (ed.): Semantik und künstliche Intelligenz : Beiträge zur automatischen Sprachbearbeitung II, Berlin 1977, pp. 113–141.

Schank, Roger C. and Peter G. Childers: The cognitive computer : on language, learning, and artificial intelligence, Reading, Mass. 1984.

Scheidgen, Helmut (ed.): Information ist noch kein Wissen, Weinheim 1990.

Schmidt, Eric and Jared Cohen: The new digital age : reshaping the future of people, nations and business, New York, NY 2013.

Schmidt, Florian Alexander: Crowdproduktion von Trainingsdaten : zur Rolle von Online-Arbeit beim Trainieren autonomer Fahrzeuge. (Study der Hans-Böckler-Stiftung, vol. 417), Düsseldorf 2019.

Schmidt, Jan-Hinrik and Monika Taddicken (eds.): Handbuch Soziale Medien, Wiesbaden 2017.

Schmidt, Siegfried J.: Der radikale Konstruktivismus : ein neues Paradigma im interdisziplinären Diskurs, in: idem (ed.): Der Diskurs des radikalen Konstruktivismus, 3rd ed., Frankfurt am Main 1990, pp. 11–88.

Schmidt, Siegfried J.: Kognitive Autonomie und soziale Orientierung : konstruktivistische Bemerkungen zum Zusammenhang von Kognition, Kommunikation, Medien und Kultur, Frankfurt am Main 1994.

Schmidt, Siegfried J.: Von der Memoria zur Gedächtnispolitik : zwischen Hypertext und Cyberspace ; was heißt individuelle und soziale Erinnerung? In: Frankfurter Rundschau, Feb. 20, 1996, p. 7.

Search engine optimization. Wikipedia, 2022, URL: https://en.wikipedia.org/w/index.php?title=Search_engine_optimization&oldid=1110413960 (visited on Oct. 2, 2022).

Searle, John R.: Kollektive Absichten und Handlungen, in: Hans Bernhard Schmid and David P. Schweikard (eds.): Kollektive Intentionalität : eine Debatte über die Grundlagen des Sozialen, Frankfurt am Main 2008, pp. 99–118.

Searle, John R.: Mind : a brief introduction, Oxford 2004.

Searle, John R.: Minds, brains, and programs, in: Behavioral and Brain Sciences 3 (1980) 3, pp. 417–457, URL: http://cogprints.org/7150/1/10.1.1.83.5248.pdf (visited on Dec. 18, 2022).

Searle, John R.: Putting consciousness back in the brain : reply to Bennett and Hacker, in: Maxwell R. Bennett et al.: Neuroscience and philosophy : brain, mind, and language, New York, NY 2007, pp. 97–124.

Searle, John R.: The construction of social reality, Harmondsworth, Middlesex 1995.

Searle, John R.: The rediscovery of the mind, 3rd ed., Cambridge, Mass. 1992.

Segal, Erich: The Britannica and its dongle, in: Times Literary Supplement, Nov. 18, 1994.

Semantic interoperability. Wikipedia, 2022, URL: https://en.wikipedia.org/w/index.php?title=Semantic_interoperability&oldid=841609884 (visited on Nov. 29, 2022).

Sennett, Richard: Authority, London 1980.

Shannon, Claude E.: A mathematical theory of communication : pt.1.2, in: Bell system telephone journal 27 (1948), pp. 379–423, 639–641.

Shannon, Claude E. and Warren Weaver: Mathematical theory of communication, Urbana, Ill. 1963.

Smith, Mark Allen: The inquisitor, London 2012.

Sokal affair. Wikipedia, 2022, URL: https://en.wikipedia.org/wiki/Sokal_affair (visited on Dec. 18, 2022).

Spies, Marcus: Unsicheres Wissen : Wahrscheinlichkeit, Fuzzy-Logik, neuronale Netze und menschliches Denken, Heidelberg 1993.

Stabile Ergebnisse bei zunehmenden Herausforderungen : Lesen muss gestärkt werden [BMBF]. Bundesministerium für Bildung und Forschung (BMBF), Dec. 5, 2017, URL: https://www.bmbf.de/bmbf/shareddocs/pressemitteilungen/de/stabile-ergebnisse-bei-zunehmenden-herausforderungen.html (visited on Dec. 18, 2022).

Stadler, Michael and Peter Kruse: Der radikale Konstruktivismus : ein Antirealismus? In: Hans Jörg Sandkühler (ed.): Wirklichkeit und Wissen : eine Ringvorlesung im Sommersemester 1991 (Schriftenreihe / Zentrum Philosophische Grundlagen der Wissenschaften, Universität Bremen, vol. 12), Bremen 1992, pp. 87–100.

Standage, Tom: Information overload is nothing new. 1843 magazine, June 21, 2018, URL: https://www.1843magazine.com/technology/rewind/information-overload-is-nothing-new (visited on Dec. 18, 2022).

Steinbuch, Karl: Die informierte Gesellschaft : Geschichte und Zukunft der Nachrichtentechnik, Stuttgart 1966.

Steinbuch, Karl: Masslos informiert : die Enteignung unseres Denkens, 2nd ed., München 1978.

Strohschneider, Stefan: Wissenserwerb und Handlungsregulation, Wiesbaden 1990.

Sühl-Strohmenger, Wilfried and Jan-Pieter Barbian: Informationskompetenz : Leitbegriff bibliothekarischen Handelns in der digitalen Informationswelt, Wiesbaden 2017.

Sweller, John, Paul Ayres, and Slava Kalyuga: Cognitive load theory, New York, NY 2011.

Taxonomy. Wikipedia, 2022, URL: https://en.wikipedia.org/w/index.php?title=Taxonomy&oldid=1100972145 (visited on Sept. 6, 2022).

Tegmark, Max: Life 3.0 : being human in the age of artificial intelligence, New York, NY 2017.

Tetens, Holm: Philosophisches Argumentieren : eine Einführung, 4th ed., München 2015.

Text REtrieval Conference (TREC), 2023, URL: https://trec.nist.gov/ (visited on Jan. 6, 2023).

Thielicke, Robert and Moritz Helmstaedter: Ein völlig neues Kapitel der Künstlichen Intelligenz. Technology Review, Oct. 12, 2018, URL: https://www.heise.de/tr/artikel/Ein-voellig-neues-Kapitel-der-Kuenstlichen-Intelligenz-4188415.html (visited on Dec. 18, 2022).

Topsøe, Flemming: Informationstheorie : eine Einführung, Stuttgart 1974.

Tufte, Edward R.: Envisioning information, Cheshire, Conn. 1990.

Tufte, Edward R.: The visual display of quantitative information, Cheshire, Conn. 1983.

Turing, Alan M.: Lecture to the London Mathematical Society on 20 February 1947, in: Brian E. Carpenter and R. W. Doran (eds.): A.M. Turing's ACE report of 1946 and other papers (The Charles Babbage Institute reprint series for the history of computing, vol. 10), Cambridge, Mass. 1986, p. 124.

Umstätter, Walter: Die Skalierung von Information, Wissen und Literatur, in: Nachrichten für Dokumentation 43 (1992), pp. 227–242.

Varela, Francisco J., Evan Thompson, and Eleanor Rosch: The embodied mind : cognitive science and human experience, in collab. with Jon Kabat-Zinn, revised edition, Cambridge, Mass. 2017.

Voorhees, Ellen M. and Donna K. Harman: TREC : experiment and evaluation in information retrieval, Cambridge, Mass. 2005.

Weber, Max: Die drei reinen Typen der legitimen Herrschaft, in: Preußische Jahrbücher CLXXXVII (1922), pp. 1–12, URL: http://www.zeno.org/Soziologie/M/Weber,+Max/Schriften+zur+Wissenschaftslehre/Die+drei+reinen+Typen+der+legitimen+Herrschaft (visited on Dec. 18, 2022).

Weinberger, David: Everything is miscellaneous : the power of the new digital disorder, New York, NY 2007.

Weisel, Luzian: Ten years after : Stand und Perspektiven der DGI-Initiative für Informationskompetenz ; Teil 1 ; Sachstand, in: Information – Wissenschaft & Praxis 68 (2017) 4, pp. 246–252.

Weizenbaum, Joseph: Computer power and human reason : from judgement to calculation, San Francisco, Calif. 1976.

Weizenbaum, Joseph: Computermacht und Gesellschaft : freie Reden, Frankfurt am Main 2001.

Weizenbaum, Joseph: ELIZA : a computer program for the study of natural language communication between man and machine, in: Communications of the ACM 9 (1966) 1, pp. 36–45, URL: https://doi.org/10.1145/365153.365168 (visited on Jan. 1, 2023).

Welzer, Harald: Das kommunikative Gedächtnis : eine Theorie der Erinnerung, München 2002.

Wenzlaff, Bodo: Vielfalt der Informationsbegriffe, in: Nachrichten für Dokumentation 42 (1991), pp. 355–361.

Wersig, Gernot: Inhaltsanalyse : Einführung in ihre Systematik und Literatur, Berlin 1968.

White, Ryen W.: Interactions with search systems, New York, NY 2016.

Wiener, Norbert: Cybernetics or control and communication in the animal and the machine, New York, NY 1948.

Wille, Rudolf: Begriffliche Datensysteme als Werkzeuge der Wissenskommunikation, in: Harald H. Zimmermann, Heinz-Dirk Luckhardt, and Angelika Schulz (eds.): Mensch und Maschine : informationelle Schnittstellen der Kommunikation ; Proceedings des 3. Internationalen Symposiums für Informationswissenschaft (ISI'92), 5.- 7.11.1992 in Saarbrücken (Schriften zur Informationswissenschaft, vol. 7), Konstanz 1992, pp. 63–73.

Willemsen, Roger: Wer wir waren : Zukunftsrede, Frankfurt am Main 2016.

Winograd, Terry and Fernando Flores: Understanding computers and cognition : a new foundation for design, Norwood, NJ 1986.

Wisdom of the crowd. Wikipedia, 2022, URL: https://en.wikipedia.org/w/index.php?title=Wisdom_of_the_crowd&oldid=1117467964 (visited on Dec. 18, 2022).

Witte-Petit, Kerstin: Der menschliche Kurswert. Rheinpfalz, Sept. 17, 2017, URL: https://www.rheinpfalz.de/artikel/gesellschaft-der-menschliche-kurswert/ (visited on Dec. 18, 2022).

Wittgenstein, Ludwig, Rush Rhees, and Anthony John Patrick Kenny: Philosophical grammar : part I, The proposition, and its sense, part II, On logic and mathematics, Berkeley, Calif. 1974.

Woolley, Samuel: The reality game : how the next wave of technology will break the truth, New York, NY 2020.

Young, John Z.: Philosophy and the brain, Oxford 1987.

Index

https://doi.org/10.1515/9783110693744-013

www.ingramcontent.com/pod-product-compliance
Lightning Source LLC
Chambersburg PA
CBHW020818300326

R18047800001B/R180478PG41927CBX00003B/1